THE **DUCATI** STORY

Also from Veloce Publishing:

www.veloce.co.uk

First published in 1996 by Patrick Stephens Limited. Second edition published in August 1998 by Haynes Publishing. This new edition published May 2018 by Veloce Publishing Limited, Veloce House, Parkway Farm Business Park, Middle Farm Way, Poundbury, Dorchester DT1 3AR, England. Tel +44 (0)1305 260068 / Fax 01305 250479 / e-mail info@veloce.co.uk / web www.veloce.co.uk or www.velocebooks.com.
ISBN: 978-1-787110-85-4 UPC: 6-36847-01085-0.

THE DUCATI STORY

SIXTH EDITION

RACING AND PRODUCTION MOTORCYCLES FROM 1945

IAN FALLOON
FOREWORD BY ING. FABIO TAGLIONI

THE CUCCIOLO

The 'Cucciolo' (or puppy) was an engine designed for Siata of Turin during the Second World War by a lawyer called Aldo Farinelli. 1945 was a very opportune time to produce such a motor: it was easily installed in a bicycle frame, thus providing cheap and economical transportation. Somehow, amidst the chaos of post-war Italy, the Borgo Panigale plant came to produce these engines, presenting their first example, the T1, at the Milan Show in September 1946. Using the FIAT foundry at Cameri near Milan, the Cucciolo was so successful that it became the cornerstone of the Ducati company's revival.

The 48 cc four-stroke Cucciolo engine was intended as a cheap, reliable, and economical unit. With only a 6.5:1 compression ratio, the 39 x 40 mm engine, with its 9 mm Weber carburettor, could run easily on the post-war low octane fuel and provide exceptional fuel economy. Perhaps the most interesting feature of the engine was that the 12 mm valves were operated by pullrods rather than pushrods. Starting was by the usual moped method of pedalling while the engine was in gear, and there were two speeds, selected by the pedals via a handlebar mounted clutch lever.

By 1948, with the injection of capital from the new controllers, the Borgo Panigale plant had been rebuilt and was operating at increased capacity. Demand for the Cucciolo was so strong that a T2 was offered in two versions, Turismo and Sport. With capacity still at 48 cc, the Turismo was detuned slightly with a 5.5:1 compression ratio to produce a mere 0.8 bhp. The Sport retained the 6.5:1 compression of the T1, and power was up to 1.2 bhp at 4,250 rpm. The valve timing was very moderate, and not particularly accurate, with the inlet opening 5°–15° before top dead centre, closing 25°–30° after bottom dead centre, and the exhaust opening 45°–35° before bottom dead centre, and closing 0°–20° after top dead centre.

The T3, which appeared at the Milan Show of 1948, was almost identical to the T2 but with fully enclosed valve gear and a slight bore increase to 43.8 mm, to yield 60 cc. More importantly, this engine was displayed in an entirely new vehicle called the Girino, an unsuccessful three-wheeled device that gave Ducati the impetus to construct their own complete motorcycle. So, with no experience in motorcycle design and construction, they went into a partnership with Aero Caproni, a company that had built aircraft before and during the war but was looking to diversify. This appeared a strange choice, because Caproni were also totally inexperienced in the field of motorcycle design and only one 60 cc motorcycle arose from this alliance. By May 1950 Caproni decided to market their own machines in an expanding, but increasingly competitive market.

In order to maintain sales of the Cucciolo, Ducati supported an attempt on some 50 cc speed records at Monza in March 1951. Ugo Tamarozzi set 12 new 50 cc world records, returning two months later with

By 1950, Ducati was producing
complete motorcycles of which
one of the earliest was the 60TL.
This example has a Caproni-style
frame. *Phil Aynsley*

co-rider Glauco Zitelli to achieve 20 more, notably the
12-Hours' at 67.156 km/h (41.73 mph). Not content
with these, a team of five riders took another
27 records in November, with Tamarozzi collecting the
final two in January 1952. These 50 cc world records
were to last five years, demonstrating to the public the
durability and reliability of the Cucciolo.

They also had the desired effect of keeping the
Cucciolo in production for several more years, with
small modifications. The final versions, the 55/r and
55/e, were marketed from 1954 as true mopeds, with
leading-link forks and swinging-arm rear suspension.
The power was now up to 1.35 bhp, but, with its
popularity waning, the little Cucciolo was discontinued
during 1956. Many thousands had been built over a

ten-year period, and while not being of a particularly
sporting orientation, they did much to establish the
name of Ducati as a motorcycle manufacturer.

THE FIRST SINGLES

Even before the brief relationship with Caproni had
soured, Giovanni Fiorio had designed another engine, a
65 cc four-stroke with pushrod-operated valves.
Introduced in March 1950 and called the 60 Sport, it
was the first real Ducati motorcycle. This engine would
form the basis of a complete range of pushrod singles
lasting through until the 125 Cadet of 1967.
The 44 x 43 mm three-speed engine produced 2.5 bhp
at 5,500 rpm, and soon became the 65TS. 1951 was a

Below: The streamlined 100 cc Gran Sport of Mario Carini and Sandro Ciceri, known as the 'Siluro', set 44 world speed records at Monza at the end of 1956. *Ducati Motor*

The dominance of the 100 Gran Sport in its class was emphasized in November 1956, when the streamlined private machine of Mario Carini and Sandro Ciceri took 44 world records at Monza. Apart from a 25 mm Dell'Orto carburettor, the engine was standard and the bike was timed at an amazing 171.910 km/h (106.8 mph). The Marianna's reliability was displayed over the 1,000 km at an average speed of 154.556 km/h (96 mph).

The first production overhead camshaft road bikes appeared in 1957 (covered in a later chapter), and not only the end of the 100 cc class, but also the final Giro d'Italia following the tragedy in the Mille Miglia car race only a week later when De Portago's Ferrari 315 ran off the road into the crowd after a tyre burst, killing nine spectators. In this last Giro d'Italia, Graziano won the event outright, with Mariannas filling the first 12 places. While the single overhead camshaft racers were now superseded by the double overhead versions, there was still one important success

left for the 125 Gran Sport, a clean sweep in the 1957 Barcelona 24-Hour endurance race. Here Bruno Spaggiari and Alberto Gandossi completed 586 laps at an average speed of 57.66 mph (92.8 km/h) on a bike intended for the cancelled Milano–Taranto race, with Gran Sports also filling second and third places. The following year Mandolini and Maranghi led home another Gran Sport dominated field: while the number of laps completed was identical, 125 cc Gran Sports this time took the first five places. The stage was set for Ducati's years of dominance in this esteemed event.

However, during 1955 Ducati had decided to contest the 125 cc Grand Prix class, and while the Marianna was ideal for street races and for establishing Ducati's reputation, a more sophisticated engine would be needed. Taglioni would also be given the opportunity to put into practice his idea for desmodromically-actuated valve operation, an idea that he had been working on since 1948.

The double overhead camshaft
125 cc Grand Prix Bialbero.
Rolf im Brahm

2 DESMODROMICS

On 25 February 1956, barely one year after the debut of the Gran Sport, a double overhead camshaft version, the Bialbero, was unveiled. It was now Ducati's intention to enter not only the Italian modified sports class with this new racer, but also the World Championship 125cc Grand Prix. This was a massive step for a small company with little racing experience. The mid-1950s was a golden age for Grands Prix in all classes, and competition between MV and Mondial in the 125 class was fierce, with DKW, Montesa, and Gilera also vying for the victor's laurels. Essentially a Gran Sport apart from the cylinder head, the Bialbero was raced in the early Grands Prix of 1956, but with little success.

While the Bialbero was significantly more powerful than the Gran Sport, initially producing 15.5 bhp at 10,500 rpm and soon increased to 16 bhp at 11,500 rpm, it was still no match for the MVs, let alone the Mondials and Gileras, and with sustained high revs its reliability suffered. The problems of valve float and the minimal valve-to-piston clearance meant there was no room for error if a rider missed a gear, so Fabio Taglioni sought to eliminate valve-springs entirely by a method of positive valve control – desmodromic valve gear. Mercedes-Benz had successfully used desmodromic valve gear on their W196 Grand Prix and 300 SLR Sports racing cars in 1954 and 1955, but apart from Mercedes only Taglioni has managed to make desmodromics work reliably and successfully.

Using the Bialbero engine from the cylinder head downward, Taglioni was able to create his 125 desmodromic racer in an astonishingly short time. Its debut at the non-championship Swedish Grand Prix at Hedemora on 15 July 1956 was one of Ducati's greatest race triumphs. Gianni Degli Antoni, on the fully-faired little desmo, easily won the 125 race, lapping the entire field. This was no hollow victory either, because the competition included a number of privately entered MVs and Mondials. While this first desmo wasn't significantly more powerful than the Bialbero, with 17 bhp at 12,500 rpm, it was the increase to over 14,000 rpm that the desmodromic system safely provided that had made the difference. A shortened big-end life was the only price paid for exploiting this capability. Taglioni's desmodromic system differed from others in that it used three camshafts mounted in a magnificent one-piece cambox

Left: Fabio Taglioni proudly showing his desmodromic 125 cc engine in the racing department in 1959. Other engines and cylinder heads are evident. *Mick Woollett*

Below: Although derived from the Marianna, the Bialbero was a real Grand Prix motorcycle. *Rolf im Brahm*

7.5 mm), and 7.4 mm for the exhaust (compared with 7.0 mm). Carburation was either a 27 mm Dell'Orto like the Bialbero, a 29 mm unit for faster circuits, or as small as 22 to 23 mm for the Italian street circuits.

Setting a precedent that would become a feature of all factory racing singles (and the later Imola twins), twin plug ignition was used. The usual 14 mm spark plug was supplemented by a 10 mm plug mounted near the bevel-gear tube, allowing the ignition advance to be reduced from 42 to 36°. Ignition was by a total loss 6 volt battery and twin 3 volt coils. The compression ratio was 10:1, and much of the lower part of the engine was shared with the Gran Sport. A five- or sometimes six-speed gearbox was fitted, but because there was no room inside the Gran Sport engine-cases for more than four, the fifth or sixth gears were mounted inboard of the clutch in the primary drive compartment. The street origins were also displayed by a blanked-off kickstart and an empty space on the left side of the crankshaft where the Gran Sport carried a generator.

Ducati hoped to create a big impression at the Italian Grand Prix at Monza in September 1956, but tragedy struck when their star rider, 26-year-old Gianni

and cylinder head casting. As with the Bialbero, the opening camshafts were carried on the outer shafts, but the desmo's closing cams were mounted on the single central camshaft, operating the valves by forked rockers. The closing camshaft was driven by a vertical shaft and bevel-gear, this being geared directly to the two opening camshafts. The 31 mm and 27 mm valves were the same size as the Bialbero, but desmodromics allowed more lift, 8.1 mm for the inlet (up from

Right: When raced during 1956 the desmo 125s were fully streamlined; Degli Antoni raced with a matching helmet. *Ducati Motor*

Below: Dave Chadwick on the start line for the 1958 Isle of Man 125 TT. *Mick Woollett*

Degli Antoni, was killed while testing at Monza in August. In the race itself none of the Ducatis performed particularly spectacularly, ending the year on a disappointing note after their magnificent display in Sweden. For 1957 it was decided to spend a year developing the desmo for an all-out assault on the Grands Prix in 1958. This also gave Taglioni time to concentrate on the production of the new overhead-camshaft road bikes. Meanwhile, a limited number of double overhead-camshaft 125s, called the 125 Grand Prix, were made available to privateers, and these featured a number of changes from the previous year, most noticeably in the frame, which now had an additional twin-loop subframe under the engine. The engine also received new crankcases. About 50 of these 125 Grand Prix racers were made between 1957 and 1959, and they were the most competitive 125 racer a privateer could buy at the time. A double overhead-camshaft Bialbero 175 cc version was also available.

While the only 1957 World Championship event that the desmos raced in was the Italian Grand Prix at Monza, this, like the previous year, was a disaster. Alberto Gandossi fell while in the lead on the first lap, bringing down most of the field. Non-desmo Ducatis were also entered for the non-championship Swedish Grand Prix (where this time they took the first five places), but in the Italian Formula 2 and 3 classes Franco Farnè and Bruno Spaggiari were virtually unbeatable. The 125 desmo now produced 18 bhp at 12,500 rpm, and, with a new double-cradle frame, was ready to take on the might of the other Italian factories.

However, before the start of the 1958 season Moto Guzzi, Gilera, and Mondial announced their retirement from Grand Prix competition. This would leave MV Agusta as Ducati's principal opposition, but with Carlo Ubbiali being joined by reigning World Champion Tarquino Provini they would be a formidable team. Ducati's own team was headed by Luigi Taveri, and consisted of Alberto Gandossi, Bruno Spaggiari, sometimes Romolo Ferri and Franco Villa, Dave Chadwick for the opening Grand Prix at the Isle of Man, and, later, trials ace Sammy Miller. The fully-streamlined 'dustbin' fairings of the previous two years were now banned, and in several pre-season events the desmos performed impressively. Ducati went to the Isle of Man with an air of confidence, and a speed advantage over the MVs.

Ubbiali on the MV won at the shorter Clypse Isle of Man circuit after Taveri retired, but Gandossi retaliated

with a win at Spa in Belgium. After the Isle of Man new, higher-lift camshafts had given the desmo single an increase to 19 bhp, and throughout the season the motorcycle was continually developed. No two were identical, with not only different petrol tanks and seats, but also crankcase castings and frames. Further Ducati victories came in Sweden and at Monza, where Spaggiari led a top-five clean sweep. His winning speed was 155.827 km/h (96.8 mph), and this was one of

Ducati's greatest triumphs. Unfortunately, while humiliating MV in front of their home crowd, Gandossi still just failed to beat Ubbiali for the 125 cc title. However, on the domestic front Ducati won all the 125 cc championships in 1958. Having proved that desmodromics worked, the factory decided to contest the 1959 series of Grand Prix and Italian Championship races on a reduced scale with both the single cylinder desmo, and the new twin. Joining Gandossi and Spaggiari were Taveri and a promising English newcomer, Mike Hailwood.

After the success of 1958, everyone expected 1959 to be a repeat performance, but, unfortunately for Ducati, this didn't materialise. Hailwood's success in 1958 on a dohc Grand Prix, along with his father Stan Hailwood's setting up of Ducati Concessionaires in Manchester as distributors, prompted the factory to loan Hailwood a 125 cc desmo single for the season. It was only Hailwood's exploits that brought any real results, and he won his first ever Grand Prix victory at Ulster in August, eventually ending up third in the 125 cc World Championship. At the end of the 1959 season Ducati retired from racing, selling off the works desmos but substituting the desmodromic heads for the dohc valve-spring type. These continued to be successfully raced for many years, often with the single down-tube Gran Sport type frame of 1956 and 1957 rather than the later full-cradle double down-tube.

There was one more interesting development to the 125 Grand Prix that needs to be documented, and this occurred at the end of the 1959 season. Australian Ken Kavanagh had successfully raced a 125 Grand Prix

during 1959 and persuaded the factory to supply him with a 220 – built out of a 69 mm bored 175 dohc Bialbero – to use to help promote Ducati in Australia in a series of races held during the antipodean summer season. Displacing 216.13 cc, and with a 9:1 compression ratio, the 220 produced 28 bhp at 9,600 rpm. Carburation was by a 29 mm Dell'Orto, and because of its success several similar 220 cc machines were later built.

RACING TWINS AND FOURS

The first indication that Ducati were interested in building larger, multi-cylindered motorcycles came at the Milan Show in December 1956, with the unveiling of a 175 cc double overhead camshaft parallel twin with exposed valve springs. This was raced by Leopoldo Tartarini in the final, 1957, Giro d'Italia, but it retired in the third stage. Originating from drawings first sketched by Taglioni in 1950, it was an interesting, if complicated design, with the pressed up crankshaft consisting of two flywheel assemblies clamped by Hirth

(radially serrated) couplings. A jackshaft was driven off the middle of the crankshaft, and this drove the twin overhead camshafts by a train of spur gears. While the 49 x 46.6 mm 175 produced considerably more power than the 175 cc single cylinder Gran Sport – 22 bhp at 11,000 rpm – the narrower power band and increase in weight to 112 kg (247 lb) largely negated this benefit. The 175 became the basis for a 125 cc Grand Prix machine first raced by Franco Villa at the Italian Grand Prix at Monza in 1958, where it finished third in that remarkable Ducati first-five clean sweep.

This 125 was intended to replace the single by producing more horsepower through increased revs, and the 42.5 x 45 mm engine produced 22.5 bhp at 13,800 rpm. A similar three-camshaft desmodromic valve system to the single allowed the engine to rev to an amazing (for the time) 17,000 rpm, but the power band was extremely narrow and the bike difficult to ride despite having a six-speed gearbox. As with the 175 twin, the 125 was also too heavy at a claimed 92 kg (203 lb), and the handling was less than satisfactory. Compared with the single, the twin (of which only

Below: One of the two desmodromic 350 cc racing twins built in 1960. Later, they were sold to John Surtees who commissioned this Reynolds frame with leading-link forks. *Rolf im Brahm*

three were built) didn't achieve much success. Breakages in the camshaft drive gear-train often occurred, with disastrous results, and the bikes were sold at the end of the 1959 season, two of them ending up being raced by Mike Hailwood.

It was during 1959 that Stan Hailwood commissioned a 250 cc version for Mike to race in 1960. Revealed to the press in February 1960, the 250 shared the same 55.25 x 52 mm dimensions with the 125 cc single, but in other respects was a scaled-up 125 twin. The power was 43 bhp at 11,600 rpm, and it was a very fast motorcycle with a top speed in the region of 218 km/h (135 mph), but it handled poorly and was considerably overweight. At about the same time, Ken Kavanagh, about to undertake his successful series in Australia, persuaded the factory to build a 350 cc desmo twin for the 1960 season. This appeared in time for Kavanagh to race at Imola in April but an accident

prevented him from riding it until the Isle of Man, by which time Hailwood also had a similar machine. With a bore and stroke of 64 x 54 mm, the 350 produced 48 bhp, but the engines vibrated badly and the bikes needed a lot of development to be competitive. At the end of the season John Surtees bought both Hailwood's 250 and 350, followed a few months later by Kavanagh's. They received new frames and leading-link forks by Ken Sprayson, and Phil Read rode a 350 at the Isle of Man in 1962 where it blew up in practice. They were raced unsuccessfully for a couple more domestic British seasons.

There was, however, to be one more multi-cylindered disaster. Seeing the limitations of a single, or even twin, at Grand Prix level, Taglioni designed a 125 cc in-line four-cylinder engine in 1958. This idea was advanced for the time, but with Ducati's withdrawal from competition at the end of 1959 the

Below: Mike Hailwood's 250 twin
as restored by Museo Ducati.

design languished until the Spanish Mototrans concern persuaded Ducati to produce it five years later, in 1964, by which time it was obsolete in a few design areas. There were four non-desmo valves per cylinder and a very wide 90° included valve angle. The double overhead camshaft 125 used a train of gears on the left side of the engine to drive the camshafts. With a compression ratio of 12:1 and four 12 mm Dell'Orto carburettors, the 34.5 x 34 mm engine produced 23 bhp at 14,000 rpm, hardly outstanding considering that the 125 cc twin had produced 22.5 bhp in 1958. Even with 12 months of development the power was only increased to 24 bhp at 16,000 rpm, and Ducati realized that it would never be competitive at Grand Prix level. Only two bikes were built, and during 1966 the 125 four quietly disappeared.

The entire parallel twin and four cylinder episode was interesting in that they were the first Ducatis designed exclusively for racing bearing no relationship to any road bikes. Because they were so unsuccessful compared to the Gran Sport derivatives none of their features ended up on the production line, but they certainly had the effect of creating a Taglioni philosophy that would prevail in the future: that of producing a motorcycle with a balance of power and weight. There was no point in an unnecessarily complex and heavy motorcycle if this did not translate into improved lap times. Also, what good was a powerful motorcycle if it did not handle well or the powerband was so narrow that it was unridable? Not only was it significant that the desmodromic Grand Prix racer was closely derived from a road bike (albeit a catalogued racer with lights), but all future Ducati success would emphasize a broad range, rather than outright power, and a balance between power and weight.

The 175 Sport of 1957 was the
first production overhead
camshaft bevel-gear Ducati.

3 PRODUCTION OVERHEAD CAMSHAFT SINGLES

(NARROW-CASE)

Following the success of the Gran Sport in the 1955 and 1956 Giro d'Italia and Milano–Taranto races, it was inevitable that the Gran Sport engine would be used as a basis for a range of production motorcycles. Given Taglioni's ability to generate designs amazingly quickly, it wasn't surprising that Ducati's first production bevel-gear motorcycle, the 175 Sport, was on display at the Milan Show in December 1956. This was followed shortly afterwards by a slightly detuned version, the 175T.

100/125/175/200

The 175 engine was to form the basis of the entire range of production singles (and also the subsequent Spanish Mototrans versions) until their demise in 1974. It differed from the Gran Sport in a number of design details, most notably in the use of enclosed, rather than exposed, hairpin valve springs. With a bore and stroke of 62 x 57.8 mm, and a compression ratio of 8:1, the 175 Sport produced 14 bhp at 8,000 rpm. The weight was 104 kg (229 lb), and though only a four-speed gearbox was used, performance was lively with a claimed top speed of 130 km/h (81 mph). The 175T had a 7:1 compression ratio and produced 12 bhp at 6,000 rpm. Top speed was 109 km/h (68 mph). The Sport featured the distinctive scalloped petrol tank that would last through to the 200 Elite.

In September 1957, 100 and 125 cc Touring and Sport versions of the overhead camshaft single were displayed, to go into production during 1958. The 125 Sport, sharing its 55.25 mm bore and 52 mm stroke with the Grand Prix, produced 10 bhp at 8,500 rpm with a compression ratio of 8:1. The 100, with the same 49.4 x 52 mm bore dimensions as the first Marianna, produced 8 bhp at 8,700 rpm. Both these Sports were styled after the F3 and weighed 100.5 kg (221.5 lb), with the 125 having a surprising maximum speed of 112 km/h (69 mph). The 175S of 1958 continued with the scalloped petrol tank, and was the first to feature the strange dual muffler that would also categorize the later 200 Elite. After about a year of production the 100 was discontinued, but the model range actually expanded during this period

The 1957 175T was similar to the Sport, but slightly detuned. *Phil Aynsley*

Below left: The 125 Sport was styled along the lines of the racing F3. *Roy Kidney*

Below right: For 1959 the 175 cc engine grew to 200 cc, and powered the sporting 200 Elite.

One of the more unusual models of this period was the 200 Motocross, only a few of this 1960 model being produced.
Phil Aynsley

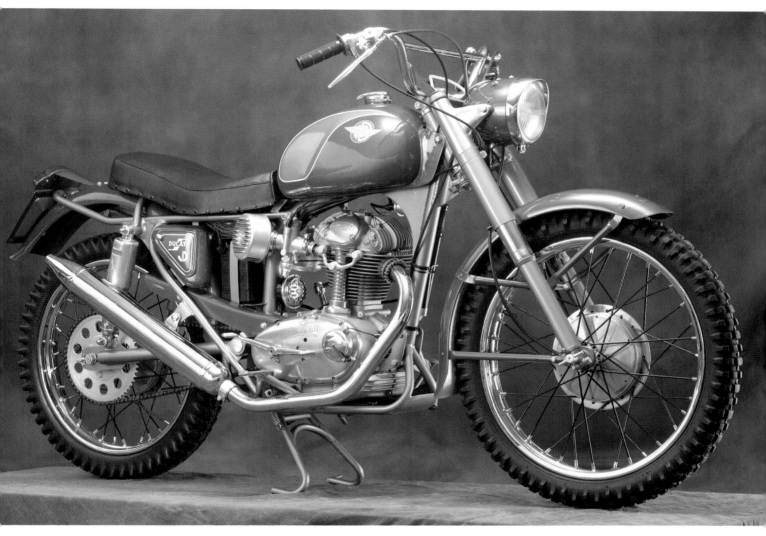

as the 125TS and 175TS were added, and the 175 grew to 200 cc. The 125 Sport remained a popular model, particularly in Italy, until 1965.

By simply boring the 175 by an additional 5 mm, to 67 mm, the 200 Elite was created for the 1959 season. With 18 bhp at 7,500 rpm, the 111 kg (245 lb) Elite had a claimed top speed of 135 km/h (84 mph). The styling followed that of the 175 Sport, but for 1959 both models received 18-inch wheels. The Elite soon gained a reputation as a first rate sporting motor-cycle and did much to establish the Ducati name in export markets. There were other 175 and 200 models for 1959, notably the Americano sharing the dual muffler and valanced mudguards. The 175 Americano was an extraordinary motorcycle with its

twin air horns, high 'cowboy' style handlebars, and chrome-studded seat. It was difficult to imagine that beneath that exterior lurked much the same engine and running gear as the 200 Elite. Another significant, if not totally successful, model was the 175 and 200 Motocross. Though this lasted only through to 1961, it was a prelude to a much more successful range, the Scrambler or SCR, later to become the backbone of the overhead camshaft line-up.

During this period a wide variety of specifications was offered with the range of 175s and 200s, much depending on the requirements of importers in specific countries. In the UK they even had different names, with the 125 Monza and Monza Super, 175 Silverstone and Silverstone Super, and 200 Super

Below: The 175 F3 was a
catalogued racer sharing little
with the production models. The
front brake was a magnesium
Amadoro. *Phil Aynsley*

Right: The first production
overhead camshaft 250 was the
four-speed Diana of 1962.
Roy Kidney

Sports and Elite being listed in 1960. For the
domestic Italian market there was also the touring
175TS and 175 'Due' Selle with an 11 bhp engine.

As the engine grew to 250 cc, the 175s and 200s
were phased out. The 125 engine eventually became
a 160, and by 1962 the 175 was discontinued. The
200 Elite soldiered on for a few more years, still
being offered until 1965, while in 1962 the 200GT
was created out of the new 250 Diana. Perceived as
an underpowered 250, this was a sales disaster, and
was dropped after only a year. The writing was on
the wall for the smaller-engined Ducatis, and the
success of the new 250 only reinforced this. The
public then, as now, wanted larger engines, with
more performance.

125/175/250 FORMULA 3

In 1958 the Formula 3 became Ducati's production
racer, superseding the Gran Sport that had been
available since 1955. If one were to make an analogy
with modern Ducatis, the Supermono would be the
closest equivalent to both the Gran Sport and the F3.

They were intended for the non-Grand Prix privateers
and were made in very limited numbers, being
assembled by racing mechanics. Also they were
extremely expensive and used unique components.
175 F3 owner Phil Schilling estimates that less than
100 of all types (125/175/250) were built over a five-
year period, perhaps some 50 of them being 175s.

Looking like racing versions of the 100 and 125
Sport, the F3 actually owed more to the Gran Sport
than the production bikes. Unlike the street bike, the
engine-cases were sand-cast rather than die-cast, and
internally the engine was completely different. From
the Gran Sport came the straight-cut primary and
bevel-gears, along with special camshaft, rockers, con-
rod, piston, clutch, and gearbox. Virtually nothing
was interchangeable with the street 125/175 Sport.
The frame was lighter, lower, and longer than the
standard model, and used different forks and shock
absorbers. The dimensions were such that neither the
petrol tank nor seat were interchangeable between the
two. However, by far the most startling differences on
the 175 and 250 were the brakes. They had the same
double-sided Amadoro front, and vented rear, brakes

that were used on the Bialbero and factory racers. These were so unusual that Phil Schilling always referred to his 175 F3 as the Ducati 'with the funny front brake'.

Interestingly, all the F3s came with complete street equipment that included a headlight, muffler, tail light, and number-plate holder, but the intention for the bike was clear. It was meant for the track. The 125 F3 featured the same engine specifications as the 125 Gran Sport (but with enclosed valve gear), and the 175 shared its 62 x 57.8 mm engine dimensions with the 175 Bialbero and 175 road bikes. The 175 F3 produced 16 bhp at 9,000 rpm, with a maximum of 9,800 rpm, and was able to achieve 100 mph (161 kph).

Given the specifications, one could assume that the 175 F3 had a spectacular racing career, but generally only factory-prepared bikes were successful. Franco Villa won the supporting Formula 3 race at the 1958 Italian GP (where Ducati had filled the first five places in the 125 Grand Prix), and Franco Farnè the Class 4 Lightweight race at Daytona in 1959. At the Barcelona 24-Hour race of 1960 eight 175s were entered, with victory going to Franco Villa and Amedco Balboni at an average speed of 59.25 mph (95.35 km/h). Most F3s were raced by privateers, but they were too expensive for many. The lightweight class eventually grew to 250, so the 175 became obsolete, and a limited number of 250 F3s were made during 1961. Pressure

from Ducati's export markets, particularly Berliner in the US, had led Taglioni to develop a 250 cc version of the 175 F3 in 1960. With a special 74 mm cast iron liner, the 250 F3 produced 32 bhp at 9,000 rpm, and Franco Villa was sent to contest a series of road races in the US. So successful was this racing effort that it established Ducati in the US as a manufacturer of reliable and competitive racing machines, and also paved the way for the release of a production 250.

By 1962, production of these beautiful and purposeful racing motorcycles was finished, but they remain as some of the best examples of Ducati's commitment to fine engineering and exquisite construction. There would be no more catalogued production racers, apart from a small number of 250 and 350 SCs Mach 1/Ss and the SCD in 1965, 1966 and 1967, until the 600TT2 of 1982.

250 MONZA, DIANA, AND SCR

Following on from the success of the prototype racing 250 F3, a 250 street bike was displayed in April 1961. This new motorcycle would form the basis of the overhead camshaft production range until the wide-case single of 1968, and was available in two versions, the touring Monza and more sporting Diana. The first Monza had high handlebars and the new engine shared

The British version of the 250
Diana was called the Daytona,
but was otherwise similar.

the same bore and stroke (74 x 57.8 mm) as the 250
F3. With a Dell'Orto UBF 24BS carburettor, and an 8:1
compression ratio, the claimed power was a pretty
un-realistic 22 bhp at 7,200 rpm. Weight was only 125
kg (276 lb), so the performance was more than
respectable for its day, and top speed was claimed to be
80 mph (129 km/h). The Diana (Daytona for the UK),
with clip-on handlebars, had a claimed power output of
24 bhp. Its weight, at 120 kg (265 lb), was slightly less
than the Monza, and top speed was in the region of
85 mph (137 km/h). There was also the option of a
larger, SS1 27A remote float-bowl carburettor for the
Diana. The styling for the 250 was completely new,
with a different petrol tank, seat, and side panels from
the 175s and 200s. The third 250 cc model to emerge
during 1962 was the 30 bhp 250 Motocross, the 250
SCR. Primarily intended for the US market, this was
based very closely on the earlier 200 Motocross.

With Ducati dubiously preoccupied throughout
1962 and 1963 with the new range of two-strokes, the
only new ohc model was the 250 Mark 3 Super Sport
for the US in mid-1963. This modified Diana was a

true production racer and offered the 30 bhp, 10:1
compression ratio engine, with the SS1 27A carburettor
and 40 watt flywheel magneto ignition, of the 250
SCR. Full racing equipment, including clip-ons, racing
guards and tyres, and a competition plate, were also
included. In April 1964 the Mark 3, Monza and
Motocross received a five-speed gearbox along with the
250GT (essentially a Diana with a Monza engine). A
few months later one of Ducati's all-time classics, the
250 Mach 1, was released.

250 MACH 1

There have been several occasions throughout Ducati's
history when one particular production model has
stood out like a beacon from the rest of the range, and
the Mach 1, first displayed in September 1964, was
undoubtedly one of these. Purely from a performance
point of view the Mach 1, based on the US 250 Mark 3
Super Sport, was outstanding, with its claim of a top
speed of 106 mph (170.6 km/h). In 1964 this placed
the Mach 1 firmly at the top of the 250 cc class, but it

Below: One of the all-time classic
Ducatis: the Mach 1.

wasn't a claim that was always substantiated. In February 1965, for instance, *Motor Cycling* could only manage a best of 83 mph (134 km/h), because the bike was too overgeared.

Of all the production street narrow-case singles, the Mach 1 was the most outstanding. It was the first top-of-the-line limited production street Ducati developed from a successful racer and offered the highest standard of performance for its day. Because of its significance, the Mach 1 justifies more detailed examination.

While Ducati had officially withdrawn from Grand Prix racing at the end of 1959, the factory continued to support various racing events that would help develop the road bike range. The most notable venue was that of Montjuich Park in Barcelona for the annual 24-Hour endurance race, and it has always been one of Ducati's

happiest hunting grounds. The first 250 had been entered in 1962, when Ricardo Fargas and Enzo Rippa took a prototype Mototrans 250 to victory, but a more significant win was in 1964 when Spaggiari and Mandolini rode a 284 cc factory prototype. With a bore of 79 mm, this was the first Ducati displacing more than 250 cc, and its success prompted the factory to release a limited number of SC (Sport Corsa) production racers. Like the F3, these had straight-cut primary and bevel gears, and special sand-cast crankcases. Those of the SC were stronger than earlier designs, and a forerunner of the subsequent wide crankcase of 1968. A 250 and 350 SC was offered in January 1965, and they had a twin spark-plug cylinder head producing 34 bhp at 8,500 rpm for the 250, and 39.5 bhp at 8,000 rpm for the 350. Because they had

been designed to be strong and reliable in endurance events, they weren't a particularly light or compact bike at 280 lb (127 kg) on a 56-inch (1,422 mm) wheelbase. The most notable feature of the SC was its double down-tube full-cradle frame and much wider engine mounts, both front and rear. The 1965 version used a Mach 1 style petrol tank, but was not particularly successful. The SC was also offered in 1966, when it had an Oldani front brake and a special fibre-glass racing petrol tank. It may not have been the ideal racer for the privateer, but its street derivative, the Mach 1, was definitely the bike that Ducati enthusiasts had been waiting for.

The Mach 1 engine had a higher compression piston, giving a 10:1 compression ratio, and had larger (40 and 36 mm) valves along with a grey coded camshaft. As with all the overhead camshaft singles, the valve springs were the hairpin type, and the valve timing figures were inlet opening 62° before top dead centre and closing 76° after bottom dead centre, and exhaust opening 70° before bottom dead centre and closing 48° after top dead centre. With an unfiltered Dell'Orto SS1 29D carburettor, the claimed power was 27.6 bhp at 8,500 rpm. The five-speed gearbox was operated by a rear-set rocking gearchange pedal, and while clip-on handlebars were specified, there was also the bizarre option of a Mach 1 with rear-set foot controls and high, touring-style handlebars.

Despite the output of the alternator being increased to 60 watts (from 40) for the five-speed 250s, the electrics remained a cause for concern, with the six-volt 25W headlight particularly poor. But Marzocchi suspension front and rear, a light weight of 116 kg (256 lb), and a short wheelbase of 1,350 mm (53.15 inches), ensured that the Mach 1 had the right ingredients for a top 250 cc sporting streetbike in the style of the 500 cc BSA DBD34 Clubmans Gold Star and Velocette Thruxton. Brakes were the 180 x 35 mm front and 160 x 30 mm rear drums fitted to the rest of the range, as were the 18-inch wheels with steel rims, but the red and silver Mach 1 was the only one with a red frame. It was also noted for a wildly optimistic 150 mph (241 km/h) Veglia speedometer.

For the US market the 250 Mark 3 continued to be the top performance model as it had been during 1963 and 1964, but for 1965 it was very much a renamed Mach 1 (with magneto ignition). The factory even claimed a higher top speed of 177 km/h (110 mph) for the Mark 3, which also came equipped with a

supplementary 100 mm white-faced Veglia tachometer and a racing plate over the headlight. The weight for the Mark 3 of 1965 was slightly less than the Mach 1 too, at 112 kg (247 lb). *Cycle World*, testing a Mark 3 in August 1965, achieved a top speed of 97 mph (156 km/h).

The Mach 1 continued in production until 1966, as did the Mark 3, now with normal foot-rests rather than rear-sets. The Mach 1 was discontinued in 1967, leaving only the Mark 3, but with battery and coil ignition rather than the flywheel magneto. However, even with the new wide-case replacement imminent, the Mach 1 (and narrow-case Mark 3) continued to be the favoured choice amongst privateer racers because they were so much lighter, and the problems of a fragile kickstart mechanism less significant. In 1969, Alistair Rogers on a Mach 1 racer gave Ducati its first TT victory – the 250 at the Isle of Man – at an average speed of 83.79 mph (134.84 km/h).

160/250 MONZA, 250GT, 250 SCR, 350 SEBRING

The importance of the US market for Ducati really became evident from 1964 with the release of a number of basically non-sporting models. The 160 Monza Junior was created out of the earlier 125 by increasing the bore to 61 mm, while retaining the 52 mm stroke, to achieve 156 cc. With an 8.2:1 compression ratio and a Dell'Orto UB 22BS carburettor, this engine was placed in the same frame as the 250 Monza, where it looked too small and out of place. The 160 also received 16-inch wheels front and rear, and there was still only a four-speed gearbox. The 106 kg (234 lb) machine was only able to reach a top speed of 102 km/h (63 mph). Most commentators couldn't understand the logic of putting a smaller engine in a 250, but Ducati kept making the 160 Monza Junior until 1966; then, in 1967, with US demand at an end, 1,800 were dumped on the UK market as part of a consignment of 3,400 motorcycles purchased by Scottish entrepreneur Bill Hannah. They were still being sold at a discount price in 1972.

The styling was altered for 1965 with a new square petrol tank, side covers and seat, and there was a similar third, and final, edition in 1966, now with a square headlight surround. Otherwise the 160

The 250 Motocross was produced primarily for the US market. *Roy Kidney*

remained unchanged throughout its production and was definitely not one of Ducati's triumphs.

The 250 Monza mirrored the 160, but for some reason the squarish styling changes happened a year later. So the five-speed 250 Monza appeared in 1964 looking identical to the earlier four-speed model, and continued unchanged through 1965. Engine specifications were the same as the first version, and for 1966 the 250 Monza shared its styling with the 160 Monza Junior.

Fitting in between the Monza and Mark 3, the 250GT was essentially a Mark 3 with the detuned Monza engine (along with battery and coil ignition), and was only available for 1964 and 1965. The final model in this range of rather mundane touring singles was the 350 Sebring. Like so many Ducati engines, the largest narrow-case single, the 350, had its origins on the race track. Franco Farnè had taken a 350 Mach 1/S racer to victory in the 350 class (and tenth overall) at an international race run in conjunction with the Sebring 12-Hour car race, in central Florida, in April 1965. Hardly a high profile event, it was, however, considered sufficiently prestigious to name the new 350 the Sebring.

Unfortunately, the production version shared little with the racer, and was in reality a Monza with a larger engine. By boring and stroking the 250 to the almost square dimensions of 76 x 75 mm, 340.327 cc was obtained. With an 8.5:1 compression ratio, and the Dell'Orto UBF 24BS carburettor of the 250 Monza, the 123 kg (271 lb) Sebring was a particularly sluggish performer with a top speed of only 125 km/h (78 mph). There were two versions for 1965, the US model almost identical to the 250 Monza, and the European model mirroring the 250GT. For 1966 the Sebring had the square styling of the 160 and 250 Monzas of that year, and, with no change in engine specification, the claimed top speed had amazingly risen to 142 km/h (88 mph).

Throughout the continuing changes to the range over this period, the 250 Motocross (SCR) remained in production, largely in the same form as it had appeared in 1962 but now with the five-speed gearbox. With a more highly tuned engine than the Monza, the Motocross had a 9.2:1 compression ratio, a Dell'Orto SS1 27A carburettor with air cleaner, and a totally open exhaust system. For 1965 there were 19-inch wheels front and rear, and the weight was 109 kg (240 lb). The 1966 version had a different headlight,

an 18-inch rear wheel, a battery to power the lights, and the weight was up to 120 kg (264.5 lb).

By 1968 the entire range of narrow-crankcase models had been superseded by the new wide-crankcase type, even though unsold stocks continued to be available long after production had finished. There had been too much emphasis placed on the mundane touring models, and problems with reliability and finish did little to endear these to the motorcycle-buying public. The only lines to continue as a wide-case were to be the 250 Monza, the Mark 3, and the Scrambler.

Throughout the 1950s and into
the 1960s, pushrod singles like
the 1958 98TS were offered
alongside the overhead camshaft
models.

4 ODDBALLS

While today the name of Ducati motorcycles is associated with the production of some of the best-ever sporting and racing motorcycles, throughout its history the company has produced a surprising variety of unmemorable products. Most of these lesser models were produced during the 1960s, being the more mundane overhead camshaft bevel-gear singles outlined in the previous chapter, and an even less noteworthy range of entry level motorcycles. These outnumbered the entire line up of ohc bikes, both in production and model range. Some had two-stroke engines, while others had four-stroke engines with pushrod-operated valves. The two-strokes were born in 1958, finally dying in 1977 with the 125 Six Days, while the pushrod singles finished in 1968. As part of a period of diversification of Ducati products that included outboard motors, lawn-mowers, and even the distribution of British Triumph cars, they were the result of poor management decisions. As would happen in the future, Taglioni refused to be involved with most of these projects, and he was ultimately proved right.

PUSHROD SINGLES

Until the advent of the Gran Sport in 1955, Ducati's road motorcycles were built around a range of pushrod overhead valve singles, which formed the basis of production until 1957, when the first overhead camshaft street bikes were released. Even after this, the overhead valve models continued to be sold in a range of capacities, and in 1957 the 85 Turismo and 85 Sport joined the 65, 98, and several 125s. At the request of Berliner in the US, the 98 cc Bronco appeared in 1959, and by 1960 the ohv model range was the 85T and S, 98 Bronco, Cavallino and TS, and 125 Aurea. The Aurea was an unusual model in that it used the twin cradle frame of the 1956 125TV, with the more sporting headlight and petrol tank of the 125 cc overhead camshaft bikes. The overhead valve motorcycles were definitely budget Ducatis, as the 125 Aurea, despite looking like a 125 Sport, only developed 6.5 bhp at 6,500 rpm from its 55.2 x 52 mm engine. The compression ratio was 6.8:1, and an 18 mm Dell'Orto carburettor was used. Performance didn't match that of the contemporary overhead camshaft 125TS with its 10 bhp.

The final pushrod single was the
125 Cadet/4 of 1967.
Phil Aynsley

TWO-STROKES

In an endeavour to expand their customer base for motorcycles, Ducati decided in 1961 to market a range of moped and lightweight two-stroke motorcycles, initially in 50 cc but later joined by an 80 cc sports model. There had been a two-stroke 48 Sport offered briefly during 1958, and the new engine was based on this design. The 50 cc range of five models started with the single speed 48 cc Brisk, and culminated in the three speed 48 cc Sport. The Brisk/1 (single speed) certainly didn't live up to its name, and was a moped of very modest specification and performance. The single cylinder 38 x 42 mm two-stroke displaced 47.633 cc, and with a 7:1 compression ratio produced 1.34 bhp at 4,200 rpm. Weighing only 45 kg (99 lb), the top speed was a mere 40 km/h (25 mph). Subsequent versions had slightly more power (1.5 bhp) and went a claimed 50 km/h (31 mph). The frame was of pressed steel, but, unusually for a moped, the Brisk had telescopic forks and a swing-arm with dual shock absorbers.

Using the same 1.5 bhp engine, but with a three-speed gearbox and dual seat, was the Piuma 48 Export. For the British market the Piuma was called the Puma, and released in 1962 with a single seat. The 48 cc Sport models were also based around the same power unit, but with a 9.5:1 compression ratio, and a larger Dell'Orto UA15S carburettor without an air filter, power was increased to 4.2 bhp at 8,600 rpm. Using a double cradle tubular-steel frame, the Sport also looked like a smaller version of the then current 125/175/200 overhead camshaft model, right down to the shape of the petrol tank and the red and gold paintwork. The basic Italian market Sport 48 was styled as the 125 Sport, with clip-on handlebars, a dual seat, and the speedometer in the front headlight. It was a real motorcycle in miniature, but some had pedals, rather than a kickstart, for starting, which looked out of place. The performance of this 54 kg (119 lb) machine was up considerably on the regular Brisk or Piuma, with the top speed a claimed 80 kph (50 mph).

Other markets received slightly different versions. There was the Sport 48 Export, identical but for a fuel tank styled along the lines of the 200 Elite, and the Sport 48 USA (called the Falcon 50) that had the Italian market version's petrol tank, but higher handlebars and a single seat. According to the factory brochures, all models had a 'voluminous toolbox'.

The 98 Bronco and 98TS used the 48 x 52 mm 98 cc engine that had first appeared in 1952. With a compression ratio of 7:1, they made 6 bhp at 6,800 rpm. Both these, and the 125 Aurea, had a four-speed gearbox, and the TS boasted a more sporting riding position. The 98s weighed 87 kg (192 lb) and the top speed for the TS was about 53 mph (85 km/h).

The Bronco continued to be produced in 125 cc form and during 1964 it received a slightly restyled 125 cc engine, with square finning, but still with the engine specifications of the 125 Aurea. Then in 1966 a new 125 cc overhead valve engine was designed, with dimensions of 53 x 55 mm. This 121.3 cc engine was installed in a model known as the 125 Cadet/4 Lusso (the 4 denoted four speeds, while lusso means 'luxury'). There was a more powerful engine (with 8.4:1 compression), able to propel the 72 kg (159 lb) Cadet to a top speed of 95 km/h (59 mph). By 1967 the Cadet/4 was joined by the Cadet/4 Scrambler, with a high-rise exhaust system and a 16-inch rear wheel. Very few were made, and production didn't continue beyond 1968.

So ended the pushrod single that had started out 15 years earlier and had been entirely eclipsed by Taglioni's Gran Sport and its successors. As with the complete range of two-strokes, these final pushrod 125s weren't missed. They have become categorized with other failures, the later parallel twins, the Giugiaro 860, and the Weber carburetted Pantahs.

Below: Although powered by an unremarkable 50 cc two-stroke, the 1967 50 SL/1 was styled like a racer and included twin fuel filler caps.

The Setter 80 (Super Falcon 80 in the US) appeared at the same time as the 48 and used a similar two-stroke engine displacing 79.807 cc. The bore and stroke were 47 x 46 mm, and with a 7.1:1 compression ratio power was 4.25 bhp at 7,200 rpm. The weight was 62 kg (137 lb), and the top speed 75 km/h (47 mph), even less than that of the 48 Sport. Needless to say, the Setter 80 wasn't a spectacular success and was discontinued during 1964. In its place was a new range built around a 94 cc engine.

Several new models joined the Brisk 48/1, Piuma 48 (three-speed), and 48 Sport (now with a fan-cooled engine). Because of Italian laws prohibiting 50 cc motorcycles to exceed 1.5 bhp and 40 km/h (25 mph), the 48SL was created using a fan-cooled version of the Brisk engine (with only 1.3 bhp at 4,300 rpm), mounted in the full cradle frame of the 48 Sport. The same motorcycle, with the new 94 cc engine in place of the 48 cc unit, became the 100 Cadet and would last, with minor changes, until 1968. The fan-cooled 94 cc engine had a bore and stroke of 51 x 46 mm, and produced 6 bhp at 7,000 rpm.

In addition to the Cadet there was also the 100 Mountaineer and two scooters, the 48 and 100 Brio.

The 100 Mountaineer was similar to the Cadet, but for a high-level exhaust, rear rack, and 16-inch wheels, while the Brio was a genuine scooter in the Vespa and Lambretta mould. Harking back to the disaster of the Cruiser, the equally uninspired Brio used the three-speed engine of the Piuma and Cadet.

Small changes occurred for the 1966 season, most noticeably with the creation of the Piuma Sport 50, which had a pressed-steel frame and used the three-speed 4.2 bhp engine of the 48 Sport. The styling was similar to that of the larger sporting Ducatis, but without the performance to match. The 49 kg (108 lb) machine had a top speed of 80 kph (50 mph). The 48SL was uprated to the 50SL. No longer with fan-cooling, and with a larger 38.8 mm bore, capacity was now 49.66 cc, and it had a four-speed gearbox. The compression ratio was 9.5:1, and the styling was similar except for the exhaust now being on the right side. Both the 100 Cadet and Mountaineer retained the fan-cooled engine, but with a foot-operated four-speed gearbox rather than the previous hand change.

While the 94 cc Brio continued into 1967 largely unaltered except for a name-change to 100/25, it still had the fan-cooled engine. The rest of the range came

The 1968 100 Mountaineer used an air-cooled cylinder head. *Phil Aynsley*

Below: The 100 Cadet, also of 1968, was similar to the Mountaineer. *Phil Aynsley*

Right: One of the last Ducati two-strokes: the 125 Regolarità. *Phil Aynsley*

5 DESMODROMICS REBORN

AND THE WIDE-CASE SINGLES

The prototype wide-case Ducati single was displayed at the Cologne Show in September 1967. This revised engine would not only improve on some of the weaknesses of the earlier design, but also allow Ing. Fabio Taglioni to make his dream a reality: the first production engine with desmodromic valve gear. Additionally, the new engine allowed for the capacity to be eventually increased beyond that of the 350 cc of the previous narrow-case, to 436 cc.

While Franco Farnè had debuted a desmodromic 250 at the Italian season opener at Modena on 20 March 1966, this bike was based on the 250 SC. It had used crankcases of a new design, with wider front and rear frame mounts, and would form the basis for future designs. There was then a full year of development, during which time Cere and Giovanardi won the 250 cc class at the FIM *Coupe d'Endurance* Imola 6-Hour race on a factory bike, but it wasn't until 1967 that the desmo single was raced again, now with an even stronger, wide-crankcase engine. Initially 350 cc, the new desmo was raced by Gilberto Parlotti and Roberto Gallina at Modena in March 1967. Soon a 250 version joined the 350, and Farnè took it to Daytona to ride in the Expert Lightweight event, but was not allowed to start as the desmodromic single was deemed to be not derived from a road-going model. These 250 and 350 desmodromic bikes were raced in several Italian early season events on street circuits with a reasonable amount of success. The 74 x 57.8 mm 250, with its 36 mm Dell'Orto carburettor, produced 35 bhp at 11,500 rpm, and the 76 x 75 mm 350, with a 40 mm Dell'Orto carburettor, 45 bhp at 10,500 rpm. In 1968, now with Bruno Spaggiari riding, the 250 and 350 desmos achieved more encouraging results, notably fifth in the Italian 350 Grand Prix, but still no outright victories. Making its debut at Rimini in March 1968 was the first 450, actually 436 cc, sharing the dry clutch, twin-plug ignition and straight cut primary and bevel gears with the smaller versions. With a 42 mm Dell'Orto carburettor, power was up to 50 bhp at 9,000 rpm.

In 1969 Gallina, Parlotti, and Spaggiari again rode the 250 and 350, with the best results being Spaggiari's two second-place finishes behind Pasolini's Benelli four at Modena and Cesenatico. While the racing results

Right: The famous glass-sided Ducati transporter with a selection of scramblers and outboard motors, 1971. *Ducati Motor*

Below: The 450 Scrambler appeared in 1969, and was extremely popular.

may not have been spectacular, they were a very useful proving ground for developing the range of street desmos. A similar scenario existed through 1970, but instead of being special factory-prepared engines, Spaggiari's 450 and Parlotti's 250 and 350 derived from the new range of road machines, and had the regular wet-clutch of these bikes. The 450 still featured twin-plug ignition, larger valves, 42 mm Dell'Orto carburettor, and a 10:1 compression ratio, but used die-cast rather than sand-cast engine-cases. It also had a reinforced swing-arm and a 210 mm Fontana front brake and weighed 264 lb (120 kg). They were entered under Franco Farnè's semi-official team quaintly called Scuderia Speedy Gonzales. Once again, while results were encouraging, particularly at Rimini, Modena, and Riccione, the new singles were no match for the multi-cylindered MVs, Benellis, Lintos, and Patons. For this reason the factory stopped development of the desmo single to concentrate on the 500 V-twin. Ironically, it was the privateers who benefited from all the factory development on the desmo racer, and Ducati singles were, and still continue to be, highly successful in the

various classes for which they are eligible. The culmination of this was Charles Mortimer's win in the 1970 250 Production TT at the Isle of Man aboard the Vic Camp Mark 3 Desmo. Here he won at an average speed of 84.87 mph (136.6 km/h).

By 1968, production of the new series of singles was underway. The wide crankcase increased the capacity of the sump to 2.5 litres (0.55 imperial gallons), and there were improved kickstart gears, a problem with five-speed narrow-case engines. There was also a larger crankpin, at 27 mm, and the drive-side main bearing enlarged to 30 x 72 x 19 mm. Because of the wider rear engine mounts and a twin down-tube rear frame section, the frame was stronger at the rear, but this was at the cost of an increase in weight.

125/250/350/450 SCRAMBLER

The first production versions of the wide-case engine appeared in early 1968 as the 350 cc Scrambler, and in

the US as the 350 Sport Scrambler. This was followed shortly afterwards by the 250 Scrambler. The Scrambler was to become the most popular of all the wide-case singles, particularly in Italy. It offered full street equipment, with no pretensions for off-road competition as had been evident in the prototype 350 Scrambler of 1967, and the 250, 350, and even the later 450 versions, were essentially similar.

This 350 cc wide-case engine shared the same dimensions of 76 x 75 mm with the 350 Sebring and 350 SC racer, and had a 10:1 compression ratio and a high performance camshaft (coded white/green). This had valve timing figures of inlet opening 70° before top dead centre and closing 84° after bottom dead centre, and the exhaust valve opening 80° before bottom dead centre and closing 64° after top dead centre. They certainly required the decompression lever operated from the left handlebar. The 250 had a 9.2:1 compression ratio and no compression release. Using 35 mm Marzocchi forks, the 1968 versions of the 250 and 350SCR had their Veglia speedometer mounted in the Aprilia headlight. They came with 315 mm Marzocchi shock absorbers, later replaced by 310 mm items, with the option of stiffer suspension available. Very soon after they were released they were restyled, with a new petrol tank and seat design that would carry through until 1974. The 350 then became the 350SSS (or Street Scrambler Sport) for the US market.

In 1969 the 450 (actually 435.7 cc) became available, and featured a new crankcase, cylinder, and cylinder head castings to accommodate the 86 x 75 mm dimensions. The reason why a full 500 wasn't created was that the 75 mm stroke was the largest that could

be used for the throw of the crankshaft to miss the gearbox pinions. To make the engine larger would have required a redesign and retool. Interestingly enough, even though the 450 shared the 75 mm stroke with the 350, the 450 used a con-rod with an eye-to-eye length of 140 mm, rather than the 136 mm con-rod that was used by both the 250 and 350. Certainly with a rod length to stroke ratio of 1.81:1, the shorter rod was not ideal for the longer stroke 350, accentuating piston acceleration.

For the 450 there was also extra gusseting along the top frame tube, exactly like Spaggiari's 1968 450 racer, and a wider chain and sprockets, allowing the use of a 5/16 x 3/8 inch final drive chain. With a 9.3:1 compression ratio, and white coded camshafts of the 250SCR, the 450SCR (and identical Mark 3) produced a moderate 27 bhp at 6,500 rpm. The valve timing was inlet opening 27° before top dead centre, closing 75° after bottom dead centre, and exhaust opening 60° before bottom dead centre, and closing 32° after top dead centre. In 1969 the US model of the 450 Scrambler was marketed by Berliner as the Jupiter. With the 450 came slightly longer (515 mm) Marzocchi forks, and these were also fitted to subsequent 250 and 350SCRs.

All the carburettors were changed during 1969, with the Dell'Orto SS1 29D being replaced by a new square-slide VHB. The 250 received a smaller VHB 26AD (from 27 mm), and the 350 and 450, a VHB 29AD. This required a new air filter and the traditional rounded muffler became the cut-off Silentium type, either long or short. At the start of 1970 the crankpin diameter was increased to 30 mm, and the Scramblers then remained unchanged until 1973, when they became very similar to the range of Mark 3 roadsters. They now had Borrani 19-inch and 18-inch alloy wheel-rims, and the 350 and 450SCR the same double-sided front brake, headlight, and instruments as the Mark 3. They also featured Marzocchi forks with exposed staunchions and new side-covers. The 250 still had the single brake and fork gaiters (though US versions differed), and all now went back to using the older rounded muffler. In 1973 they received the Ducati Elettrotecnica electronic ignition, and finally a larger, 32 mm diameter crankpin in 1974.

For a short while during 1971 a 125SCR was actually built in Bologna with a narrow-case Spanish Mototrans five-speed engine, complete with Spanish Amal carburettor. This wasn't a success and was soon discontinued, but the final 250 Scramblers of 1974 also used Spanish-built engines.

250/350/450 MARK 3 AND MARK 3 DESMO

Soon after the 350 and 250 Scramblers appeared with the new wide-crankcase engine in 1968, so did the Mark 3 and 250 Monza. The Monza was of similar specification and styling to the unremarkable narrow-case version, but the Mark 3 was now quite distinctively styled with a twin filler petrol tank (like the two-stroke 50 SL/1). The 250 engine remained in the same state of tune as it had in the Mach 1, with the same grey-coded camshaft, 10:1 compression ratio, and Dell'Orto SS1 29D carburettor, while the 350 Mark 3 had the even more highly tuned (white/green camshaft) 350 engine from the 350SCR.

For the wide-case Mark 3s the weight was up from the earlier models, at 128 kg (282 lb), so the 250 didn't perform as strongly. Only 143 km/h (89 mph) was claimed for the 250, a far cry from the Mach 1 and Mark 3 of 1965–67. While the 350 Mark 3 was considered the performance model with its top speed of 170 km/h (106 mph), waiting in the wings to enhance Ducati's reputation was Taglioni's engineering *tour de force*, desmodromic valve gear.

During 1968, Fabio Taglioni's dream was fulfilled: Ducati produced the first production motorcycle engine with desmodromically-operated valve gear. Unlike the 125 Grand Prix desmos with their three camshafts, only one was used, incorporating both opening and

closing lobes, and hairpin valve springs were retained to assist in starting. These were from the 160 Monza Junior, and lighter than standard, but were still considerably stronger than the small closing springs fitted to the later desmo twins. Apart from the cylinder head the engines were identical, and there really wasn't much of a performance differential between the two models in standard trim. The desmo engine was fitted to the 250 and 350 Mark 3, creating two new models, the 250 Mark 3 Desmo, and the 350 Mark 3 Desmo. These were virtually indistinguishable from the regular Mark 3 apart from a 'D' on the side-panels and different colours.

All the Desmos used the same white and blue coded camshaft with the inlet valve opening 70° before top dead centre, closing 82° after bottom dead centre, and the exhaust valve opening 80° before bottom dead centre and closing 65° after top dead centre. The performance was up on the Mark 3, with 150 km/h (93 mph) claimed for the 250D, or 160 km/h (99 mph) with megaphone exhaust. The 350D became the fastest production Ducati single offered with its top speed of 180 km/h (112 mph) with megaphone exhaust, but with the standard silencer the maximum speed was 165 km/h (103 mph). Several options were available for the Desmo, these being a high, touring-style handlebar, or a racing uprating kit containing a racing camshaft, a range of main jets, a megaphone, and a full racing fairing. The 1968 models, with their twin filler petrol tanks, Dell'Orto SS1 carburettors, and auxiliary white-faced Veglia tachometer, were amongst the finest Ducati singles, and each bike was provided with a test certificate. All they needed were rear-set footpegs to go with the clip-on handlebars.

With the release of the new 450 engine in the Scrambler in 1969, it wasn't long before there was also a 450 Mark 3 and 450 Mark 3 Desmo. The 450 Desmo used the same camshaft as the other Desmos, and the lower, 9.3:1 compression ratio of the 450 SCR. All the 450s had the new type of Dell'Orto VHB 29 square-slide carburettor, a single filler petrol tank, and the cut-off Silentium muffler, and soon these were shared with the 250 and 350 Mark 3 Desmo. The 450 also had an individual speedometer and tachometer, rather than the headlight-mounted speedo and white-faced Veglia, and these too would become standardized throughout the range of Mark 3s and SCRs during 1970. For the US, Mark 3s and Desmos were fitted with a Scrambler petrol tank and the higher

police forces. The T and TS (differentiated only by their camshaft) had a shorter and rounder petrol tank, valanced mudguard, and panniers. Rather heavy at 160 kg (353 lb), the performance wasn't too exciting either, with 140 km/h (87 mph) claimed for the TS and only 128 km/h (80 mph) for the T. The only redeeming feature of the T and TS was in the use of a 12-volt electrical system, and they were discontinued during 1973.

One rather unusual model of 1974 was a 239 cc Mark 3 built specifically for the French market to circumvent taxes on motorcycles over 240 cc. With a 72.5 mm piston, these 239s also used a Dell'Orto PHF 30 mm carburettor, and had regular coil valve springs replacing the hairpin type, along with 12-volt electrics. The 239 also received the reinforced 450 frame, and in many ways was the most developed of the overhead camshaft singles.

250/350/450 DESMO 1971–74

The Mark 3 Desmo became an even more sporting motorcycle with the creation of a new Desmo single for 1971 and 1972. This was the model nicknamed 'The

Silver Shotgun' by the Australian magazine *Two Wheels* in their long-term test of a 450 in January 1974. While the 250, 350, and 450 cc desmodromic engines were unchanged (apart from larger timing side main bearings), the rest of the motorcycle was considerably updated. Most obvious was the metalflake silver paint scheme for the fibreglass petrol tank, side covers and solo seat, but the Desmo was now a genuine cafe racer with rear-set footpegs to complement the clip-on handlebars.

Most of the improvements came with the running gear. Borrani 18-inch alloy wheel-rims replaced the previous steel type, and the front brake became a Grimeca double-sided single leading shoe instead of the rather weak single leading shoe that had been fitted from 1957. The forks were considerably uprated from the previous spindly 31.5 mm units, with a new type of 35 mm Marzocchi fork with exposed staunchions. As expected, the performance was similar to that of the earlier Mark 3 Desmos. *Motociclismo* managed a maximum speed of 158.632 km/h (98.57 mph) from their totally standard 450 Desmo test bike in 1972.

For some reason the silver Desmos have become an endangered species and not too many are to be seen

Another classic: the 450 desmo of 1971, known as the 'Silver Shotgun'.

Below: For 1973, the desmo single was restyled along the lines of the 750 Sport.

these days. This is probably because they were mainly sold on the local market, and is a pity because I prefer these to the later yellow type. They had a more pleasing Aprilia headlight (with the speedometer mounted in the shell), the white-faced racing Veglia tachometer on its individual bracket, and more attractive levers and controls. They still used contact breaker and coil

ignition, the smaller tail-light of the 750GT and 750 Sport, and I find the styling of the seat more in keeping with the overall design.

The Desmo single was given to ex-racer Leopoldo Tartarini (of Italjet) for a slight restyle for 1973. Thus appeared the distinctive yellow colour scheme, to match the 750 Sport, along with a new seat incorporating the tail-light. This final version featured electronic ignition, by either Ducati Elettrotecnica or Spanish Motoplat, and the larger 32 mm crankpin. They also received a revised instrument panel with Smiths instruments, and a new style of CEV headlight. With the new colour scheme came replacement of the fibreglass petrol tank by one in steel.

In all other respects the specification was identical to that of 1971–72, but in 1974 Ceriani 35 mm forks, with a 280 mm Brembo disc and 08 caliper, replaced the Marzocchis and their Grimeca double-sided single leading shoe drum brake. These forks were not fitted to any other models in the Ducati range and were unique to the Desmo single. Because of the use of the front disc brake and 750 style hub, the 18-inch WM2 Borrani had 40 spokes rather than the 36 of the drum-braked versions, and the fibreglass front mudguard was bolted, rather than clamped, to the fork legs. New con-rods

Below: A few 750GTs were fitted
with an electric start and by 1973
the fuel tank and side covers
were steel rather than glass-fibre.
Nico Georgeoglou

slipping. It wasn't long before the factory racing bikes were using a dry multi-plate clutch, but it would be over ten years before these made it to the production line.

With two tower shafts of bevel gears driving the single overhead camshaft in each cylinder head from a set of bevel-gears originating at the crankshaft, and primary drive by helical gear, there wasn't a chain in the engine (at least until the advent of an electric start version first displayed early in 1972). All bearings were ball or roller and every shaft, be it crank, gearbox or bevel, was shimmed individually for the correct end float or backlash. This was truly an engine from a different era, designed without any concession to

production economics. It was so labour-intensive to assemble (particularly the bevel-gears, which had to be set up individually from the crankshaft) that it took up to eight hours to assemble one engine at the factory and two days for a racing one. Consequently it wasn't possible to produce many, and over the four-year production period (1971–74) only 6,159 were made, around 1,500 a year including 750 Sports and 750SSs. Even contemporary Italian manufacturers were moving towards less expensive engines in the early 1970s. Moto Guzzi was building a pushrod twin and the Laverdas had chain primary drives and cam chains like British bikes and Hondas. The Ducati singles and twins, and the MV fours, were really the only bikes left

with their roots in the great racing designs of the 1950s. However, a beautiful engine is worthless if placed in a mediocre chassis, and this is where Ducati came up trumps. The Seeley-inspired frame using the solid sand-cast engine as a stressed member, though not light, was strong, and utilized mainly straight tubes. Steering was slow due to the 29° fork rake and the 60.2-inch (1,530 mm) wheelbase, but stability was unquestioned. The wheelbase length, which resulted from the long engine, was considerably greater than that of the contemporary 500GP Twin racer. In a time when most large bikes used forks with tiny diameter staunchions and small diameter plastic swing-arm bushes, the 750GT was very advanced with its 38 mm staunchions and large bronze bushes. Not only that, but Taglioni had designed the bike with his typical commitment to balance and symmetry. The crankshaft was placed exactly mid-way between the axles and on the same line, and high quality components such as Borrani alloy rims were fitted to reduce unsprung weight.

All these factors contributed to many commentators at the time claiming that no bike in the world handled better than the 750GT. The testers at *Cycle* magazine in the USA were particularly enthusiastic about the Ducati 750. To quote from their road test in October 1972: 'When the right-side peg nicks down in an 80 mph sweeper and the bike never bobbles … you know that a motorcyclist designed this machine, and he got it right'. Admittedly, the quality of certain components, such as the Aprilia switchgear and the general standard of chroming, was questionable. However, features like the straight pull spokes laced to strong cast hubs, Tommaselli throttle, and stainless steel guards, showed that Ducati had different priorities when it came to building bikes.

It may have handled better than any other bike, but to those brought up on British motorcycles it looked long and weird. By the standards of the day the single opposed piston Lockheed front brake was excellent (most calipers at that time were floating piston types), but even though weight was moderate at 185 kg (408 lb), it was down on power compared to a Norton Commando or Triumph Trident. With heavy 8.5:1 pistons, and tiny 30 mm Amal carburettors (made in Spain) with extremely restrictive air cleaners, the bike was slow. A rider was hard-pressed to coax more than 180 km/h (112 mph) out of it, even though the factory claimed 200 km/h (124 mph). Maximum power was quoted as 55 bhp, and maximum revs as 7,800 rpm.

With a dealer network that was very poor outside Italy, the bike proved a slow seller until its victory at Imola in April 1972. As Ing. Fabio Taglioni observed in 1974: 'When we won at Imola we won the market too'.

The GT, rather than the singles, became the mainstay of the production line-up, but it underwent numerous changes during its manufacture. The very first few examples built in 1971 featured a twin leading shoe rear brake. Those up to engine number 404 had engine-cases with a bolt through the sump (this was also to mount the forward-set foot-rests of the first prototype). The very earliest bikes also had a clutch cover without an inspection plate, and the engine-cases were sand-cast. The first 500 bikes were considered pre-production. In 1972, new paint schemes appeared, the silver frame and metalflake paint giving way to a black frame and red or black fibreglass petrol tanks. Veglia instruments replaced the Smiths. There were new seats, and the rear tail-light from the singles.

Problems with the kickstart lever cracking the engine cover led to the installation of a longer kickstart shaft, and new lever after engine number 1500. By now, with Berliner serious about distributing the bikes, US versions had appeared, slightly different to their European cousins. Larger tail-lights and higher, wider handlebars were the most notable alterations.

Some commentators have made the observation that the 750GT appeared with a random selection of equipment from 1974, but this is incorrect. All bikes can be dated from the range of brakes or suspension fitted, bearing in mind that at Ducati batches of engines are always made separately to the bikes, and engine and frame numbers do not coincide. There was nothing random about the way the bikes were assembled, though the shipment of bikes from Italy may have been less methodical. By mid-1973 the glass-fibre fuel tank had been replaced by a steel one, with a new colour scheme, and the Lockheed front disc and master cylinder had given way to an Italian Scarab that was essentially a Lockheed copy.

Earlier, the Smiths instruments had been replaced by Veglia, the tachometer in particular becoming a rather unreliable electronic type. I can remember that the 750GT I bought in 1973 had three of these replaced under warranty. The tacho drive on the first series had been similar to the singles, with a floating drive mounted on the front camshaft end cover, and was rather prone to leaking oil. In addition new camshafts were fitted at this time, with the same opening and

The final year for the 750GT was 1974, and these appeared with a centre-axle fork. All the carburettors this year were Dell'Orto.

closing specifications but a new profile, and the new type of Dell'Orto PHF 30 AD and AS carburettor of the type fitted to the 750 Sport. Though these didn't help the bike develop any more horsepower, they certainly aided starting, and they didn't leak fuel as much as the Amals. The stainless guards now made way for a painted steel variety.

At this point – late 1973 – about 2,500 bikes had been built (GTs and Sports), and they all featured the leading axle Marzocchis, which were painted black for the European market but rendered as polished alloy for the USA. Some of these had an electric start mounted over the clutch cover, but they were unusual and it is rare to see one today. The next stage in production demonstrated the greatest variety, which was caused by variability in supply from Ducati's sources of proprietary components.

In the search for a shorter wheelbase, the racing bikes had moved away from the leading axle forks during 1973, and this filtered through to the production line. By early 1974 some GTs appeared with 38 mm centre-axle Cerianis and a single Brembo 280 mm cast iron front disc and forward-mounted 08 caliper. They still had the Borrani wheel-rims, and had

reverted to a cable-driven Veglia tachometer with the drive housed in a one-piece cover from the front camshaft. As supply from Ceriani became difficult, Marzocchi also produced a centre-axle fork, but with a Scarab brake caliper mounting for the 278 mm iron disc. These Marzocchis had modified top triple clamps to provide the same trail as the centre-axle models, and steel rims rather than the Borranis. Marzocchi also produced a centre-axle fork with a forward-mounted Brembo 08 caliper, but fewer GTs had this arrangement.

By now not only had the Borrani rims disappeared, but quieter Lafranconi mufflers had replaced the loud, but lovely, Contis. The valve adjustment followed the practice established by 860 of being by screw and locknut, rather than shim. All engines from mid-1974 had the higher crowned rocker covers, whether they were GT, Sport, or SS, irrespective of their method of valve adjustment. Also, the revised primary ratio of the 1974 750 Super Sport was standardized throughout the range. With 32 teeth on the crankshaft and 70 on the clutch drum, the ratio was now 2.187:1, and helped alleviate problems of clutch slip. This ratio was retained until the advent of the Mille in 1985.

The final examples shared much in the way of ancillary components with the 860 that was in production simultaneously. They had the revised CEV switch-gear and throttle, with the ignition switch now placed under the tank, not between the tank and seat. They also shared the 860 wiring loom and 860 instrument panel with the intriguing 'city/country' horn button switch. The last models had lost a lot of the individual features of the original and it set a precedent that Ducati was to follow in the future. Often it is the earliest examples of particular models that are the most appealing. Throughout the subsequent history of the marque this has happened time and again.

By late 1974, US legislation was making left-side gear shifts mandatory, so the round-case engine was phased out to make way for the square-case 860 that had a left-side gearshift by a crossover shaft behind the engine. The round-case was also too expensive and time-consuming to manufacture, and by 1975 its production had ended, though, like the last singles, it continued to be sold until stocks had run out. Interestingly, demand occurred again three years later, in 1978, when the Australian importers, Frasers in Sydney, requested a batch of both 750GTs and Sports. The factory responded by building 40 GTs and 23 Sports out of spare parts. These, along with some police bikes, were the last of the round-case models.

For some reason the GT has become one of the forgotten members of the Ducati family. Considering the exotic nature of the engine, and its beautiful castings, it is surprising how little status it has in the Ducati classic hierarchy. Once again it comes down to the sporting heritage. Ducatis are perceived as sporting motorcycles, not touring bikes. However, it is

The first production 750 Sport used a 750GT frame, and only a few were manufactured.
Thorsten Schulze

had been displayed, largely based on the GT but with clip-on handlebars and rear-set footpegs, and a more highly-tuned engine. The first prototype was shown to Italian concessionaires in 1971 by the then Ducati directors, Arnaldo Milvio and Fredmano Spairani. It was little more than a sporty GT with a deeply-scalloped tank, and a second prototype appeared in early 1972. This was black with a white frame, had Nippon Denso instruments as on the Honda 750, 32 mm Amal carburettors with no air cleaners, and unique curved Conti mufflers. Braking was by a single Lockheed disc up front, and a single Lockheed rear disc. Alternative versions were also shown, some with a half-fairing, twin Lockheed front discs, and Veglia instruments. The colour scheme was the one eventually chosen for the production bikes, yellow with black frame and 'Z' stripes. By the end of 1972 the 750 Sport was in production, and today it is one of the most sought-after of the older Ducatis. There is no denying that Ducati got it right with the Sport.

The first production Sports used 750GT frames with the wide rear sub-frame, Veglia instruments, single Lockheed 278 mm iron disc, and the single rear drum brake as on the GT. The strange curved Contis never made it to production, and by 1973 the frame was replaced by a neater-looking one with a narrower rear sub-frame. All 750 Ducatis at this time came with leading axle Marzocchi forks, but there were a number of details that differentiated the Sport from the GT. It must also be remembered that the 750 Super Sport had not yet appeared, and the 750 Sport was the company's top-performance, and top-of-the-line, model.

The appearance of the Sport created quite a stir in the motorcycle press. Everyone was still amazed by the MV-beating performance of the 750 Desmos at Imola, so naturally the bike was expected to perform considerably better than the GT, and they were not disappointed. With only minimal changes to the engine the 750 Sport now vied for the title of the best-performing 750 on the market. Not only was this a respectably fast bike for its day but it probably handled best too.

The 1973 version looked stunning with its yellow fibreglass tank, seat, and matching guards contrasting with the black-painted engine side-covers. I can clearly remember seeing one in 1973 and thinking how narrow the bike was compared to Honda 750 fours and Kawasaki triples. As a factory option a small half-fairing was available, but as this was only frame, and

important to remember that even the most revered sporting Ducatis had more humble origins. Historically the 750GT is perhaps one of the most important Ducatis ever, the first of the long line of highly successful 90° V-twins. They were also powered by an engine rated by Taglioni as his best design.

DUCATI 750 SPORT

When Ing. Fabio Taglioni conceived the 750 Ducati in 1970, he always had it in his mind to develop this design as a sporting motorcycle. An early prototype 750 cc engine carried 35 mm carburettors and spun to 9,500 rpm, far removed from the eventual 750GT, and indicating that sometime in the future a higher performance version would appear. Even before the historic Imola victory in 1972, prototype 750 Sports

One of the classic sporting
Ducatis, the 1973 750 Sport,
with black engine cases and a
leading axle fork.

Right: By 1974, the 750 Sport
had a centre-axle fork and
polished engine cases.

not steering head, mounted, its effectiveness looked
better than it was. At high speed it moved around
unnervingly, and with all the instruments and the
headlight still mounted on the fork legs and triple
clamp, no advantage could be made of any reduced
steering inertia. Another problem was caused by the
clip-on handlebars being splayed out at an
uncomfortable angle because the petrol tank lacked
sufficient clearance on full lock. Starting was by
kickstart only, using a revised, swinging out lever, and
fold-up foot-rest. This was a far more satisfactory
arrangement than the kickstart on the GT, which more
often than not resulted in bruised shins.

However, it was in the engine department that the
Sport really showed most improvement over the GT.
While engine changes consisted purely of lighter (by
around 70 gm) slipper, pistons matched to a
correspondingly lighter crankshaft, and larger
carburettors without air cleaners, the change was
dramatic. The very earliest models also had milled and
polished con-rods, but without the dual strengthening
rib around the big-end that characterized the later 750
Super Sport rods. The increase of compression to 9.3:1
was much better suited to the quite radical camshaft
profiles of the GT, and the use of the new type of
Dell'Orto PHF 32 mm carburettor with unfiltered
velocity stacks allowed the engine to breathe more

freely. While power was only up to a claimed 60 bhp,
the difference in performance between a GT and Sport
was considerable. In all other respects the Sport engine
was identical to the GT, despite various claims of hotter
camshafts and larger valves.

The cycle parts were identical to the GT, except that
the rear 305 mm long Marzocchi shocks were without
the top spring covers. All the guards were fibreglass,
like the seat and petrol tank, and were of dubious
quality. In the search for lightness even the rear
number-plate holder was made of plastic. Wheels with
19-inch Borrani WM2 front and 18-inch WM3 alloy
rims were the same as for the GT, as were the single
278 mm iron disc and single drum rear brake. With
these early Sports no provision was made for any
pillion passenger, and like the GT, Scarab brake
components appeared during 1973, as did the
electronic tachometer. They were still an
uncompromised sporting motorcycle, with no provision
for turn indicators.

By 1974 the 750 Super Sport had entered
production, and the Sport was no longer the range
leader. Changes in specification began to mirror those
of the GT. First there were Ceriani centre-axle forks
with a single Brembo front disc. Then, in deference to
the UK market, where fibreglass petrol tanks were
illegal, came a steel tank in the same shape. Some of

these had appeared in 1973 on US market Sports. During 1974 the black-painted cases were replaced by polished cases like the GT and SS. Also like the GT, Marzocchi centre-axle forks with a Scarab front disc were fitted throughout 1974, still with the flat triple clamps, but unlike the GT Brembo-equipped centre-axle Marzocchis were not specified. While engine specifications remained unchanged except for a longer-stemmed inlet valve and the use of the revised primary drive, the very last 750 Sports featured a range of differences. To pull the widely splayed clip-on handlebars back to a better angle, they became offset forward of the forks. This was a considerable improvement over the strange riding position of the earlier models, and made the bike more similar in feel to the 750 Super Sport. The switch-gear and wiring mirrored the final 750GTs and first 860s, with the boxy CEV items and two-into-one throttle. The last item was definitely a retrograde step as throttle action was poorer and the cables were under more stress. The last Sports also featured a dual seat as an option. US models now had indicators and large tail-lights, but fortunately the Borrani alloy rims stayed. The earlier Sports, while essentially the same, were a purer display of the sporting concept.

As a sporting motorcycle, the 750 Sport was superb. Lighter than the GT, at 182 kg (401 lb) due to the widespread use of fibreglass, and with more power, it was a stronger performer. Handling was the same, but the riding position lent itself to more spirited riding. To quote *Cycle* magazine in its June 1974 issue: 'The 750 Sport has a great engine packaged with a brilliant chassis'. *Cycle* went on to say: 'The Ducati 750, in any of its three incarnations, is still the best handling street machine available.' Elsewhere, too, praise was heaped on this motorcycle. The Australian magazine *Two Wheels* stated in October 1974: 'The Ducati 750 Sport is not just a good bike – it is a truly exceptional motorcycle'. In England, *Motorcyclist Illustrated* said, in July 1974: 'The Ducati Sport stands level with the very best that history can offer to match it, and as a sporting machine probably better than almost any other big roadster in production'.

Fifteen years later Ducati acknowledged the importance of the Sport when they released the Nuovo 750 Sport, a bike that was unfortunately only a shadow of the original. The round-case 750 Sport epitomizes the very best of Ducati, uncompromised engine and chassis performance, equal to the best in its day. If it hadn't been for the 750 Super Sport, or if it had possessed desmodromic rather than valve spring heads, the 750 Sport would have a higher status among *Ducatisti*. As it is, not many Sports were made and they are amongst the most desirable street Ducatis.

The 1973 Imola 750 racer was considerably more compact than that of the previous year's, here ridden by Bruno Kneubühler who crashed out after setting the fastest lap. *Mick Woollett*

7 IMOLA AND THE DESMODROMIC 750

April 23, 1972 was the day when a brace of specially-prepared desmodromic 750 racers took on the best the world's manufacturers had to offer, and trounced them convincingly. It was the inaugural Imola 200, the 'Daytona of Europe', for Formula 750 machines, racing 750 cc machines with production-based motors. The win at Imola marked the transition for Ducati, from a relatively small and unknown Italian manufacturer, primarily of small-capacity single-cylinder bikes, to that of a marque equal to any other. Within Italy, and to certain *cognoscenti* in other countries, Taglioni and Ducati were respected for technical excellence and innovation. Yet, in production terms, Ducati was a minor manufacturer of motorcycles. Imola changed that.

The impetus for developing a racing 750 had occurred back in July 1971. In a one-off ride, Mike Hailwood was to race a prototype Formula 750 machine at Silverstone in August 1971. However, although Hailwood tested the bike, and recorded a sixth-fastest practice lap for the F750 race, he elected not to race it in the event, telling *Motor Cycle* that 'it did not handle well enough. This isn't surprising because it is only three weeks old and has never been raced before; it just needs a bit of sorting out. It should be good then'.

This 750 was more closely related to the 500 racer than the 750 street bike that had only just gone into limited production. The sand-cast crankcase was identical to that of the 500 Grand Prix bike, but it had the bore and stroke, 80 x 74.4 mm, of the production bike. It also had the dry clutch and six-speed gearbox of the 500, and a single overhead camshaft driven by bevel-gears. This was also the first 750 twin with desmodromic valve gear, and it reputedly allowed 75 bhp to be developed, with the engine revving to 11,500 rpm, using 40 mm SS Dell'Orto carburettors. The frame, likewise, was from the 500, being one of the batch made by Colin Seeley earlier that year. Up front, only a single Lockheed disc graced the Marzocchi leading axle front end, and this was insufficient for the more powerful 360 lb (163 kg) machine. The handling problems mentioned by Mike Hailwood were obviously the result of slotting a 750 engine into a 500. The bike would need to be redesigned for the inaugural Imola 200 the following year.

Below: Paul Smart's 1972 750
Imola racer was built out of a
750GT. *Ducati Motor*

With the support of Fredmano Spairani, Fabio Taglioni was given the brief to make an all out assault on this important race. It was being heavily promoted, and nine different factories had entered works-supported teams. In order to assess the level of competition, Taglioni made the trip to Daytona in March 1972, and came away impressed by the well developed Japanese racers. He realized that he couldn't tackle them head-on, he didn't have the resources. Utilizing proven technology from the 350 Desmo and 500 racers, he aimed to build a balanced machine, with handling and braking matched to usable horsepower.

Upon his return from Daytona, serious work began on developing the Imola bikes. Surprisingly, Taglioni started with standard 750GT street bikes. They had 750 engine numbers, indicating that bikes were just taken off the production line and into the racing department. The frames still had centre-stand mounts. They also had machined production leading axle Marzocchi forks, but there was more to these bikes than met the eye. The engines, while using standard 40 mm inlet and 36 mm exhaust valves, used

desmodromic valve control enabling the engine to run to 9,200 rpm. These were the first bikes to use the 'Imola' desmodromic camshafts with figures of inlet opening 65° before top dead centre and closing 95° after bottom dead centre, and exhaust opening 95° before bottom dead centre and closing 60° after top dead centre. Inlet valve lift was 12 mm. Power of 84 bhp at 8,800 rpm was claimed at the rear wheel, but more importantly it was the spread of power that was so advantageous. At 7,000 rpm the engine was said to make 70 bhp. Compression was up to 10:1 and these engines still used the wide, 80° included valve angle. They also used the first versions of the new 40 mm Dell'Orto PHF concentric carburettor.

In order to keep combustion temperatures down, an oil-cooling system was fitted that cooled the oil to the cylinder heads, and dual plug ignition installed with an additional 10 mm Lodge spark-plug. This enabled ignition advance to be cut back to 34° before top dead centre. With the alternator removed from the right side of the crankshaft, total loss battery and coil ignition, still by dual points, was employed. Since his experience

with electronic ignition on the 500, Fabio Taglioni was wary of employing it on the 750 for Imola, and was also worried about heat build-up inside the fairing over such a long race. Thus the condensers were mounted on the front frame down-tubes, away from the heat of the engine.

Apart from the stronger connecting rods machined out of solid billet, 50 gm lighter than standard, the lower end of the engine was early 750GT. There were straight cut primary drive and clutch gears (with a drilled clutch basket to save weight), but it had the same gearbox. There was no six-speed gearbox, or dry clutch, as on the 500 racers. The primary drive ratio differed from the GT and the later SS, being 31/75, or 2.419:1. Further weight was saved by completely removing the kickstart mechanism, which also served to increase ground clearance on the right side. Braking was uprated to two Lockheed front discs, and a rear 230 mm disc replacing the road bike's drum. With only left-side calipers in stock from the street bikes, these were used all round, the right-side front having an unusually long brake hose. A high-rise exhaust pipe was on the left, but not on the right. Imola had predominantly left-hand corners, but ground clearance was still a problem because racing tyres required an 18-inch front wheel instead of a 19-inch. Total dry weight of these racers was 392 lb (178 kg), and they were reputed to pull the tallest available gearing, giving 169 mph (272 km/h).

Seven bikes were built. To ride one of them, Ducati had approached firstly Jarno Saarinen, Renzo Pasolini, and then, in February, Barry Sheene. All had declined, not feeling that the Ducati would be competitive. Ducati already had the evergreen 39-year-old Bruno Spaggiari, who had raced every factory bike since the 1950s, and knew the Imola circuit intimately. To partner Spaggiari would be the younger Ermanno Giuliano, who had raced the 500 Ducati throughout 1971. English rider Alan Dunscombe, who had already been racing a modified 750GT for English importer Vic Camp, filled the third berth. Spairani now only required a top-line F750 racer to ride the last bike, and, through Vic Camp, managed to secure Paul Smart at the last minute. Originally planning to ride a Triumph Triple, the deal fell through, and reluctantly Smart flew to Italy. While a 750 Desmo with Sport bodywork had been tested at Modena in March, with further tests by Spaggiari with revised bodywork on 6 April, it wasn't until 19 April that the Imola racers were started up for

Below: Bruno Spaggiari was Ducati's veteran rider in 1972 and still raced with a pudding basin helmet. *Mick Woollett*

Bottom: Paul Smart won the 1972 Imola 200, and with this win Ducati changed forever. *Mick Woollett*

the first time at Modena, too late to correct any defects. However, Taglioni was quietly confident. Smart had equalled Agostini's lap record, set on a 500 cc MV Agusta Grand Prix bike. In their specially-constructed glass-sided transporter, all seven Ducatis – two each for Smart and Spaggiari, one each for Dunscombe and

Below: Paul Smart and Fabio
Taglioni accept the trophy from
Dott. Francesco Costa.
Ducati Motor

Giuliano, and one spare – were transported the 40 km (25 miles) to Imola.

On race day, 70,000 spectators crammed into Autodromo Dino Ferrari at Imola. With works machines in abundance from MV Agusta, Honda, Norton, Moto Guzzi, Triumph, and BSA, alongside works-supported Kawasaki, Laverda, Suzuki, and BMW, they had hopefully come to see the Italian factories beat the Japanese teams that had dominated Daytona. The best riders in the world were there too: Giacomo Agostini, Phil Read, Roberto Gallina, Walter Villa, Ray Pickrell, Tony Jeffries, John Cooper, Percy Tait, Ron Grant, and Daytona winner Don Emde. In practice, Spaggiari, followed by Smart, had set the fastest time. With its fast sweeping curves – some smooth, others bumpy – and its up-and-down topography, Imola seemed to suit the Ducatis. Unlike Daytona this was no mere horsepower circuit. This was Imola before the advent of chicanes, a fast European circuit in the traditional style.

Agostini, on a specially-prepared 750 MV, led at the start. This MV, while still with the shaft-drive of the road bikes, had a Grand Prix style frame with 500GP

forks and brakes. At the end of the fourth lap Smart overtook Agostini, followed a lap later by Spaggiari. From then on the two Ducatis were untroubled out in front, and in the final five laps they were both racing for the lead. Spaggiari nipped in front, but on the final lap his bike started to misfire as he was low on fuel. He ran wide on a sweeper, allowing Smart to take a comfortable victory. It had been a great day for Ducati. It wasn't so bad for Paul Smart either, as he took home 7,080,000 Lire in prize money. Spairani was so excited that he donated the winning bike to Smart. Spaggiari's bike ended up being sold to Ron Angel, Ducati distributor in Victoria, Australia, where it was campaigned by Kenny Blake during 1973. The race speed over 200 miles had been an astonishing 97.76 mph (157.35 km/h), with the fastest lap of 100.1 mph (161.11 km/h) being shared equally by Smart, Spaggiari, and Agostini.

After the race, Ducati promised 'Imola' replicas, but these were slow to appear. In the meantime the 750 racers were displayed at selected events around the world as part of a promotional exercise for the 750 road bikes. In June, three bikes were entered at

Below: Spaggiari at Imola in
1974, now with a full face
helmet. His best result this year
was an eighth in the first leg.
Mick Woollett

Daytona, followed in July by the Canadian GP at
Mosport, where they were raced unsuccessfully by
Bruno Spaggiari and Percy Tait. Then in October,
Smart won the Greek GP on the island of Corfu.
Meanwhile, Smart had raced his own bike at various
races in England throughout 1972, with moderate
success. One was also taken to South Africa to race
over the northern winter, where local rider Errol
Cowan had some reasonable results in highly
competitive fields that included Giacomo Agostini.

For 1973, despite the replacement of Arnaldo Milvio
as general manager by Ing. de Eccher, Taglioni was
given the authorization to build brand new racers,
considerably removed from the street bikes. He knew
that the 1972 bikes were too close to the road bikes to
be competitive against the new wave of two-stroke
Yamahas and Suzukis, so a completely new bike was
designed, this time a real racer. As Formula 750
regulations only stipulated that the crankcases of the
production bike must be retained, he designed a
shorter, lighter frame, and a more powerful and
compact engine. The frame featured eccentrics in the
swing-arm bosses for chain adjustment, along with

positions in the swing-arm to select one of three
different wheelbases. The chain adjustment system
ultimately found its way through to the next generation
of road frames, the 860GT, yet the wheelbase selection
remained peculiar to this 1973 racer. Also, to shorten
the wheelbase even further, the distinctive Marzocchi
leading axle forks were replaced with those of a centre-
axle type after Spaggiari complained of front end
instability at the first test session at Modena. Thus,
without the time to experiment further, the centre-axle
Marzocchis were installed along with the flat triple
clamps of the leading type. Though it meant an
enormous trail increase (to nearly 6 inches), and despite
reservations, it cured the wobble, and the bike
subsequently handled well. Taglioni was so impressed
with this suspension set-up that when the production
750SS appeared the following year it had this front end
on the standard frame. Indeed, this front end geometry
was fitted to the entire range of 750/900 Super Sports
throughout their nine-year model life.

As he was still committed to the 90° twin, Taglioni
needed more horsepower as well as a lighter, shorter
bike. Here, by taking the 86 mm pistons of the 450 racer

Spaggiari's 750 in the pits at Imola in 1974. Although outclassed, this was a magnificent machine.

of 1970 that were readily available, he was able to shorten the stroke to 64.5 mm. This enabled revs to increase by 1,000 rpm, from the 9,200/9,500 rpm of the 1972 bike to 10,200/10,500 rpm. To take advantage of this more oversquare bore/stroke ratio, a new head was designed with a 60° included valve angle, rather than the 80° that had been a feature of all previous Ducatis. Preparation was left to the last minute, this time due to the endless strikes that occur in Italy from time to time. Because of delays in signing the 1972 metal-workers' contract, it wasn't until March 1973 that the strikes ended and work could begin on the new engine, barely a month before the Imola 200. The cylinder heads, new camshafts (now giving 14 mm of intake valve lift), connecting rods, and rockers were all specially machined out of solid billets or castings, and a new vented dry clutch took the place of the previous oil-bath type. Carburettors remained the same 40 mm Dell'Ortos of the previous year, but instead of the unusual one-up, one-down exhaust system, both exhausts were now the high-rise type. Weight was down significantly, to 325 lb (147 kg). Front brakes were now forward-mounted Italian Scarab, a Lockheed pattern that would also eventually be seen on the 750 Super Sport.

On the dyno, the engine power dropped off at 9,500 rpm, yet in testing Spaggiari reported it happy to rev beyond 10,400 rpm. These problems with the Ducati dyno room meant that no one knew exactly how much power this new engine actually made, but claims in the region of 93 bhp were made. While testing at Modena, Spaggiari set an absolute record, beating Agostini's previous best on the MV 500 by 0.3 seconds, and demolishing the 750 record, set by Smart in 1972, by two seconds. With only three days to go before the race, the last engine was finished. It had to be run-in during qualifying and ended up in Spaggiari's bike.

Race day was 15 April 1973, and even without the presence of Giacomo Agostini and his MV, 100,000 people streamed in to see the second Daytona of Europe. The Ducati team consisted of three riders, Bruno Spaggiari, Bruno Kneubühler, and Mick Grant. There was also another Ducati, entered under the NCR banner for the first time, but it wasn't a short-stroke racer, and was a prototype for the production 750 Super Sport to be released later in the year. Ridden by Claudio Loigo, it finished 15th. Even without Agostini, the competition was much stronger, particularly with Jarno Saarinen on a Yamaha 351 two-stroke, and the

before and since. Now the fibreglass 'Imola'-shaped tank was replaced by a 750 Sport style steel one, and the Conti silencers by the Lafranconis of the 860. Indicators on stalks appeared from the fairing along with new Aprilia switch-gear and an ignition switch mounted on the dashboard. 32 mm Dell'Orto carburettors and air-cleaners were fitted onto the now cast aluminium inlet manifolds, and Veglia instruments replaced the Smiths. No longer did the engine breathe directly into the atmosphere, but into a catch-tank moulded into the fibreglass seat. The gearshift was also moved to the left via the sloppy crossover shaft arrangement of the 860, the gear-selecting mechanism still residing in the right outer cover like the 750 (and the singles). The rear brake lever was thus moved to the right. It wasn't a very tidy conversion and the rubber foot-rests and levers were clumsy. While a display bike that appeared in early 1976 had a blue frame, colours for the production models were the same as for 1975, but with different graphics on the tank.

To fit a Super Sport with quiet mufflers and small carburettors really destroyed the character of the bike, but fortunately many came with the 40 mm Dell'Ortos and Contis packed in the crate. This restored the power to that of the 1975 bike, as the engine specifications were still the same. The 900SS was a strong-performing motorcycle, even if weight was up from the 750 to 414 lb (188 kg). *Cycle* magazine, testing a 1977 (the same as 1976) bike in July 1978, achieved a standing quarter mile time of 12.91 seconds at 104.16 mph (167.6 km/h) with Lafranconis and 32 mm carburettors. The kitted bike ran 12.4 seconds at 109 mph (175 km/h). *Cycle* 'marvelled at its almost hydraulic power.' *Revs* in Australia tested both the standard and kitted versions in 1977, coming away with the conclusion that, with the 40 mm Dell'Ortos and Contis, Ducati had created an engine that was 'truly brilliant – a real credit to the Italian motorcycle industry'. They achieved a 17% overall power increase over the detuned version, with even greater gains in the mid-range. The engine was

For 1979 the 900 Super Sport
gained an attractive black and gold
colour scheme while the wire-
spoked wheels made way for a
cast-alloy type. *Nico Georgeoglou*

obviously designed to run in this trim. Even today, the
900SS is a brilliantly-performing motorcycle and it is
no wonder that it is considered an all-time classic.

A lot of the details of the 1976–77 bikes were tidied
up in 1978. The SD900 Darmah had just gone into
production with a revised left-side gearshift and Bosch
ignition. It also had a new big-end with a larger, 38 mm
crankpin and correspondingly smaller rollers in an
effort to improve reliability. These changes were now
incorporated in the Super Sport, which still retained its
kickstart and alloy Borrani rims. By now, with full
production underway, the polished rockers
disappeared, but the 1978 bikes were better than in
1976–77. The gearshift was improved, as the crossover
linkages tended to develop a lot of slop with wear, and
the footrests and levers were neater. The engine was
also smoother, with the Bosch ignition and its revised
ignition advance. Unfortunately it now needed a fully-
charged battery. The earlier system was notable in that
it was self-generating, and if required the bike could be

run without a battery at all. A dual seat was also listed
as an option at this time.

In parallel with the 900SS, production of the 750SS
continued, although on a much smaller scale. The
1975–77 bikes were identical to the respective 900,
save for the silver fairing, smaller pistons and 750
bearing-covers on the cylinder heads. The last 750SSs
appeared in 1979, with the Bosch ignition and
Goldline Brembo 08 calipers. They were the last
Ducatis with Borrani rims, as by now the 900SS was
fitted with alloy Speedlines. Very few were made, and
total production for the 750SS was only about 1,000
over five years.

During 1978 the 900SS appeared with a black and
gold paint scheme along with the alloy wheels of the
Darmah. This mirrored the striping of the previous
year, but with gold stripes over a black petrol tank. The
engine remained as before, with the option of 40 mm
Dell'Ortos and Conti mufflers. The Speedline wheels
were prone to cracking and soon replaced with alloy

The final 900SS of 1981/82 with
Silentium mufflers, FPS wheels
and a restyled seat.

FPS ones. By now some Super Sports had the 40 mm carburettors they deserved, and the use of alloy wheels meant a 280 mm disc was now fitted at the rear. The small CEV tail-lights made way for the larger US-style ones.

The final 900SS was shown at the 1980 Bologna Show and released during 1981, now with a dual seat only, a black frame with silver bodywork, and new decals. There were lots of detail changes, but unfortunately quality control could have been better at this time. Bikes appeared with incorrect speedo drives and 'A' pistons in 'B' barrels. Some had a handle on the frame to help in putting the bike on the centre-stand, and others had early petrol tanks and front guards. Its Silentium silencers were better-looking than the Lafranconis, but still not a Conti replacement. Yet the engine and running gear remained the same, so the basic ingredients were still there. Unfortunately, the constant modernization of the Super Sport had also diminished its original appeal as a race replica. While

the last bikes had better paint and fibreglass, much better electrics, cable-mounted chokes, even locking petrol caps, they lacked the raw appeal of the original, and lost a lot of the character. They also became hard to sell and in 1982 were dumped at bargain prices in markets like Australia.

So, ten years after Imola the same basic bike remained in production, but time had caught up with it. Buyers now wanted electric start and an easier bike to live with. The Super Sport had already evolved into the Mike Hailwood Replica and they both merged to become the S2. But now we are a long way from Imola. The early 750 and 900 Super Sports reflected the very best of the Italian concept of a sporting motorcycle, genuine unadulterated race replicas built irrespective of regulation and, to some extent, cost. However, the later bikes were inevitably compromised by increasing legislation, fashion, and economics, and they were no longer race replicas. The next generation of race replica Ducatis lay in another bloodline, the Pantah.

A restyled seat appeared on the
Darmah for 1979, and it lost the
kickstart.

This Mille engine was placed in the identical 900 MHR running gear. The earlier bikes had black-painted forks, but these were painted red on final examples, along with a red front guard. As it had the S2 frame and suspension it suffered from the same deficiencies. The first examples appeared in mid-1984, and when tested by *Motorrad* in November they achieved 214 km/h (133 mph). The bike also weighed in at 240 kg (529 lb) wet. When compared to their test of the 1974 750SS, which achieved 216.7 km/h (135 mph) and weighed 202 kg (445 lb) wet, one must wonder at the progress over ten years.

With the Cagiva take-over, the days of expensive bevel-gear engines were numbered, and by the end of 1985 the Mille was finished. This year saw a prototype built using a 16-inch front wheel and M1R Marzocchi forks, and Massimo Tamburini, formerly of Bimota, developed a new frame of square-section tubing, with a single shock rear end and 16-inch wheels, for the Mille engine. However, nothing ever came of these. I saw a Mille MHR with the new Cagiva-inspired Ducati lettering at the factory at the end of 1985, but by now production had ended. It was unfortunate, because, with development, this engine had potential. All it really needed was more up-to-date running gear, but economics had forced its hand. It was a difficult time for Ducati with Cagiva taking control, and production was at an all-time low. Some remained unsold into 1986, and they were to be the last of the illustrious line of bevel-gear Ducatis.

Arguably the most attractive
Pantah: the first 600SL Pantah
of 1981.

11 RACING PANTAHS AND THE 750F1

As the racing success of the 900NCR waned, the Pantah took over, and during 1980 two 600 cc race-kitted Pantahs were prepared by Franco Farnè. These were campaigned successfully in the Italian national junior championship by Vanes Francini, Paiolo Menchini, and Guido Del Piano, and were based on the standard SL frame but with Marzocchi racing suspension. The red and yellow bodywork was similar in style to that of the 900NCR, and power from the 583 cc engines was up to 70 bhp at 9,800 rpm. Then, for the 1981 season, Fabio Taglioni released his *tour de force*, the TT2.

The prototype TT2 was tested in Spain over the winter by Angel Nieto (14 times World 50 cc and 125 cc Champion) and successful Ducati endurance racer Salvador Canellas. So good was its design that, at its debut race meeting on 29 March 1981, the TT2, in the hands of Sauro Pazzaglia, won the opening round of the Italian TTF2 series at Misano. However, even as the TT2 was making its presence felt on Italian circuits, Sports Motorcycles' Steve Wynne and Pat Slinn had prepared a modified 500SL Pantah for Tony Rutter to race in the Isle of Man Formula 2 event in June 1981. Originally promised two factory bikes that didn't materialise, they had found an insurance write-off, installed a factory race kit, sent the frame off to Ron Williams of Maxton for some extra bracing, and signed up Isle of Man veteran Tony Rutter. Rutter won at an average of 101.91 mph (164 km/h), with a fastest lap of 103.51 mph (166.58 km/h). Ducati were pleased enough with this victory to offer Rutter a TT2 factory bike for the next round at Ulster on August 22. In atrocious conditions, Rutter finished second to secure the 1981 World Formula Two Championship.

The TT2 marked the return of the factory to official competition after an absence since 1975. By using an 81 mm bore capacity was increased to 597 cc, almost the class limit, and a completely new frame was designed by Taglioni and made by Verlicchi. Weighing only 7 kg (16 lb), rear suspension was by a cantilever and single Paioli shock absorber. This frame was exceedingly compact and strong, being heavily triangulated around the steering head, and comprising essentially straight tubes. It bolted to the engine in four places, still using the latter as a stressed member, with butt-fitted bosses rather than flat tabs as on the SL. The

The line-up of factory racing
Pantahs in 1980. *Ducati Motor*

18-litre fibreglass petrol tank was encased by this frame. Fitted with 35 mm Marzocchi racing forks with magnesium sliders and 280 mm Brembo front discs, the racer weighed in at a mere 270 lb (122 kg). It was also extremely compact, with only a 55-inch (1,395 mm) wheelbase. The 18-inch Campagnolo wheels were 2.15 inches wide on the front, and 3.00 inches on the rear.

In the engine department, the TT2 was pure factory racer. The 81 mm Borgo pistons only had moderate compression of 10:1, but valves were larger at 41 mm inlet and 35 mm exhaust. These valves were operated by desmodromic camshafts giving 12 mm of intake lift and 10 mm of exhaust. Italian regulations permitted the use of 40 mm Dell'Orto carburettors, but for the TT World Championship, standard 36 mm carburettors needed to be retained. Claimed power was 76 bhp at 10,750 rpm. There was much evidence of weight saving – exposed camshaft drive belts, a magnesium primary drive cover, and hydraulically operated dry clutch. A lightweight two-into-one

exhaust system was also used. Internally most gears were drilled for lightness and ignition was still by electronic Bosch BTZ, with the small battery mounted in the rear tailpiece. Because Italian regulations required an electric starter, both this and the 200 watt alternator were retained.

The TT2 was a very effective racing machine, in the best Taglioni tradition of achieving maximum results through a balance of power and weight. It was light, athletic, slim, had a wide power-band, and Taglioni was especially proud of the specific fuel consumption figures of 187 gr/HP/hr – less than a diesel! Just how effective it was as a racer was displayed by Massimo Broccoli in October 1981 at the final round of the Italian 500 series at Mugello. On a TT2 sleeved down to 500 cc, he finished seventh in a field of 500GP Suzukis and Yamahas. Broccoli had already secured the Italian TT2 championship ahead of the Kawasaki-powered Bimota KB2s. In its first full year the TT2 had won the two championship series that it had contested.

A triumph of form and function,
the TT2 was minimalist in
execution, and totally effective.
Roy Kidney

The TT2 was even more successful in 1982. In the Italian TT2 championship Walter Cussigh won every round on his factory TT2, and the now 40-year-old Tony Rutter again won the World TT2 Championship. For the Italian events power was up to 78 bhp at 10,500 rpm using 41 mm Malossi Dell'Orto carburettors, and Cussigh favoured a 16-inch Campagnolo front wheel with a 3.25–4.50 Michelin front tyre. Rutter still used the 18-inch wheels, preferring them to the 16-inch type on the bumpier street circuits. At the Isle of Man he was considerably faster than the previous year, winning the Formula 2 race on the factory bike at an average speed of 108.50 mph (174.61 km/h), with a fastest lap of 109.27 mph (175.85 km/h). He was timed at 144 mph (232 km/h) at a speed trap at the Highlander. With the World Championship now extended to three rounds, Rutter scored perfect points on his factory bike. He won at Vila Real in Portugal at an average speed of 86.69 mph (139.51 km/h), following it at Ulster with a win at 100.73 mph (162.1 kph).

During 1982 a limited number of production TT2 replicas were built for privateers. These were very close to the factory bikes but lacked items such as the magnesium primary drive cover and hydraulically-operated dry clutch. They still had the racing magnesium Marzocchi forks and 18-inch Campagnolo wheels. The engine had the same valve sizes as the factory racer, and valve timing figures of inlet opening 74° before top dead centre and closing 92° after bottom dead centre, and exhaust opening 100° before bottom dead centre and closing 64° after top dead centre. Still only using 36 mm Dell'Ortos, power was a claimed 76 bhp at 10,750 rpm. The TT2 also had straight cut primary gears, with a higher ratio than the street bikes. 36/70 teeth gave a ratio of 1.94:1. The five-speed gearbox had the same ratios as the street bike, except for fifth gear being moved closer to fourth. The final drive was considerably lower, at 3.15:1, with 13 and 41 teeth sprockets. Like the factory racer, an oil-cooler was mounted in the fairing, cooling oil to the

Tony Rutter was the TT2's most successful exponent, winning four successive World Championships. *Mick Woollett*

750TT1

With the possibility of the World Championship TT2 class disappearing completely, Ducati hastened development of a 750 cc TT1 version of the Pantah for 1984. As previously mentioned, both TT1 and World Endurance were becoming limited to 750 cc, so a longer 61.5 mm stroked crankshaft was homologated with the 650SL Pantah. Even as far back as March 1982 a 750 cc version of the TT2 had been raced by Jimmy Adamo for Reno Leoni at the Daytona 200, finishing 13th overall. This bike had produced nearly 95 bhp at 10,250 rpm, with a top speed of almost 155 mph (250 km/h). The following year at Daytona, this time in the Battle of the Twins race, Tony Rutter took the 750 TT1 to third place. Then, in July 1983, at Ducati's happy hunting ground, Montjuich Park, a TT1 won the now non-championship 24-Hour race with Benjamin Grau, Enrique de Juan, and Luis Reyes. Prepared by Franco Farnè, the 135 kg (298 lb) racer produced 86 bhp at 9,000 rpm, but the riders limited this to 8,000 rpm during the race, and 83–84 bhp. In front of 250,000 spectators they completed 708 laps, compared to the second-place French Kawasaki's 690.

While Tony Rutter still raced the 600TT2 in 1984, and won the Formula 2 World Championship for the fourth successive year, he also campaigned a 750 cc version of the same bike in Formula 1. He failed to win the Isle of Man F2 race, coming second, but won at Vila Real (at 90.81 mph, or 146.14 km/h). Trevor Nation, also on a 600TT2, came second in the championship. In Formula 1, Rutter managed third overall on the new Ducati during the 1984 season, and the 750 had limited success in endurance racing. At the non-championship Le Mans 24-Hour race in April, a 750 TT1 ridden by Marc Granie, Philippe Guichon, and Didier Vuillemin finished fourth; there were only 18 finishers from a field of 54. They followed this up with a fourth at the Österreichring 1,000 km race, third in the Liège 24-Hours at Spa, and fourth at the Mugello Six-Hours. They finished fifth in the final placings. The works bike of Walter Villa and Walter Cussigh came fourth at the ADAC Eight-Hour race at the Nürburgring, but was plagued with problems throughout the season.

The TT1 differed slightly from the TT2. It still had the cantilever swing-arm, but this was wider to accommodate wider wheels, and was painted red and

cylinder heads in a similar system to that of the Imola racers a decade earlier. Because it still had the electric starting mechanism, weight was 130 kg (286 lb). Rear suspension was not Paioli as in 1981, but a Marzocchi PVS 1 remote reservoir gas shock absorber. Only about 20 of these bikes were made in 1982.

Racing results for the TT2 in 1983 weren't quite as spectacular as the previous year. Tony Rutter again won the World TT2 Championship, but not quite as convincingly. At the Isle of Man he headed a Ducati one–two with Graeme McGregor, at an average speed of 108.20 mph (174.13 km/h), with a fastest lap of 109.44 mph (176.12 km/h). At the other two rounds at Ulster and Assen he could only manage second, but it was enough to win the championship again. Another batch of TT2 replicas was built for 1983, virtually identical to the previous year, but now with a Campagnolo 3.50 x 16 inch front wheel to complement a rear 3.50 x 18 inch. Malossi modified 41 mm smooth bore Dell'Orto carburettors were fitted, and power was up to a claimed 78 bhp at 10,500 rpm.

Below: The author test riding the
first production 750 F1 in 1985.

headlight was fitted in the full fairing, and it had
16-inch gold-painted Oscam wheels. Claimed power
was 70 bhp at 9,000 rpm, with dry weight at 165 kg
(364 lb). Other features were a hydraulic clutch and a
two-into-one exhaust system. 36 or 40 mm Dell'Orto
carburettors were specified, and the compression ratio
was a high 10.4:1.

In mid-November 1984, photographs of mock
production bikes appeared, now with an 18-inch rear
wheel, and in February 1985 the 750F1 was premiered
at the Sydney Motorcycle Exhibition. It still didn't
have the fully-floating Brembo 280 mm front discs and
260 mm rear, but the engine was painted black and
had a Conti two-into-one exhaust system, claimed to
meet all noise regulations. The red frame, sourced
from the TT2/TT1, had been widened to accommodate
the camshaft belt covers and an adjustable steering
damper fitted to complement the 16-inch front wheel.
Even before the bike had gone into production there
was controversy surrounding the fitting of a 16-inch
front wheel.

When the first production models appeared during
1985 they were a confusing mixture of good and bad.
The engine was only an over-bored 650 Pantah, still
with the 37.5 and 33.5 mm valves of the 500. The oil-
cooler lines were cheap rubber hoses crimped into
place, yet the brake discs were full-floating iron
Brembos. Basic air-assisted Marzocchi 38 mm
suspension was used at the front and a Marzocchi
adjustable shock absorber at the rear (which was still a
cantilever rather than rising rate), yet an aluminium
petrol tank was fitted. It was also the very last Ducati
to feature the old Giugiaro graphics that had first
appeared on the 860 in 1975. The rear seat and tail
section was much larger and uglier than on the TT1
and TT2, designed to locate the 14Ah battery, and a
dual seat at a later stage.

While still using the 36 mm PHF Dell'Orto
carburettors of the Pantah, the 750F1 received new
camshafts along with 9.3:1 88 mm pistons. Valve timing
was now inlet opening 29° before top dead centre,
closing 90° after bottom dead centre, and exhaust
opening 70° before bottom dead centre, closing 48°
after top dead centre, and power was only a claimed
62.5 bhp at 7,500 rpm. The primary drive ratio was
altered, more in line to that of the TT2, to 36/71, or
1.97:1, and the 750F1 also received the fifth gear ratio
of the TT2 at 0.97:1. A 300 watt alternator provided
electrical power. Weight was up to 175 kg (386 lb), but

it was still a much more compact motor-cycle than the
preceding Pantah. The wheelbase was only 1,400 mm
(55 inches), and a far cry from the older bevel-gear
bikes with their 60-inch wheelbase. Compared to the
racer, steering rake was increased to 28°, with
corresponding trail of 5.2 inches, making the F1 a
relatively slow steerer in the traditional Ducati fashion.
Performance wasn't particularly outstanding for its day,
and didn't even match the 750SS of over ten years
earlier. *Motorrad* tested the two bikes back to back in
November 1985 and found the older bike accelerated
faster and had a higher top speed. The 750F1 managed
206 km/h (128 mph) but was considerably punchier in
the mid-range. I rode one of the first examples and,
after the heavy feel of the last Mike Hailwood Replicas,
was pleasantly surprised by the light weight and
responsiveness of the F1. The F1 was a generation
ahead when it came to steering and handling. Despite
only a cantilever rear suspension system, the light
weight and short wheelbase made the F1 a surprisingly
quick road bike for its power output. Just like the
magnificent TT1 and TT2 racers, it managed to match
much more powerful bikes with its better balance and
power characteristics. The only problem with the F1

The 1986 750F1 was an
improved machine over the 1985
version. *Two Wheels*

was that, because it was derived from the TT2, it was a very small motorcycle and the riding position was consequently cramped for larger riders.

By late-1985 F1s were being displayed with the new Cagiva graphics and logo. Some of these were silver and red, but they were all interim models before the arrival of the significantly improved 750F1 for 1986. Following racing experience with the TT1, the original 500 type crankcase, which had always cracked around the drive side main bearing under the stress of racing, was finally strengthened, with extra webbing between it and the gearbox mainshaft bearing. Straight cut primary gears now took power to a hydraulically-operated dry clutch and a new, stronger gearbox was fitted with 30° wider gears. The crankshaft was strengthened around the big-end journal with new connecting rods. The oil-cooling was now full-flow, rather than just a cylinder head bypass, and, in keeping with the larger capacity, valve sizes were increased to the 41 and 35 mm of the TT2, necessitating a move to smaller 12 mm spark-plugs. Along with slightly revised camshafts (about 8° retarded), and an increase in compression to 10:1 using higher-domed pistons, power went up to a claimed 75 bhp at 9,000 rpm. The new camshaft timing was, inlet opening 39° before top dead centre, and closing 80° after bottom dead centre, and exhaust opening 80° before bottom dead centre, and closing 38° after top dead centre. The same Dell'Orto PHF36 carburettors were used, with small foam air-filters.

The engine was certainly an improvement, and so was the front suspension. 40 mm Forcella-Italia forks, with provision for a wide range of adjustment in damping and preload, were vastly superior to the non-adjustable 38 mm Marzocchis. Also, the rear 260 mm disc was no longer the fully-floating type, and the 22-litre aluminium petrol tank became an 18-litre steel one. As has often been the case at Ducati, some things improve, but other details exhibit cost-cutting when models are revised. However, the instrument layout with the white-faced Veglias was a welcome relief from the Nippon Densos that had by now become dated, and still carries through to today on the Super Sport line. The styling of the rear seat was improved, but it still looked awkward from some angles, and the red Oscam wheels mirrored the racing TT1.

Cycle magazine summed up the 750F1 succinctly in February 1987 when it said 'the F1 allows a very competent street rider to understand how a race bike feels because the engine will help him rather than

intimidate him'. For the F1 still didn't possess exceptional horsepower. When *Cycle* tested an F1 in June 1988, it only achieved a standing quarter-mile time of 12.70 seconds at 103.1 mph (166 km/h). Perhaps the most disappointing aspect of the new 750 engine was the vibration, which after a long ride would leave you with numbed wrists. Somehow, the short-stroke 750 engine never managed to feel as smooth and relaxed as the earlier bevel-gear examples.

For 1987 and 1988 the 750F1 continued to be marketed in small numbers beside the new range of Cagiva-inspired Ducatis. From bike number 1505 the Japanese Kokusan ignition, that had first appeared on the limited edition 750 Montjuich, replaced the Bosch system. Also, the last versions had a locking fuel cap and a dual seat. However, by now the F1 was an anachronism within a Ducati range that was becoming increasingly Cagiva-influenced. To quote *Cycle* magazine again, the 750F1 was 'the last true fundamentalist Ducati'.

750 MONTJUICH, LAGUNA SECA AND SANTAMONICA

To celebrate the win by Grau, de Juan, and Reyes in the 24-Hour race at Montjuich Park in 1983, a limited edition race replica F1 in the finest Ducati tradition was announced at the end of 1985, and displayed at the Milan Show. As usual it had taken long enough to appear, but like the first 750SS of 1974 many thought it worth the wait. Though essentially a 750F1, the Montjuich was tuned considerably with hotter camshafts, Dell'Orto PHM40ND carburettors, and a less restrictive Verlicchi two-into-one *Riservato Competizione* exhaust system. Even though it still only had the cantilever rear end, the swing-arm was Verlicchi aluminium, and in a carry-over from the 750TT1 both front and rear wheels were 16-inch. The wheels were lightweight composite Marvic with magnesium hubs and spokes, and Akront aluminium rims. Rim sizes were much wider than the standard F1 at 3.50 x 16 and 4.25 x 16, and shod with Michelin 120/60V16 and 180/60V16 tyres. Other detail differences included a 22-litre aluminium fuel tank like the first 750F1, four-piston Brembo 'Gold Line' racing calipers with fully-floating discs all round (280 mm at the front and 260 mm rear), a vented dry clutch, and different front guard. While the prototype featured a

The 1986 750F1 Montjuich was a true race replica in the best Ducati tradition.

centre-stand, the production models saved a few kilos by only specifying a side-stand. The relationship between the Montjuich and F1 was similar to that which existed between the original 750SS and 750 Sport: a limited production bike that offered higher performance through engine modifications, better brakes, and less weight.

However, this is where the concept of the two bikes differs. The Montjuich was created and sold as a limited edition item, each of the 200 bikes having a numbered plaque on the petrol tank. It was only several years later that anyone realized how rare the original 750SS was, and by that stage many had been raced and ruined. Still, there were many detail differences to the Montjuich, and it was both lighter and significantly more powerful than the standard F1. Starting with the engine, the Montjuich received new camshafts with timing figures of inlet opening 67° before top dead centre, and closing 99° after bottom dead centre, and exhaust opening 93° before bottom dead centre and closing 70° after top dead centre. With 137° of valve overlap, these camshafts had more than the racing TT1, and inlet duration of 346° was also slightly more than the TT1. These were the fiercest camshafts ever fitted to a street Ducati, and as such the Montjuich was peakier than expected. Along with the larger carburettors and racing exhaust system, the camshafts lifted claimed power for the Montjuich to 95 bhp at 10,000 rpm. Unlike the earlier 750SS, the lower half of the engine was standard 750F1. There were no polished crankshafts or con-rods, and the 10:1 pistons and barrels were identical to the F1. The Montjuich had an aluminium clutch drum and slightly different gearbox internals, to accommodate the outboard countershaft sprocket. Rather than the Bosch ignition that had been used since 1977, a Kokusan system was used for the first time.

To compensate for the 16-inch rear wheel, the final-drive gearing was altered to 15/43, or 2.87:1, and a narrower, 5/8 x 1/4 inch chain was used. The Montjuich also used a better-quality Marzocchi rear shock absorber, but tests still criticized it for being underdamped. Claimed dry weight was a mere 155 kg (342 lb), but *Motorrad* weighed their test bike in at 178 kg (392 lb) fully wet, still much less than any other two-cylinder street Ducati. *Moto Sprint*, in April 1986, managed 221 km/h (137.3 mph), with 75 bhp at 10,000 rpm. *Cycle World* also put theirs through a standing quarter-mile in 11.87 seconds, at 113.52 mph (182.7 km/h).

12 THE CAGIVA TAKE-OVER

During the early 1980s, when Ducati was under the VM Group of industries, production levels were low and the plant was very unprofitable. Although 5,665 motorcycles were produced in 1982, these proved to be difficult to sell. By 1983, production had dropped further, to 3,909, and would reach an all-time low of 1,765 in 1984. The situation was so bad that the future of Ducati motorcycle production looked very bleak, then in a surprise move the managers of the VM Group started negotiations with the relatively unknown Cagiva company from Varese. On 1 June a press statement was released in Milan announcing a joint venture.

Cagiva had been built in 1978 out of the ashes of AMF-Harley Davidson (formerly Aermacchi) by the two Castiglioni brothers, Claudio and Gianfranco. Their move from manufacturing combination locks for briefcases and a wide range of fasteners and electrical hardware to motor-cycles was a brave one. However, within four years they were producing 40,000 motorcycles a year from their converted aircraft hangars on the foreshore of the Lago di Varese, north of Milan. These motorcycles were predominantly of small capacity (less than 350 cc), so in order to expand their range into larger varieties it was easier to buy engines from outside than develop new ones. The initial agreement called for Ducati to supply engines for a range of Cagiva-badged motorcycles for seven years, with an option for automatic renewal. There were to be 6,000 engines for 1984, 10,000 in 1985, and 14,000 in the following years, with production of all Ducati motorcycles to cease by the end of 1984.

Production of the Cagiva range of Ducati-powered motorcycles was initially very slow, so Ducati persuaded their parent group, VM, to allow the continuation of motor-cycle production for another year. Then, during 1985, Cagiva bought Ducati, and with it pledged to maintain the Ducati name with a completely new range of bikes. Later they also bought Husqvarna and Moto Morini, and today the Cagiva group is the largest manufacturer of motorcycles in Italy.

750 AND 906 PASO

When Cagiva acquired Ducati in 1985, they also inherited a production line-up with an uncertain future. The Mille engine had reached the limit of its development, but there was still development life in the Pantah range of engines. The biggest problem facing Ducati at this time was that they were not profitable, and there was no new investment, a scenario similar to that which had afflicted the British motorcycle industry in the 1970s. Even before the Castiglionis bought Ducati, the bevel-gear engines had been considered too expensive to produce. Taglioni had indicated as much back in 1977, but the future seemed to be with smaller-capacity motorcycles at that stage, so the bevel-gear engine continued for a few more years. Cagiva immediately decided to concentrate on the Pantah, which by that time had only been developed to a maximum of 750 cc. The initial contract had called for Ducati motors to be installed in Cagiva motorcycles, and several models appeared under this agreement, notably the 650 Alazzurra and the Elefant off-road bike. The 750 Pantah motor had made it to the F1, but the Castiglionis were determined to develop a completely new type of Ducati. The future of the Ducati marque lay in the radical Paso of 1986, not the traditional-style 750F1.

To the traditionalist, the announcement and display of the 750 Paso at the Milan Show of 1985 was a surprise – it was such a huge departure from the hard-edged, sporting F1 style. However, underneath all the bodywork was a vastly more modern motorcycle. It may not have been a race replica, but it promised to be the first Ducati that was a complete package. While the 750F1 was an excellent sporting motorcycle, as delivered from the factory it had poor rear suspension and inferior Michelin A48/M48 tyres, as was traditionally the case with Ducatis, even the race replicas, and the Paso was the first to break with this tradition.

The origins of the Paso only went back to 1984. When Cagiva entered into the agreement with Ducati, they also approached Bimota in Rimini to develop a new motorcycle around the Pantah engine. Massimo Tamburini (the 'ta' in 'Bimota') had broken with Giuseppe Morri (the 'mo' in the name) and set up on his own with Roberto Gallina, the former Italian racing champion and manager of the Suzuki HB Grand Prix team. He had been involved with the design of the TGA1 Suzuki Grand Prix with which both Marco Lucchinelli and Franco Uncini had won the 1981 and 1982 500 cc World Championships, and was approached by Cagiva to design a new chassis for the Mille (outlined in Chapter 9). Soon Tamburini was to

become head of the Cagiva research and development department, and when he considered the Bimota Pantah, later the DB1, too impractical for mass-production, he began work on a completely new frame for the Pantah engine (Bimota later put the DB1 into limited production). Tamburini called his new design the Paso, in memory of his friend and Grand Prix racer Renzo Pasolini, tragically killed in an accident at Monza in 1973.

Departing from more recent Ducati practice, Massimo Tamburini's cradle for the 750 Pantah engine did not use the engine as a stressed member. It was closely modelled on the frame that Bimota had designed for Yamaha, which had eventually become the FJ1100. Built from square-section tubing, but with an aluminium swing-arm with eccentric chain adjustment, both the wheelbase and steering geometry were altered from the 750F1. The swing-arm was lengthened by 60 mm, and the steering head angle pulled in to 25°, to give a wheelbase of 1,450 mm (57 inches). Trail was much less than the F1, at 103 mm (4 inches) rather than 133 mm (5.24 inches). The lower cradle unbolted to ease engine removal, but more importantly the new frame allowed access to the rear cylinder head to aid servicing of the desmodromic valve gear. There was no attempt to make the engine and frame visually appealing as they were to be completely covered by bodywork, but unclothed the Paso was one of the messiest looking Ducatis.

With the latest Marzocchi 42 mm M1R forks, and Öhlins CA 2508 rear shock absorber operating through a 'Soft Damp' rising rate linkage, the Paso had much more sophisticated suspension than any previous street Ducati. The Marzocchi forks were unusual in that the right fork leg controlled the rebound damping only, while the left fork leg looked after the compression stroke. Adjustment for rebound damping was provided by an external four-position knob on the right leg, which had initially appeared on the TT1 and TT2, and also on the Cagiva 500 cc Grand Prix bike. The rear Öhlins featured hydraulically adjustable spring preload. The wheel sizes were also a considerable break with tradition, with 3.75 x 16 and 5.00 x 16-inch Oscam wheels shod with the first new-generation low-profile Pirelli MP7 series radial tyres. The use of such wide tyres also required the engine to be offset to the left for the chain to clear the rear tyre.

There were also many changes to the engine. In a departure seen on the Cagiva Elefant a year earlier, the

The 750 Paso, with its full-
coverage bodywork, represented
a significant departure from the
traditional Ducati.

rear cylinder was rotated so that both inlet manifolds faced each other between the cylinders. The advantage of this was that both inlet tracts could now be of equal length, and straighter. They would also lend themselves to downdraught carburettors. Unfortunately, the choice of carburettors available for such a layout was limited, and Cagiva chose to adapt a Weber automotive type.

This 44DCNF 107 twin-barrel carburettor, 44 mm wide at the throttle and 36 mm at the venturi, was problematic and the cause of many complaints and factory jetting revisions. Despite problems with an off idle and mid-range flat spot, backfiring when hot, and throttle hesitations, the factory persevered with the Weber until 1991, seemingly oblivious to these problems. Finally they got the new engine right when they fitted the Mikuni carburettors for the 1991 season.

In other respects the engine was much the same as the 1986 750F1. It had the larger valves and slightly retarded valve timing (39/80/80/38), together with the stronger engine cases and gearbox, and a hydraulically operated dry clutch. All Pasos had the Kokusan ignition with the coils mounted on the left side of the frame, and there were two oil-coolers, one on each side of the fairing. Considering that the engine was now effectively silenced by the Silentium mufflers, the claimed power of 72.5 bhp at 7,900 rpm was very respectable. Where the Paso really did suffer in comparison with the F1 was in its weight. The claimed dry weight was 195 kg (430 lb), but *Cycle* weighed their test bike at 495 lb (224 kg) wet, a full 69 lb (31 kg) heavier than the F1.

The top speed achieved by *Motociclismo* in December 1986 was only 204.2 km/h (127 mph). However, sheer performance was not what the Paso was about. This was a refined sports tourer aimed at appealing to a broader range of riders than traditional Ducatis. The press loved it. *Motorcyclist* in the US in February 1987 said that 'the Paso represents a truly streetable version of the exotic Italian sport bike.'

There were many other changes incorporated in the Paso. A fuel pump kept the Weber supplied, and features like a fuel level gauge and much more modern switchgear put the Paso on a par with Japanese bikes. The styling, with totally enclosed bodywork and no clear fairing screen, was original, and eye-catching. However, while in many respects the Paso did bring Ducati up to date, as a sporting bike it still could not match a 750F1. I had the opportunity to test one of the first 750 Pasos in company with an F1, and the Paso was a disappointment. It understeered badly, and throttle response was vastly inferior to that provided by the 750F1's Dell'Orto PHM36s.

By 1987 the Öhlins rear shock absorber had been replaced by a much harsher Marzocchi unit, but in 1988 only small changes occurred. The triple clamps and handlebars were now painted black, and a fold-out handle was fitted to help in putting the bike on the centre-stand. In addition to red, there was now also the option of blue or white paintwork. The 750 Paso continued through until 1990, by which time it had the revised silencers from the new model 900SS, and the Weber had received numerous jetting modifications.

The importance of the Paso lay not in whether or not it was a superior motorcycle to the Ducatis of the past, but in the incorporation of new ideas within the traditional framework. For the first time since 1980, when the entire range had desmodromic valve gear,

The 906 Paso appeared in 1988
with different colours from the
750, but offered no real
improvements.

Right: Another misguided
marketing attempt was the 1986
Indiana, aimed at the US market.
Ducati Motor

there was a genuine commitment to aid servicing. The new frame design not only aided access to the rear cylinder head for valve adjustment, but Massimo Bordi's assistant, Gianluigi Mengoli, also simplified the rocker layout by incorporating a spring clip on the opening rocker shaft so that the rocker could be moved sideways to allow shim removal. No longer did the opening rockers and pins need to be removed. Unfortunately the 750 Paso still did not appeal to the traditional Ducati buyer, and ultimately suffered a similar fate to that of the 600TL and 900 Darmah. It was sold off at heavily discounted prices in 1990, by which time it had been superseded. Still, it provided a strong basis for further development during 1988, and by 1989 had evolved into the 906 Paso.

Most of the changes between the 750 and the 906 occurred in the engine, which was now based on the new 851 'large crankcase' eight-valve engine detailed in the next chapter. With a six-speed gearbox rather than the 750's five-speed, the new bike was called the 906, the '6' indicating the six speeds. Actual capacity of the new engine was 904cc, for while the bore of 92 mm was shared with the 851, an extra 4 mm of stroke, to 68 mm, gave additional displacement. With an extra 6.5 mm of stroke over the 750, con-rod length also grew, from 124 mm to 130 mm. The con-rod length to stroke ratio was still 1.9:1, despite the necessity to keep

the cylinder and head as short as possible. Big-end bearing size increased to 42 mm from the 40 mm on the 750. In other respects, too, the 906 was a marriage of the 750 and 851: the water cooling for the cylinders and heads of the 851 was coupled with the two-valve desmodromic heads of the 750 and similar Weber 44DCNF 116 twin-choke downdraught carburettor with slightly revised jetting (160 rather than 150 main jet). The dual oil-coolers of the 750 went, to be replaced by a single radiator. Valve sizes were up to 43 mm inlet and 38 mm exhaust, and in the search for more performance there were new camshafts yet again. These featured steeper ramps and higher lift, but less overlap. Valve timing was now inlet opening 20° before top dead centre and closing 60° after bottom dead centre, and exhaust opening 58° before bottom dead centre and closing 20° after top dead centre. Valve lift was increased considerably from the 750, to 11.1 mm for the inlet (9.35 mm on the 750) and 10.56 mm for the exhaust (8.50 mm on the 750). Despite a slight reduction in the compression ratio to 9.2:1, the claimed power went up to 88 bhp at 8,000 rpm. The combustion chamber also came in for some redesign at this stage, to become the 'tri-spherical' type.

The 750's Kokusan ignition with progressive advance was replaced by a Marelli Digiplex inductive discharge type, powered by a new 350-watt alternator, up from the 750's 300-watt type. The clutch and all the gearbox and primary drive ratios were shared with the 851, as were the water pump, thermostat and radiator. Despite the very similar external appearance of the 750 and 906 Paso, there were a few changes to the frame and suspension. To prevent the front wheel hitting the longer front cylinder, a 20 mm-longer Marzocchi M1R 42 mm fork was fitted, with 15 mm less travel, and revised fork offset brought the trail back to 96 mm (3.8 inches). The rear suspension was identical to the later 750 Paso, with a Marzocchi shock absorber connected to the 'Soft Damp' rising rate system. The 16-inch Oscam wheels were the same as the 750, as were the Brembo brakes. Unfortunately, despite the power increase the downside to all this extra engine sophistication was in the claimed increased weight of 10 kg, to 205 kg (452 lb).

In many ways the 906 represented an even greater departure from the traditional Ducati philosophy of reducing power and weight to achieve a balanced motorcycle. This was demonstrated clearly in contemporary road tests of the 906, for while the new, larger engine produced more mid-range torque, overall

technology 851 series backed up with a successful racing programme in World Superbike, and on the other was the development and refinement of the F2 Pantah racing bike that had first appeared in 1981. As there was no longer any use for a racing version of the two-valve Pantah, the air-cooled line was to remain a street bike with all the racing duties going to the water-cooled eight-valve series, which was marketed to appeal to the traditional Ducati owner who wanted a less complex motorcycle than the water-cooled and electronically fuel-injected eight-valve 851.

The 1989 900SS had shown promise but was still a flawed motorcycle. The revision that occurred during 1990 was not major, but was enough to create one of Ducati's modern classics. The desmodromic 904 cc air- and oil-cooled engine remained essentially the same but for the stronger crankcases that were standardized throughout the range that year. The biggest change was in the use of Mikuni 38 mm B67 (B73 for the US) constant-velocity carburettors, matched to equal-length inlet manifolds, a first for carburetted Ducatis. While not vastly improving the power output, throttle response almost matched that of the fuel-injected 907IE. The new 900SS also saw the return of the Kokusan ignition rather than the Marelli Digiplex.

While the frame was still similar, in order to quicken the steering the rake was reduced from 27° to 25°, with much less trail at 103 mm (4.1 inches). A new aluminium swing-arm reduced the wheelbase to 1,410 mm (55.5 inches) and was attached to a slightly longer Showa GD 022-007-OX shock absorber that raised the rear end and provided 65 mm (2.56 inches) of travel, still without any linkage. The Marzocchi M1R front forks went, and were replaced by a set of multi-adjustable 41 mm Showa GD 011 upside-down forks. The 17-inch Brembo wheels were same as the previous year, but larger 320 mm front disc brakes were now fitted, together with the 245 mm rear disc. In a further concession towards ease of maintenance, the newly styled steel fuel tank flipped up to allow access to the battery and air-cleaner. The oil-cooler was no longer mounted in the fairing, but on a bracket cast into the front cylinder head exhaust valve rocker cover; this was a very vulnerable position, right behind the front wheel. While the new aluminium swing-arm did not resolve all the previous cracking problems, the chain adjustment bolt also proved to be a weak point on the new model and was modified the following year.

The riding position was also completely revised, with higher clip-on handlebars and lower footpegs. A newly styled petrol tank, fairing and seat completed the redesign, which was first exhibited at the Cologne Show in September 1990. Two versions were offered, one with a half fairing clearly showing the engine and exposed oil-cooler, and one with full fairing. While the 900SS still had basically a traditional air-cooled engine, this engine was not the aesthetic delight that the earlier engines had been. However, it was a Ducati that carried on the tradition of the earlier 900SS by generating impressive performance through low weight and high torque. It lacked the high horsepower and technological complexity of even the 851, let alone Japanese four-cylinder motorcycles, but on the road it almost matched them and was easier to ride.

From 1991, power was now stated as at the rear wheel, rather than the crankshaft, so the claimed power for the 900SS was 73 bhp at 7,000 rpm. The claimed weight for the half-faired version was 180 kg (397 lb), but the on-the-road weight was about 200 kg (440 lb). The fully faired version weighed slightly more, at 183 kg (403 lb). Performance was similar to the 1989 900SS. In January 1991 *Motociclismo* put their test bike through the speed trap at 219.0 km/h (136 mph), and *Cycle*, in September 1991, managed a standing quarter mile time of 11.64 seconds at 114.72 mph (184.6 km/h), faster than a 907IE and not too far short of the 851. *Cycle* summed up the 900SS with the comment, '… this is the superlative sport bike that the Ducati faithful knew was at the heart of the original Pantah, the TT2, and the F1'. So good was the 1991 900SS that it continued as the mainstay of the Ducati range, virtually unchanged, until the end of 1997.

For 1992 only minor graphics changes, a passenger rear seat cowling, black-painted wheels, revised footrests brackets, and gold Brembo P4.30-34 front brake calipers (though these were fitted to 1991 bikes from No 1601) differentiated the two models. For the US, a black option with white wheels was available. There were even fewer changes for 1993. The frame was now bronze, and there was a new set of graphics, with a gold rather than black-bordered Ducati logo, and 'Desmodue' being termed for the Supersport line. In 1994 the wheels also became bronze, the fork was an uprated Showa, also fitted to the Superlight, and the clutch and brake reservoirs were remotely mounted. A larger-diameter front axle stiffened up the front end, and the foot controls and supports were now black. These changes lifted the claimed dry weight to 186 kg (410 lb). The 1995 model had an oil temperature gauge added to the instrument panel, the rear brake caliper was underslung, and there was a new windshield. These minimal differences from year to year show that the basic motorcycle was right when it was released in

1991. During 1995 7,195 Supersports were manufactured, down slightly on the 7,597 of 1994, and considerably less than the peak year of 1992, when 8,545 Supersports were built.

In November 1990 at the Bologna Show, two months after the new 900SS was displayed at Cologne, a smaller 750SS was shown, to be released during 1991. Using the five-speed 750 engine of the 750 Sport, it also featured a hydraulically operated dry clutch with the actuating system of the earlier 750, rather than the 900 type that operated from the left-side crankcase. While still using the Mikuni carburettor, they were the slightly different 38-B70 type. The 750SS used what Massimo Bordi termed the 'small crankcase', or the Pantah crankcase. This was used for all engines of 750 cc and less, and thus could not accommodate the six-speed gearbox of the newer 'big crankcase' family unless it was for the 350 cc or 400 cc versions that used narrower gears. The 750SS did not have the external oil-cooler of the 900, and had completely different valve timing. These new desmodromic camshafts would be standardized throughout the entire small crankcase family, including the 350, 400 and 600 Super Sport, as well as the later 600 Monster. The inlet valve opened at 31° before top dead centre, and closed 88° after bottom dead centre, while the exhaust valve opened at 72° before bottom dead centre and closed at 46° after top dead centre. Valve overlap, at 77°, was more like the Ducatis of the past, and the valve lift for the 41 mm and 35 mm valves much less than the 900, at 9.35 mm and 8.50 mm. Claimed power was 60 bhp at 8,500 rpm (at the rear wheel).

The 1991 750SS was only fitted with a single front 320 mm disc brake, and was the first Ducati to use the new gold Brembo P4 30/34 caliper. Following the practice of the racing Brembos, the new caliper used four pistons, but with the leading piston being of a smaller (30 mm) diameter than the trailing one (34 mm). The 750SS also used a smaller Brembo rear wheel, at 4.50 x 17. The front forks were still 41 mm upside-down Showas, but the non-adjustable GD 031 type. Weight was down to 173 kg (381 lb) and, like the 900, the 750 was offered with a choice of full or half fairings. With the full fairing, weight went up to 176 kg (388 lb), while the on-the-road weight (half-faired) was still a very light 417 lb (189 kg) as tested by *Motorcyclist* in April 1992, making the 750SS easily the lightest 750 cc bike on the market. A month earlier, in March 1992, *Cycle World* had put their test 750SS

Joining the 900 Supersport was
the similar 750 Supersport. This
1992 version has a half fairing.
Two Wheels

through the standing quarter mile at 12.10 seconds and
108.17 mph (174 km/h), noticeably faster than both
the 750 Sport and earlier 750F1 that shared a similar
engine. In the US the half-faired 750SS was sold as an
entry level Ducati for a bargain $7,350 in 1992, but
was less attractively priced in other markets. Top speed
was, however, down on the 900SS, with *Moto Sprint*
managing 208 km/h (129 mph).

The next year saw the 750SS receive the oil-cooler of
the 900SS, together with the black-painted wheels; as
with the 900SS, there was also the option of metallic
black and white wheels. The engine was unchanged but
for the clutch, which now became a hydraulically
operated wet type, a modification that would find its
way to all the small crankcase models. 1993 saw that
year's revised colours and graphics of the 900SS, and
for 1994 the 750SS received double 320 mm front
discs, a steel swing-arm instead of the 900SS's
aluminium type, along with the bronze wheels and
larger-diameter front axle. The 750SS continued largely
unchanged for 1995, but for the replacement of the
Showa GD 031 forks by a new type of upside-down

Marzocchi. There was no 750SS for the US market
after 1994, and a hybrid model was marketed; called
the 900CR, it was essentially a 900SS engine mounted
in the more basic running gear of the 750SS.

Alongside the 750SS in 1991 there was a new model
400 Supersport Junior, replacing the unusual 1990
Japanese market version. There was also a 350 Sport
for the Italian market. These bikes used identical
running gear to the 750, and also came with the option
of half or full fairing. The 66 x 51 mm 350 had 10.7:1
compression and produced 36 bhp at 10,500 rpm,
while the 70.5 x 51 mm 400 with 10:1 compression
made 46 bhp, also at 10,500 rpm. Both engines still
used the large 38 mm Mikuni carburettors of the larger
bikes, but they produced flat spots under full throttle,
not unlike the Weber-carburetted models. The exhaust
system was a two-into-one, exiting on the right side,
and, unlike the previous 400SS, the wet clutch was now
hydraulically operated. The colour scheme of the SS
Junior seemed to be a year behind the larger bikes, with
the black-painted wheels coming in 1993, together with
the bronze frame and steel swing-arm.

The 1992 900 Superlight, while not especially fast, was still a magnificent riding machine.
Rolf im Brahm

For 1994 the 350 was discontinued and replaced by a 27 bhp version of the 400 for the German market. The various changes to the 750SS that year also appeared on the Junior, and the almost identical 600SS was added to the range, in 33 and 53 bhp versions. While building the SS Junior was undoubtedly a useful method for the factory to increase sales, the physical proportions of the bike were that of the 750SS, so it really ended up being a considerably underpowered motorcycle. *MO* magazine in Germany, testing a 1993 400 cc model in March of that year, still managed a respectable top speed of 175 km/h (108.7 mph), but the bike weighed in at 190 kg (419 lb). Coupled with the general lack of mid-range power that the small engine provided, testers were not over-enthusiastic about the Junior. Also, by this time the Japanese market was becoming less important for Ducati, being overtaken by Germany, and the sales of the 400 slowed. For 1995 the 400SS Junior was no longer offered, but reappeared in 1996 and 1997 for the Italian market.

The last 600 Ducati had been the 600SL of 1984, and the 600SS released for the 1994 season resurrected the same 80 x 58 mm, 583cc, five-speed engine. With the valve timing and Mikuni carburettors of the 350/400/750SS, the new 600 made 53 bhp at 8,250 rpm (at the rear wheel). While it seemed that the 600SS was merely an update of a ten-year-old design, it was actually a significant improvement, reflecting ten years of subsequent development of the Pantah engine. Also offered as a 33 bhp for some markets, in 53 bhp form it was a superior model to the asthmatic 350 and 400SSs from which it was derived. This was shown in the performance. *MO* magazine, in December 1994, managed 197 km/h (122.4 mph) from their 182 kg (401 lb) wet test bike. The 600SS continued virtually unchanged in 1995, but for the use of new 41 mm upside-down Marzocchi forks, the right leg no longer having the provision to mount an additional brake caliper.

900 SUPERLIGHT

Following the success of the numbered series of 851 (888) Sport Production bikes in 1990 and 1991, a numbered series of 900 Supersports was planned for 1992. To be called the 900SL, or 900 Superlight, originally 500 bikes were to be made, but this eventually became 1,317, with 300 bright yellow ones going to the USA. However, unlike the 888SPs, the

Superlight had the standard 73 bhp 900SS engine, frame and suspension. The lightweight parts on the bike took the form of carbon-fibre mudguards, vented clutch cover, and 17-inch Marvic composite wheels of the type fitted to the 750 Montjuich, Santamonica, 851 Strada of 1988, and Japanese market 400SS of 1989. Other main differences were a single seat (with minimal padding), high-rise exhausts, and fully floating 320 mm Brembo front discs. The Superlight was only offered with a full fairing, and with a claimed weight of 176 kg (388 lb) it was indeed a light bike, being significantly lighter than any comparable bike in its class.

Performance was similar to the regular 900SS. However, *Motorrad*, testing Superlight No 537 in June 1992, only managed a top speed of 204 km/h (126.7 mph). *Cycle World*, in August 1992, put their test bike No 253 through a standing quarter mile at 11.74 seconds and 113.78 mph (183.1 km/h), almost identical to their 1991-test 900SS. On the scales the Superlight failed to match the factory claim of being 7 kg less than the 900SS. *Cycle World*'s example weighed in at just 5 lb (2.3 kg) less, 409 lb (185 kg) dry, or 436 lb (198 kg) wet. Also, despite the presence of a numbered plate on the triple clamp, too many Superlights were built for them to benefit from any rarity value. They also offered few advantages over a standard 900SS except for the wheels and carbon-fibre guards.

The next year saw the release of Superlight II, but this model was unfortunately a step backwards. Repeating a scenario so often typical of Ducati, the first model was the best, with subsequent versions losing many of the special detail touches. First to go were the Marvic wheels, replaced by the regular Brembo type, now painted bronze to match the frame. There was no longer a vented clutch cover, and even the fully floating Brembo front discs were replaced by the normal steel variety. The only concession made to differentiate the Superlight II from the normal 900SS was the use of a fully floating rear brake linkage, with a carbon-fibre torque arm; breakages of this on some early models of both the Superlight II and 888SP5 saw its replacement by an alloy item. All these changes pushed the claimed weight up to 179 kg (395 lb), though *PS* weighed in their 1993 test bike at 200.5 kg (442 lb) wet, only 3 kg up on the 1992 model. Massimo Bordi admitted to me in 1993 that the Superlight of that year had been a mistake, and many details were rectified for 1994.

While cosmetically the 1994 Superlight III was very similar to the Superlight II, there were quite a few changes. First, the fully floating Brembo front discs returned and, instead of the regular clutch cover, a carbon-fibre one appeared. There was a new, stronger swing-arm, and the suspension was uprated through the use of the 41 mm higher-specification upside-down Showa forks that had appeared on the 1993 888SP5. The brake and clutch fluid reservoirs were remotely mounted, and the colours were now red or yellow. Weight was up yet again, to 182 kg (401 lb) dry, but the Superlight III was a more attractive proposition than the II had been. The Superlight IV of 1995 was almost identical, but for the addition of an oil temperature gauge and the new windshield, both shared with the 900SS. Each year production was reduced, and only 578 Superlights were produced in 1995.

The Superlight was no longer offered for the US market in 1994. In its place was the 900SS Sport Production, a Superlight III with a dual seat and low exhaust pipes. These 175 bikes also came with a serialised plate, and they were again offered in 1995. The lack of any passenger accommodation was one of the limitations of the Superlight, and in many markets they had to be discounted. While the sporting purist preferred the single seat, most buyers required a pillion, and for that reason the regular 900SS consistently outsold its more expensive and glamorous partner. If the Superlight had been a genuine limited edition bike, like the 888 Sport Production series, offering improved engine performance with better-quality suspension, it might have been more successful. As it was, for most buyers there were few benefits over a standard Supersport to justify the additional cost.

M600/900 MONSTER

By the end of 1992, with the end of the 907IE, the entire Ducati range was one of sporting motorcycles. These were the successful lines of the Supersport Desmodue, and Desmoquattro, so there was some surprise when a completely different Ducati was released at the Cologne Show in October 1992. Called the M900, and nicknamed *Il Mostro* ('the Monster'), it was the brainchild of Miguel Galluzzi, and was neither a sporting nor touring motorcycle. Neither was it a cruiser like the unsuccessful Indiana, but underneath its minimalist styling lay a truly competent sporting motorcycle in the best Ducati tradition. The Monster was probably the first successor to the original 750GT,

Launched in 1993, the iconic 900M Monster has become Ducati's most successful motorcycle.

a light motorcycle with a race-bred frame, torquey engine, and an upright riding position. It was also released at exactly the right time, and was immediately successful, though production was delayed until mid-1993 because of component supply problems. The Monster became a fashion statement, even being bought by such notables as Barry Sheene and Damon Hill.

The Monster seemed to be a 'parts bin special'. The engine was the identical 73 bhp air/oil-cooled unit of the 900SS, but the oil cooler was now mounted above the front cylinder. The frame was a modified 851/888 with 24° of fork rake and 104 mm (4 inches) of trail, and the same rear suspension linkage (without ride height adjustment). As this was the same frame that had been used to win three consecutive World Superbike Championships, it was obviously understressed by the 900SS motor. The non-adjustable 41 mm inverted Showa forks of the 750SS and a Boge rear unit were fitted, but the front brakes were the same dual 320 mm Brembos of the 900SS, as were the 17-inch Brembo wheels. The M900 was a curious mixture. There was no tachometer on the basic instrument panel, but parts of the bodywork (like the side panels) were carbon-fibre. The low weight of 184 kg (406 lb), and the low seat height of 770 mm (30.3 inches), contributed to a compact and manoeuvrable package. The US magazine *Motorcyclist*, testing a Monster in October 1993, put their example through a standing quarter mile in 11.78 seconds, at 112.0 mph (180 km/h). Their measured top speed, despite the poor aerodynamics, was 128 mph (206 km/h). This was with the same (15/37) final drive gearing as the 900SS, but there was also the option of a 39-tooth rear wheel sprocket. Even fully wet, the Monster only weighed 199 kg (439 lb), and certainly performed much more strongly than the old 750GT or any of its derivatives such as the 860GT, GTS or 900SD Darmah. Despite limited ground clearance due to the low mufflers, it also handled considerably more adeptly on its shorter, 1,430 mm (56.3-inch) wheelbase.

The M900 continued unchanged through 1994 except for the addition of black as well as red paintwork. For 1995 it mirrored the rest of the range by gaining the bronze frame and wheels, together with grey timing belt covers and rear sprocket cover. The mufflers now featured a chamfer to increase ground clearance.

During 1995 a small number (30) of special M900s, called the 'Club Italia', were manufactured for members of this exclusive club at the instigation of the Castiglioni brothers. Members included Piero Ferrari, Michele Alboreto and Clay Regazzoni. Not for sale, they were fitted with many higher-specification components such as an Öhlins rear shock absorber, fully floating iron Brembo discs, a leather seat, and fully adjustable Showa forks.

So successful was the Monster concept that in 1994 a 600 version, in red or yellow, was released. Using the same motor as the 600SS, but with the 900M two-into-two exhaust system, and the same single 320 mm disc front brake, the 600M was also made in 33 bhp as well as 53 bhp versions. Dry weight was 174 kg (384 lb), and the 600M tested by *Motociclismo* in September 1994 managed a top speed of 176.0 km/h (109.4 mph). With a standing 400-metre time of 13.592 seconds, at 156.36 km/h (97 mph), the 600M performed very similarly to the 750GT of more than 20 years earlier. In 1995 the 600M received the minor changes of the 900M, and at the 1995 Milan Show the only new Ducati model displayed was the 750 Monster, identical to the 600 but for the larger engine and an oil-cooler.

The Monster soon established itself as a particularly important model in the Ducati line-up, and with demand for naked motorcycles increasing it continues to be so.

Marco Lucchinelli on his way to
victory on the 851 prototype in
the Daytona Battle of the Twins
race of 1987.

1990

Reverting to the 888 (from the larger 919), the factory bikes were sufficiently well developed for Raymond Roche to win the World Superbike Championship. With more power (130–134 bhp at 11,000 rpm) and less weight, at 147 kg (324 lb), by the end of the season it was also the improvement in reliability that clinched the Championship. Additionally, there was an improvement in tractability, with more mid-range power due to revised camshafts. Significantly, the 1990 engine made a useful 110 bhp at 8,000 rpm, which was reflected in the results, with Roche winning eight and team mate Giancarlo Falappa one, before he crashed heavily during qualifying at the Österreichring. They still suffered crankcase failures, but most of the electrical problems had been eliminated. It had been found that a faulty rpm sensor had been the cause of most of the electronic failures.

Visually, the 1990 bike was little changed from the previous year. It still used Öhlins suspension, with a revised rear linkage, and by the end of the year had

Below: Roche won the 1990 World Superbike Championship on the 888 cc factory bike.

more upswept exhausts with carbon-fibre mufflers. Other carbon-fibre parts appeared, such as a seat/tail section and front guard, in order to get the bike closer to the class minimum weight of 140 kg (309 lb). Starting the season at 157 kg (346 lb) with oil and water, by Monza in October the bike weighed a significant 10 kg (22 lb) less. A smaller, curved radiator raised the cooling temperature to 70–75°C because it had been found that sometimes the bikes had been running as cool as 40°C. An electronic tachometer was also used occasionally, and would appear again in 1991.

A limited number of 888 Corsa Roche Replica (formerly Lucchinelli Replica) racers were again available to selected dealer teams. These incorporated many of the developments that had occurred during 1989, setting a pattern that was to follow in subsequent years, and meant that the privateer bikes would always be one year behind the factory. The Roche Replica of 1990 had the upper outer tube Öhlins forks, Marvic magnesium wheels, and lightweight parts such as an aluminium sub-frame and magnesium

primary drive cover. As with the factory bikes, the
computer was housed in a bracket off the steering
head. The claimed weight was 158 kg (348 lb), and the
engine used larger (34 mm and 30 mm) valves, and a
new inlet camshaft. Developed from the previous
racing season, this opened the inlet valve at 53° before
top dead centre, closing 71° after bottom dead centre.
Intake valve lift was up 1 mm to 11 mm. The exhaust
camshaft was the same as before, and was shared with
the Sport Production series. Compression ratio was up
to 12:1. The Roche Replica also used a completely
different gearbox, with different ratios.

Alongside the Roche Replica of 1990, Ducati
released possibly their most significant street bike since
the 750SS of 1974, and certainly the most significant
new street Ducati since the Cagiva take-over in 1985.
Called the 851 Sport Production 2, this motorcycle was
considerably removed from the 1989 Sport Production,
and was the closest street bike to a factory racer
available. In essence, it was a Roche Replica with lights
and treaded tyres. Primarily aimed at the Japanese
market, then Ducati's prime export destination and a
market obsessed with race replicas, the SP2 was
displayed at the Tokyo Show at the end of 1989.

Still called an 851, the SP2 was similar to the 1989
Sport Production but with an overbore to 94 mm to
take the displacement up to 888 cc, as with the racing
bikes. With the same 33 mm and 29 mm valves, and
the same camshafts, power was up to 109 bhp (at the
rear wheel). In the engine department there were still
the Pankl con-rods, a polished and lightened
crankshaft, polished rockers, oil cooler and vented dry
clutch. Both the inlet and exhaust systems were
considerably less restrictive, with no inlet air box and
larger-diameter exhausts. The gearbox had the same
ratios as the 1988 851 Superbike (lower third, fourth
and fifth than the Strada), and there was a return to
twin injectors per cylinder. However, while the frame
was identical to that of 1989, this bike had the same
suspension as the works racers, the Öhlins FG9050
42 mm upside-down forks and an Öhlins DU8070 rear
unit. The quality of these components alone justified
the price differential between the SP and the Strada, but
there were many other differences besides the extra
power. Like the 888 Corsa, the rear sub-frame was
lightweight aluminium, there were fully floating iron
320 mm Brembo discs, and a carbon-fibre rear guard.
The SP2 had moved further away from the Strada to

become a true limited-edition race replica. Styling was very similar to the Strada, and apart from the suspension the most visible distinguishing marks were Agip and Michelin stickers on the fairing, and a numbered plaque on the top fork yoke. Dry weight was up from the SP1, largely due to the forks, at 188 kg (414.5 lb) from 180 kg (397 lb).

Performance of the SP2 dramatically eclipsed any previous street Ducati, even the 851 Strada. *Motociclismo*, in April 1990, managed an impressive top speed of 255 km/h (158 mph) from SP2 No 74. *Cycle* magazine also found the SP2 a strong performer, making 96.4 bhp at 9,000 rpm on their dyno in December 1990. *Motorcyclist*, testing the same SP2 No 50 in July 1991, powered through the standing quarter mile in an impressive 10.72 seconds at 128 mph (206 km/h). The SP2 was barely street legal in many countries, and the larger-capacity exhaust system with minimal muffling produced sounds reminiscent of the older Super Sports with their Contis, or the 750 Montjuich with its Verlicchi competition system. The racing-specification Öhlins forks transformed the handling of the 851 Strada, and the SP2 was one of the most confidence-inspiring motorcycles to ride at high speeds. *Cycle* thought it a fantastic motorcycle, claiming it to be 'perhaps the best production race bike money can buy'. To put the SP2 into perspective, they hailed it as 'one of the most desirable sporting motorcycles since the original Ducati 750SS', a statement with which I whole-heartedly agree.

In rather typical Ducati fashion, the Strada was softened slightly for 1990 with the addition of a dual seat. As the Strada and Sport Production 851 lines developed they diverged, and the performance gap between them increased. By 1990 the relationship was similar to that which existed in 1974 between the 750 Sport and 750SS, and also in 1986 between the 750F1 and 750 Montjuich. The higher-performance versions were made in more limited numbers (about 500 SP2s), and sold at a price almost 50% higher. However, in the case of the 851 series the performance difference was far more considerable between the SP and the Strada, as there was a genuine 20% power difference, and the SP had better-quality suspension, less weight, and improved weight distribution.

The 1990 Strada continued essentially unchanged in the engine department, but the Pankl con-rods were replaced by the standard Pantah style. The addition of the dual seat with a stronger sub-frame increased the

weight to 506 lb (230 kg) as tested by *Cycle World* in June 1990. Performance, however, had not suffered, and their test bike posted a standing quarter mile time of 11.26 seconds at 121.29 mph (195 km/h), with a measured top speed of 150 mph (241 km/h).

1991

An indication of the outcome of the 1991 World Superbike Championship was demonstrated at an international Superbike race in Mexico in December 1990. Doug Polen and Raymond Roche were on factory 888s, and Polen won both legs. Recently having left the Yoshimura Suzuki team, Polen had only tested the Fast by Ferracci Ducati at Daytona a week before the Mexico race.

For 1991 there would still be the two factory bikes, for Raymond Roche and Giancarlo Falappa, but also support for Polen and Stéphane Mertens. Polen was racing for Eraldo Ferracci, an Italian who had spent 25 years building racing bikes in the US, and who had enjoyed moderate success with Ducati 888s in 1990 in the AMA series with rider Jamie James. In comparison to the factory effort, Ferracci operated on a much smaller budget, and Polen was contracted to Dunlop rather than Michelin tyres. He also teamed up with the legendary veteran Ducati tuners, Giorgio Nepoti and Rino Caracchi of NCR.

Both the factory and two supported riders had bikes close to the class minimum of 140 kg (309 lb). Through the considerable use of carbon-fibre for radiator, exhaust and fairing brackets, as well as the airbox and air ducts, rear-brake torque-arm and fuel tank, the works machines weighed 143 kg (315 lb). Other modifications such as a smaller rear disc (190 mm in carbon or steel from 216 mm in steel), smaller calipers, titanium exhausts and Termignoni carbon-fibre mufflers, also contributed to the weight reduction. An important by-product was the improvement in weight distribution, with more front weight bias. In January 1992 the Japanese magazine *Bikers Station* put the Fast by Ferracci 888 on the scales: total weight was 146.5 kg (323 lb), and weight distribution was 51/49% front to rear.

By getting close to the allowable minimum weight, Ducati were now making the most of the regulations that gave two-cylinder motorcycles a 25 kg (55 lb) advantage over their four-cylinder opposition. These regulations came in for increasing criticism from the

Below: Doug Polen
demonstrating the style that took
him to two World Superbike
Championships.

Right: The 1991 SP3 was similar
to the SP2 but for a carbon-fibre
front guard and upswept
exhausts. This is the author's
example.

Japanese teams, but the credit still had to be given to
Ducati for designing and developing a twin-cylinder
motorcycle capable of competing with 750 cc four-
cylinder bikes. When the regulations were drafted in
1987, it had appeared inconceivable that a twin could
become as dominant as the Ducati did during the 1991
season. So good had the 888 racer become that Ducati
won 23 World Superbike races, and they were only
beaten once. Doug Polen himself was so dominant on
the Fast by Ferracci Ducati that he won 17 races. He
even held the outright lap record for a while at Jarama,
Spain, during 1991. To emphasize the superiority of the
Ducati 888, Davide Tardozzi on his Team Grottini bike
won the European Superbike Championship, with four
wins from six starts.

The Fast by Ferracci bike used the 888 cc engine
with 36 mm and 31 mm valves, and with 11.8:1
compression produced 133 bhp at 11,500 rpm. The
camshafts used by Ferracci had more lift, but less
duration than even the SP, with the inlet opening 48°
before top dead centre, closing 68° after bottom dead
centre, and the exhaust valve opening 68° before
bottom dead centre and closing 40° after top dead
centre. A new crossover exhaust system contributed to
the extra 3 bhp, and more upswept exhausts,
homologated on the SP3, together with some changes
to the front fairing, improved aerodynamics. Roche's

bike sometimes featured different specifications, but all
the racing engines now used modified crankcases that
solved the crankcase cracking problem of 1990. There
was now more extensive webbing and ribbing around
the base of the cylinder. Engine problems early in the
season were solved by drilling an oilway up the Pankl
con-rod to the gudgeon pin. Whereas the FBF bike still
used the Öhlins upside-down forks as fitted the
previous year and to the 1991 Corsa and SP, Roche had
a new type of Öhlins fork. Braking was usually by a
combination 320 mm steel and carbon disc with
Brembo calipers, and wheels a Marchesini 3.50 x 17
front, and 6.25 x 17 rear. With slightly less steering
head angle, at 23.5°, the wheelbase was shortened
slightly to 1,420 mm (55.9 inches).

The 50 Corsas made in 1991 included many of the
modifications of the factory bikes. Using a carbon-fibre
seat-tail unit together with a carbon-fibre petrol tank,
the weight was down to 155 kg (342 lb). The computer
was now housed in a carbon-fibre bracket
incorporating the air intake and supporting the
electronic tachometer. The engine was largely
unchanged from 1990 (but for the stronger
crankcases), and the claimed power (at the rear wheel)
was 128 bhp. Wheel sizes were up to 3.75 x 17 front,
and 6.00 x 17 rear. The frame, brakes and suspension
were identical to 1990.

The SP3 was slightly restyled for 1991. Even though it was still called an 851, the 888 cc SP3 now had upswept mufflers, carbon-fibre front mudguard and black wheels, a revised air intake system and, like the SP2, was also made in small numbers (about 500), with a numbered plaque on the top triple clamp celebrating the winning of the 1990 World Superbike Championship. With the Agip and Michelin stickers and the white racing plate on the rear seat, it was the closest replica yet and really looked like a street version of the 1991 factory racers. The claimed power of the SP3 was slightly up on the SP2, now 128 bhp at 10,500 rpm at the crankshaft, or 111 bhp at the rear wheel. All 1991 models received the stronger crankcases, and the SP3 a specially machined and polished crankshaft. While most of the engine and gearbox specifications were unchanged, one area where the SP3 was improved over the SP2 was the clutch, a notorious area of weakness; it now had eight driving plates, and could also be retrofitted to the rest of the 851 range. Still with the Öhlins FG9050 upside-down forks, the SP3 was fitted with a slightly different Öhlins DU0060 rear unit. Front brakes were the same fully floating 320 mm iron Brembo with four-piston calipers, but the front master cylinder diameter was increased from 15 mm to 16 mm. Other minor changes from the SP2 included a degasser in the aluminium fuel tank (reducing the

capacity to 17 litres from 20 litres), and remote location of the front brake and clutch reservoirs. Claimed dry weight was still 188 kg (414.5 lb) and essentially the two models were identical.

As expected, the performance of the SP3 was similar to that of the SP2. *Moto Sprint* achieved a top speed of 261.1 km/h (162.2 mph) with a 0–400-metre time of 10.78 seconds at 207.664 km/h (129 mph). *Motociclismo* managed 106.82 bhp at 10,250 rpm, at the rear wheel, so just like the SP2, the SP3 was a powerful motorcycle. Wet weight for the SP3, as measured by *Moto Sprint*, was 202.1 kg (445 lb). Being fortunate enough to have some experience of riding an SP3, I can confirm that these motorcycles were superb sporting bikes. Despite being a modern, computerized device, there was still a lot of the rawness of previous race replica Ducatis in the SP3.

The 851 Strada for 1991 gained Showa GD011 upside-down front forks, but also the Öhlins DU0060 rear unit of the SP3. Engine specifications remained unchanged but for a slightly lower compression ratio of 10.5:1, with the claimed power being 91 bhp at 9,000 rpm at the rear wheel. Dry weight went up to 199 kg (439 lb). Visually it was little changed from the dual-seat 1990 bike, and was still red with white wheels. The front brake and clutch reservoir were now remotely located, as with the SP3, and the diameter of the front brake master cylinder was also increased to 16 mm. The eccentric adjustment for the ride height was also deleted from the Strada, though it remained on the SP. The machined rear suspension rocker arm was also replaced by a forged item. As tested by *Cycle* in September 1991, the 851 covered the standing quarter mile in 11.23 seconds at 120.80 mph (194.4 km/h). *Motorcyclist*, in November 1991, weighed the 851 Strada at 220 kg (485 lb) wet, and managed a top speed of 149 mph (240 km/h).

1992

Although Ing. Bordi had talked during 1991 of a new bike with a longer-stroked engine in a Massimo Tamburini-designed frame with a single-sided swing-arm, the 888 had proved so competitive that it continued virtually unchanged from the previous year. Whereas the street 851 and 888SP4 had a revised frame, footpeg brackets and styling, the factory racers and 888 Corsa still used the 1991 frame and bodywork.

Doug Polen was now riding for the official Ducati team, alongside Giancarlo Falappa. With sponsorship from Italian sunglasses manufacturer Police, the team was managed by another former Italian World Champion, Franco Uncini; he replaced Marco Luchinelli, who had been arrested and imprisoned for drug offences during 1991. Unfortunately, due to the bad publicity, this resulted in considerable lost sponsorship. Uncini had a long association with Ducati, having raced a 750SS during 1975 and 1976 for Bruno Spaggiari's team in the Italian Championship. Raymond Roche now found himself a privateer, electing not to become part of the Police team, but still with a factory bike, and tuned by ace tuner Rolando Simonetti. More often than not, Roche's bike was the fastest of all the Ducatis and allowed him to come from the back to win the race after one of his traditional poor starts. Other factory machines were supplied to Stéphane Mertens, Davide Tardozzi and Daniel Amatriain.

There were very few changes to the all-conquering 1991 888. With yet another new clutch and a new exhaust camshaft design, the power was up slightly to 135 bhp at 11,800 rpm. The new exhaust camshaft allowed safe revs to 12,000 rpm, and different valve sizes of 35 mm and 30 mm were tried, along with variable-length inlet tracts on Roche's bike. The biggest changes came in weight saving, not just in carbon-fibre parts, but also now within the engine. Narrower

gearbox gears (6 mm to the Corsa's 10 mm), hollow camshafts and more titanium and magnesium helped to get the weight down to 142 kg (313 lb), and the shape of the Pankl con-rods was slightly altered to eliminate some of the breakages of the past. All bikes now used the new type of 42 mm Öhlins fork that Roche had used the previous year. The type of disc rotors varied, Polen generally using US-made C-CAT carbon discs, and Roche the regular 320 mm steel Brembo type.

Due to some difficulties within the team, Doug Polen had a slow start to the season, and the Ducatis were nowhere near as dominant as they had been in 1991. Polen won nine, Roche six, and Falappa four races (out of a total of 26), but the most impressive was probably Carl Fogarty's win in the second leg at Donington on one of the production Corsas. However, Polen again won the World Championship, with Raymond Roche second, but it was obvious now that the 888 was nearing the end of its competitive life.

The weight-saving programme of the factory racers passed down to the 888 Superbike Racing (Corsa) for 1992. Still using the 1991 frame and bodywork, but with more carbon-fibre, the weight was reduced to 150 kg (330 lb). The engine now had magnesium primary drive, ignition, and camshaft covers, and, while power was still quoted at 128 bhp at 11,000 rpm, the Superbike Racer received the revised exhaust camshaft, still with 9 mm of valve lift, but with the valve opening at 71° before bottom dead centre, and closing 45° after top dead centre.

The suspension was the new type of 41 mm Öhlins forks with magnesium triple clamps, as used on the factory bikes, together with an Öhlins shock absorber as before. The 320 mm front brakes were also uprated to the latest Brembo racing type with a 19 mm PS13B master cylinder and P2105N 30 and 34 mm calipers. The rear disc was now a smaller 190 mm unit (from 210 mm). All the frame dimensions remained unchanged from 1989, but for a slight increase in trail to 98 mm (3.86 inches). The limited number of 1992 Superbike Racers made (30) were much more competitive bikes than in previous years, as witnessed by Fogarty's consistently good results on his privateer Corsa. While they were no more powerful, they were much lighter, even if there was 7 kg (15.4 lb) between the Superbike Racer and the factory bikes.

In 1992 the first signs of cost effectiveness became evident, even with the SP series. While the factory racers and Corsas still used the old frame with

Carl Fogarty and Giancarlo Falappa, and Fabrizio Pirovano was Davide Tardozzi's new rider. Other factory 955s went to James Whitham, riding for the British Moto Cinelli team, and occasional World Superbike rides to Troy Corser, the Australian 1993 Superbike Champion, now riding for Eraldo Ferracci in the US AMA Superbike series (on a 955 cc-engined 1994 Corsa). After Falappa injured himself badly while testing, Mauro Lucchiari replaced him in the Ferrari team.

A new type of 46 mm Öhlins upside-down fork was used, together with an Öhlins rear unit. The new airbox, with 58 mm intakes and larger valves of 37 mm and 31 mm, allowed the 955 engine to develop 150 bhp at 11,000 rpm. Titanium valves were tried, but were the cause of several engine failures throughout the season. The 955s also used titanium Pankl con-rods, and Omega 11.6:1 pistons. The weight was right on the minimum 145 kg, and 290 mm carbon front brakes were gripped by the latest type of Brembo racing caliper.

It was a lot to expect the new bike to be totally competitive immediately, and there were some initial problems in the handling department. Race results confirmed that the 955 still needed some development;

winning just 12 out of the 22 World Superbike Championship races, it was nowhere near as dominant as in the past. However, some of this was probably due to injuries to Carl Fogarty and, more seriously, Giancarlo Falappa. By the end of the season most of the factory 955s had a 25 mm longer swing-arm, together with a different rear shock leverage ratio to improve rear-end traction. Fogarty received a special swing-arm, while lesser teams such as Moto Cinelli had to fabricate their own. Fogarty eventually came back from breaking his wrist at Hockenheim to win the World Superbike Championship with 10 victories. It had been an impressive debut season for the new 955.

Rather than using the new 916 as a basis, the 30 1994 Corsas owed much to the 1993 926 cc factory racer. As a thoroughly developed machine, this was still a surprisingly competitive piece of equipment, as was so ably demonstrated by Austrian rider Andreas Meklau with his two second place finishes at the Austrian round at Zeltweg. There were quite a few differences from the previous version, most noticeably the use of a 96 mm piston to give 926 cc. With a claimed 142 bhp at 11,500 rpm, the 926 used the lighter titanium Pankl con-rods,

While the trademark trellis frame continued on the 916, there was a single-sided swingarm, and spectacular attention to detail. *Rolf im Brahm*

Right: The 916 rewrote the rules for styling and twin-cylinder performance, and became the most important model ever in Ducati's history. *Rolf im Brahm*

1 mm larger inlet valve (37 mm), and new, stronger crankcases. The use of lighter Omega pistons and crankshaft assembly improved the response of the larger engine, overcoming criticisms of the past. The frame was altered too, with the steering head angle now 22½°, and the trail 102 mm (4.02 inches), and there were new Brembo P4.32-36 front brake calipers, with a 19 mm master cylinder, together with thinner discs. At the rear no torque-arm was now fitted, and other changes mirrored those of the factory 926 of 1993, including a new airbox and larger-bored exhaust, 42 mm Öhlins suspension and steering damper, a new crankcase breather and tank, and five-spoke Marchesini wheels with rim sizes of 3.50 x 17 and 6.00 x 17. The final version of the old design may have been overshadowed in 1994 by the 916 and 955, but it was still a very impressive racing motorcycle, and one that could be purchased by privateers.

When the 916 was released in early 1994, it received incredibly favourable press reports and, as in the past, a Sport Production version was made available. By 1992, with the 888/851, the Strada and SP lines had

become quite diverged, but in 1993 the gap had closed again as the SP5 had not received the racing Öhlins front forks. With the 916 the gap closed even more: there was virtually no difference in weight, and while the SP made higher rpm horsepower, at the expense of the lower end, the performance differential was nowhere near as great as it had been between 1990 and 1992. The 916SP had the same higher-specification engine of the SP5, still with twin injectors per cylinder, and the same valve sizes of 34 mm and 30 mm, together with the titanium Pankl con-rods of the Corsa. With 11.2:1 compression, the claimed power was up to 131 bhp at 10,500 rpm (at the crankshaft). The titanium con-rods (still with a length of 124 mm) allowed the maximum engine rpm to be increased to an impressive 11,500. Unlike the previous SP, the 916 version used the 350-watt alternator of the Strada, and no longer had the close-ratio gearbox.

The chassis was also identical to the 916 Strada, except for the use of an Öhlins DU3420 rear shock absorber. All the bodywork, together with wheels and front suspension, was the same, and there was no

carbon-fibre airbox as was initially indicated, the
carbon-fibre parts being limited to the front and rear
guards, chainguard, and the Termignoni mufflers. The
SP had adjustable brake and clutch levers, but the frame
was identical to the Strada, down to the aluminium sub-
frame, an item previously reserved for the SP series only.
While the claimed dry weight was 192 kg (423 lb), the
German magazine *PS*, in their test of August 1994,
weighed their bike at 207 kg (456 lb). Their 916SP also
reached 259 km/h (161 mph). As with previous SPs, the
916SP had the fully floating iron 320 mm front discs,
and a white number patch on the seat.

The 916 Strada, released at the Milan Show in
October 1993, was the most significant new model
Ducati since the 851 (even more so than the
Supermono a year earlier). While the engine was not
very different from previous versions, the 916 was
designed as a total package, with, for perhaps the first
time at Ducati, an attempt to make the bike easy to
service. The front forks were 43 mm Showa GD051,
supported in a massive 80 mm steering head, with
especially sturdy triple clamps. Everywhere there was

the most spectacular attention to detail, from the
machining of the top triple clamp with its steering
damper, to the levers and controls. The wheels, shared
with the SP, were three-spoke Brembo in sizes of
3.50 x 17 and 5.50 x 17, mounted with either Pirelli or
Michelin tyres, the rear a larger 190/50-ZR17. Perhaps
the weakest aspect in the 916 Strada specification was
its Showa GD052-007-02 rear shock absorber, which
was criticized for being under-damped.

In the engine department the 916 Strada was a
combination of the 888 Strada and SP, having the
external oil-cooler and the Pankl (non-titanium) con-
rods. The clutch was the 15-plate 888 Strada type, as
was the six-speed gearbox, and the camshafts were also
the milder Strada, still with 33 mm and 29 mm valves.
With a single injector per cylinder, claimed power was
109 bhp at 9,000 rpm (or 114 bhp depending on the
source), at the crankshaft. However, in reality the 916
was a considerably faster bike than its power figures
would suggest. Improved aerodynamics over the 888,
and a claimed dry weight of 198 kg (436 lb), saw the
916 Strada approach the performance of the much

Carl Fogarty totally dominated
the 1995 World Superbike
Championship on the 955 of
Ferrari's Ducati Corse.

more highly tuned 888SP models: *PS*, in July 1994, saw 256 km/h (159 mph). The wet weight was 211 kg (465 lb). For an engine not that different from the 888 Strada, the 916 Strada produced considerably more power, 104.3 bhp at 9,000 rpm on *Cycle World*'s dyno in July 1994. They also managed a standing quarter mile time of 10.72 seconds at 130.62 mph (210 km/h), figures approaching that of the 888 Sport Production. The 916 won every 'Bike of the Year' award in 1994, but *Motorcyclist* magazine in the US summed it up in their test of September 1994: 'The essence of the new 916 is its intoxicating blend of sound, looks, feel and the way it turns street riding into an almost religious experience.'

While most of the attention was centred on the 916, the 888 Strada also continued to be offered as a 1994 model, alongside the 888LTD for the US market. The 100 examples of the 888LTD were built in September 1993, prior to the commencement of the production of the 916, and each was fitted with an identification plaque, like the earlier Sport Production series. While they had carbon-fibre mudguards, much of the LTD was the same as the 888 Strada, including the engine, bronze-painted wheels, larger-diameter (25 mm) front axle, and black anodized footpeg brackets and controls. The LTD retained the SPO's Öhlins rear shock absorber with eccentric ride height adjustment, and made 95.8 bhp at 9,000 rpm, at the rear wheel, on *Cycle World*'s dyno in June 1994. This was enough to propel it to a top speed of 157 mph (252.6 km/h), and through a standing quarter mile in 10.81 seconds at 128.02 mph (206 km/h). The 888LTD also

convincingly won *Cycle World*'s comparison with its four-cylinder Japanese opposition.

The final 888 Strada also received the bronze wheels and larger-diameter front axle, together with braided steel front brake lines. Some testers claimed that this final version was the best of all the Stradas, but it was overshadowed by the 916.

1995

For the 1995 season the minimum weight was increased by 2 kg (4.4 lb) to 147 kg (323 lb) for twin-cylinder and 162 kg (356 lb) for four-cylinder bikes, still maintaining the 15 kg differential. However, with more development of the 955 cc factory racers over the winter, they immediately started to dominate the 1995 World Superbike Championship, so dominant in the first three rounds that the FIM increased the weights for twins for the fourth round at Monza to 155 kg (341 lb), and reduced the fours to 160 kg (352 lb). With Carl Fogarty and Mauro Lucchiari riding for Virginio Ferrari's Ducati Corse, there was also Alfred Inzinger's Austrian Promotor Team of Troy Corser and Andreas Meklau, managed by Davide Tardozzi. Additionally there was Fabrizio Pirovano (Taurus Ducati), and ex-GP rider Pierfrancesco Chili riding the Team Gattalone's customer 955 Corsa. In the US former World 500 cc Champion Freddie Spencer rode the Fast by Ferracci 955 in the AMA series.

One of the most significant changes for 1995 was the controversial banning of carbon discs, so all the factory bikes now used 320 mm iron front Brembo discs. Winning 13 of the 24 races, Carl Fogarty dominated in a style reminiscent of Doug Polen in 1991, and he easily won the Championship from Troy Corser with four wins.

The 955 cc engine remained virtually unchanged apart from new valves, rockers, camshafts, and the occasional use of a 996 cc engine with 98 mm pistons. With more emphasis on reliability, the horsepower, according to Virginio Ferrari, was 141–145 at the rear wheel at 12,000 rpm. There were detail modifications to the rear suspension linkages and steering head angle, but generally the increase in weight hurt the lap times compared to the previous year. Ducati's big advantage was in their use of telemetry so that they could fine the suspension very quickly.

The customer 916 Racing was essentially the 955 cc bike that Fogarty had raced the previous year, and even main bearings, oil pump flow was increased on the Supermono to 3.3 litres/minute every 1,000 rpm, from 2.6 litres/minute/1,000 rpm on the twin, and as with the larger Corsas the engine side covers were magnesium, and the clutch cover carbon-fibre. The six-speed gearbox was unique to the Supermono, with closer ratios than any of the twins.

Because Bordi adopted the horizontal cylinder of the V twin, making the *doppia bielletta* out of the vertical cylinder, he rediscovered the benefits of a low engine pioneered by Moto Guzzi as long ago as 1921, and developed to its ultimate fruition by Ing. Giulio Carcano with his racing single-cylinder Guzzis. The 250s and 350s in particular were incredibly successful against larger, more powerful bikes by virtue of their superior agility, lighter weight, and better weight distribution. These bikes won eight 250 and 350 cc World Championships between 1949 and 1958, demonstrating the advantages of balance and finesse over sheer horsepower.

The Supermono also confirmed these benefits convincingly. At race tracks around the world Supermonos, with more like 62 bhp at the rear wheel (as on *Cycle World*'s dyno), consistently turn in lap times similar to 100-plus bhp 600 Supersports. They have also proven to be exceptionally reliable, with brilliant handling. *Cycle World*, testing a Supermono in September 1993, managed a standing quarter mile in 11.44 seconds at 122.11 mph (196.5 km/h) with the single-exit Termignoni exhaust. Using the optional twin-exit with a revised EPROM as supplied with each bike would have undoubtedly produced even more performance. Fully wet, their test bike weighed 301 lb (136.5 kg), and *Sport Rider* achieved a top speed of 144 mph (232 km/h) in April 1994.

In 1995 a Supermono followed earlier Ducati singles by winning the Single Cylinder TT on the Isle of Man. After finishing a close second in 1994, New Zealander Robert Holden took his Supermono to an easy victory with a fastest lap of 111.66 mph (179.7 km/h). Set to repeat the feat in 1996 on a 572 cc 1995-spec Supermono, Holden was tragically killed during TT Formula 1 practice on a 916 Corsa. In practice for the Singles TT he had set a time 6 mph faster than his nearest competitor. Holden's death resulted in immediate abandonment of Steve Wynne's Sports Motorcycles team for which he rode, a team that had enjoyed an association with racing Ducatis for many years, including Hailwood's 1978 TT Formula 1 victory.

While the few racing bikes that were built were initially meant to herald a range of Supermono street bikes, nothing has transpired, although Massimo Bordi has indicated to me on several occasions that he would still like to see it in production, particularly in Supersport form. I saw prototype air-cooled four-valve cylinder heads lying around the factory in 1993, but these have now been consigned to the museum. Looking closely at the engine, it is obvious that provision was made for an electric starter, and the cases are even drilled and tapped for a clutch cable. Still, there was no provision for the mounting of a sidestand on the engine cases and these will be redesigned if the bike does go into production. It also seems likely that the plain main bearings will return to the previous ball type. For now, the Supermono lives only as the racing bike, leaving the handful built as rare examples of a superb and fascinating motorcycle. With production only reaching about 50 bikes by mid-1995 (although about 80 engines had been built), another series of 20 was constructed at the end of that year. These had new numbered plaques indicating that they were from the 1995 series. As a finite item, the Supermono is the rarest of all current Ducatis.

In every respect, the Supermono represents the pinnacle of the Ducati philosophy created by Ing. Taglioni with the first desmodromic singles way back in 1956. Not content with mainstream solutions to solve a problem, Ducati have continued to be different, this time with the adoption of its unique balance system. In a manner reminiscent of earlier Ducatis, superior racetrack performance is achieved, not through sheer power, but through a more balanced overall package.

There is no doubt that without Cagiva, Ducati would have disappeared entirely, swallowed up within an Italian Government conglomerate. Unfortunately, ominous signs that not all was well started to appear during 1994 and 1995. Partially constructed bikes were to be seen at the factory waiting for delivery of components from outside suppliers. By 1996 there were waiting lists for all models all around the world. Fortunately, even though Ing. Taglioni had now retired, the management was still dominated by engineers. Massimo Bordi was General Manager of Cagiva Motorcycles, and his protégé, Claudio Domenicali, operated the racing department. These three engineers represented the past, present and future of Ducati, and it was to be the engineers that would keep the company alive through its next crisis.

The 1996 World Superbike
Championship went to the
final round and was won by
Troy Corser on the 996 cc
Promotor Ducati.

result was not decided until the final race. This time Paolo Casoli on the Gio.Ca.Moto. 748SP, with three race wins, was triumphant by 1 point over the Yamaha-mounted Vittoriano Guareschi. So competitive was this class of racing during 1997 that these were the only two riders to win more than one race.

As expected, the 916 Racing for 1997 incorporated many of the improvements that had appeared on the factory racers during 1996. Within the engine there was an increase in displacement to 996, and the new crankcases with wider cylinder head studs homologated with the 916SPS. Compression with the 98 mm pistons was increased slightly from 11.8:1 to 12:1, and claimed power was also marginally higher at 155 bhp at 11,000 rpm. While the valve sizes were unchanged, as was the inlet camshaft, there was a new exhaust camshaft. The timing figures were now exhaust opening 69° before bottom dead centre and closing 47° after top dead centre; valve lift was still 10.5 mm. In line with the 1996 factory bikes there were now 54 mm exhaust pipes, and an increase in fuel pressure to 5.0 bar via a pressure regulator. The primary drive was also changed to the 32/59 of the 1996 racers.

Other changes also reflected the continual development of the factory bikes. The airbox had a greater capacity and was fed by a larger air intake in the fairing. Smaller changes were evident throughout the motorcycle: a larger oil radiator, thicker front brake discs, a new rear wheel hub assembly, and new attachments for the handlebars. While 46 mm Öhlins front forks were still used, the triple clamps now had adjustable offset. Thus, while the trail was previously 97 mm, this could now be adjusted within a range of 96.6–109.2 mm. With a new Öhlins rear shock absorber, rear shock travel was increased from 65 to 74 mm, translating into 136 mm of rear wheel travel.

Perhaps the most important new model for 1997 was the 916SPS. This was intended as a very limited production motorcycle alongside the 916SP, purely to homologate the new crankcases for World Superbike and FMI Sport Production. However, there was more to the SPS than merely new crankcases and larger pistons, as 36 mm inlet valves (up from 34 mm) were used, together with new inlet and exhaust camshafts. With 10.8 mm of inlet valve lift, the valve opened 14° before top dead centre and closed 73° after bottom dead centre. The exhaust valve now opened 57° before bottom dead centre, closing at 23° after top dead centre with 9.8 mm of valve lift. The compression ratio was

marginally increased to 11.5:1 and claimed power was up to 134 bhp at 10,000 rpm. The gearbox ratios for third, fourth, fifth and sixth gears were also altered for the SPS, being shared with the 748BP and SP. The SPS also received the new primary drive gears (32/59) of the 916 Racing and the same titanium con-rods. Unlike the single-injector Desmoquattros, the SPS continued with the Weber Marelli 'P8' CPU, but the throttle bodies remained at 50 mm.

Visually similar to the 916SP, and sharing the chassis and running gear, the 916SPS had all the performance equipment associated with limited-edition Sport Production Ducatis: cast-iron fully floating 320 mm front brake discs with steel brake lines, Öhlins shock absorber, and larger-diameter exhaust pipes with carbon-fibre leg-shields. All 916SPSs came with carbon-fibre Termignoni mufflers and an alternative chip. Continuing a trend started back in 1974 with the 750 Super Sport, the 916SPS was the standard by which all sporting motorcycles were judged. It was also the fastest Ducati to date, the Italian magazine *Motociclismo* in April 1996 managing a top speed of 270.1 km/h (168 mph) in standard form, or 275.4 km/h (171 mph) with the performance kit that included the Termignoni mufflers and revised computer chip. Horsepower, too, was impressive: 122.59 bhp at 9,500 rpm, increasing to 124.35 bhp at 9,500 rpm with the performance kit. In production racing the 916SPS was immediately competitive, winning the production race at the North West 200 and coming second on the Isle of Man. Unanimously named 'Bike of the Year' by magazines around the world, it was initially intended to continue the 916SP alongside the SPS, but demand for the latter was so strong that it soon replaced the smaller bike. Rather than a proposed production series of only 200, nearly 800 916SPSs were built during 1997. With the injection of capital from TPG, overall production was significantly increased during the year, 8,500 Hypersport 916/748s being constructed.

After a hiatus during 1996, the 916 Senna was again produced as a limited edition of 350 during 1997. As in 1995, the Senna had red wheels and steel grey bodywork, although this time a lighter colour than before. No Sennas were produced with the yellow wheels intended for the 1996 version. Although it had the Öhlins shock absorber, fully floating cast-iron brake rotors and a carbon-fibre front mudguard, the Senna retained the standard 916 engine of the Biposto and Strada. All Sennas came with a numbered plaque

The 916SPS was built specifically to homologate the crankcases for the 996 racer.

on the top triple clamp, but suffered in much the same way as the 900 Superlight. For a premium price they offered no performance advantage over a standard bike and too many were built for them to qualify as a very limited edition.

The 916 Strada and Biposto continued essentially unchanged – why alter something that was so successful and desirable? Even with an increase in production there were insufficient to satisfy demand. The US still received a solo-seat 916 with an Öhlins shock absorber, but it was otherwise identical to the European Biposto. There were also no changes to the 748SP and 748 Biposto. Only available in yellow, the former was manufactured in similar numbers to the 916SPS, but with fewer special parts. At the Cologne Show of 1996 a hybrid 748S was displayed. This red solo-seat 748 used the standard 748 Biposto engine (without oil-cooler) in a 748SP chassis. It never made it to the production line.

Now into its seventh year of production, the Supersport was starting to look a little dated. For several years there had been talk of a replacement, but the financial difficulties of 1995 and 1996 had meant further delays to this project. With a new commitment to the Supersport line, the specification was upgraded for 1997 in order to maintain sales. Overall Supersport sales had been falling from a high of 8,545 in 1992, and while 3,741 were built in 1997 (plus 500 1998-model Final Editions), numbers were well down on those of the Hypersport and Monster. The Superlight was no longer offered, and most of its special features made their way to the 900 Supersport.

Although now at the end of its production run, the Supersport for 1997 was a thoroughly developed machine. In 900 guise especially it offered a number of more appealing features over the earlier models. The engine specifications of all Supersports were unchanged except for bimetallic inlet and exhaust valves to better suit unleaded fuel. The oil radiator on 750s and 900s was now mounted above the front cylinder, similar to that of the Monster, and a heating kit was installed on all front carburettors to minimize icing in cold weather, which had always been a problem on Mikuni-carburetted models because of their long inlet tracts.

As there was no Superlight offered for 1997, the 900 Supersport received the fully floating rear brake and carbon-fibre front mudguard. There were also steel brake and clutch lines for Europe, and adjustable brake and clutch levers. The clutch cover was grey, and standard equipment included Michelin Hi-Sport tyres. Offered in red or yellow, the 900 Supersport shared its new bodywork with the 750 and 600 Supersport; the fairing had revised graphics, with an air intake and internal sound-absorbing panels. Other improvements for 1997 were the increased steering lock to 28° either side, and a more comfortable seat. Cosmetic changes included anodized aluminium footrest plates.

With unchanged specifications, the 900 Supersport continued to offer a balanced package with the less extreme riding position of the Hypersports 916/748, and for many it still offered enough performance. The Italian magazine *Super Wheels* of March 1997 managed 220.856 km/h (137 mph) with a standing 400 metres at 11.777 seconds at 182.426 km/h (113 mph). Significantly, however, the measured dry weight was 189.8 kg (418 lb). The gradual development of the Supersport over a seven-year period had also seen it become a thoroughly refined sporting motorcycle, without the demands placed on the rider by the race replica Hypersports. It still appealed to those who wanted a simpler, lighter sports bike, without a racetrack orientation. Unfortunately the market also perceived the Supersport to be old-fashioned; just as had happened with the earlier bevel-gear Supersport, Ducati had let what was once their most successful model run too long and sales were suffering as a result. It was not really a case of the motorcycle being obsolete, but more the continual emphasis placed by the press on new products. Also the Supersport was coming under increasing pressure in the marketplace from the Honda VTR1000F and Suzuki TL1000S 90° V twins. These new bikes were priced in Supersport territory but offered more performance, albeit without the character and breeding of the Ducati model.

For the United States there was once again the 900 Supersport SP and CR. As the regular Supersport for Europe incorporated most of the previous Superlight features, the SP now only differed in the use of the fully floating Brembo cast-iron front brake discs, carbon-fibre rear mudguard, and numbered plaque. US bikes did not receive the steel brake lines. The 900CR continued as before, still essentially a 900 engine in a 750 Supersport chassis. Although only 60 750 Supersports had been manufactured during 1996, production was back to reasonable levels in 1997, and 1,146 were built. As with the 900, the oil-cooler was mounted in an upper position, and all the alterations to the steering lock,

valves, carburettor heating kit, fairing, seat, and graphics also made it to the 750. The 600 Supersport also continued, again incorporating these changes, and all Supersports were available in yellow or red.

Of all the existing models, the M900 Monster came in for the most modifications during 1997. Previous 900 Monsters had shared engines with the Supersport, but now the 900M received a de-tuned engine to improve low-down power, better suiting its role as a city bike. The 900 engine had always been slightly unhappy running below 3,000 rpm, so to help cure this the cylinder head received smaller valves, now 41 and 35 mm, and there were new camshafts. New and much more sophisticated computer programs that came with the TPG involvement now enabled the development department to design desmodromic camshafts much more quickly. Whereas in the past there had only been a few desmodromic camshaft profiles, 1997 saw a range of camshafts for different models. The M900 in this lower state of tune now had a camshaft that opened the inlet valve 12° before top dead centre, closing it 70° after bottom dead centre. The exhaust valve opened 56° before bottom dead centre, closing 25° after top dead centre. Valve lift was unchanged at 11.76 mm and 10.56 mm respectively. Claimed power was reduced to 77 bhp at 7,000 rpm, but more significantly the lobe centres of the camshaft were retarded for better low-down power characteristics.

Other engine changes from the Supersport were carried through to the new M900 engine: sintered steel valve seats and bimetallic inlet and exhaust valves for better compatibility with unleaded fuel, and the carburettor heating kit to prevent icing.

Complementing the lower state of tune on the M900 was a new Kokusan ignition system and revised jetting for the Mikuni 38 mm carburettors. Elsewhere the specifications were unchanged, except for the small front fairing that had featured on the projected Special Edition Monster of 1996. Colours for the M900 of 1997 were black or red. As expected, ultimate performance was reduced with the lower-tuned engine, the 1997 M900 managing a top speed of 196.3 km/h (122 mph) in a test by *Motociclismo* in April 1997; earlier M900s had achieved around 206 km/h (128 mph). *Cycle World*, when testing an M900 in November 1997, found it also to be slightly slower over a standing quarter mile at 11.98 seconds at 108.53 mph (175 km/h).

An M900 Solo with front cast-iron disc brake rotors and a single seat was also intended for 1997. Displayed at the Cologne Show in 1996, as with the Special Edition of a year earlier it was not put into production due to negative dealer response. This M900 Solo was almost identical to the M900 Police, which also had a solo seat. The silver M750 and red and yellow M600s continued as before.

Below: The first sport-touring
Ducati since the 907IE, the ST2
was the first new model
introduced after the TPG
takeover.

To help promote the Monster in Italy, Ducati supported the 'Ducati Monster Cup 97'. Organized by Techna Racing in Rome, six races were held, with identical Gio.Ca.Moto. M900s being allocated by lot for the series. The yellow racing Monsters had a solo seat, belly-pan, and 916-style Gianelli exhausts. Monsters had always been particularly popular in Italy, and the strength of the local market saw Monster production outstripping both the Hypersport and Supersport, with 10,000 units in 1997.

Although it was originally intended to release it during 1996, the ST2 was also delayed due to the production difficulties experienced by the company that year. First displayed at the Cologne Show at the end of 1996, the ST2 was Ducati's first exploration of the sport-touring category since the 907IE of 1991–92. Historically this had not been the most successful area for Ducati as it meant competing directly with the Japanese. The company's past was littered with some rather dismal forays into this area, the 860GT and Paso in particular. While some other examples were excellent motorcycles, notably the 750GT, Darmah and 907IE,

after initial success they never achieved the sales that were expected. Many of the earlier attempts at sport-touring motorcycles had suffered particularly from poor reliability and incomplete development. Early reports suggested that the ST2 was a finely developed machine, but still had considerable competition.

One of TPG's objectives was to expand into wider market segments, and the ST2 fitted this bill comfortably. With progress already well advanced by the time of the merger with Cagiva, it took only a short time to construct another assembly line for the ST2. Production began in April 1997, and during that year 4,300 ST2s were manufactured.

Development of the ST2 was facilitated by utilizing as many existing parts as possible. Thus the basic frame was from the Monster (originally 851/888) constructed of ALS450, in concert with a swing-arm with a 916-style linkage. The 43 mm Showa front forks were also similar to the 916, but with more fork travel (130 mm), as was the new-generation Brembo front wheel. With 24° of fork rake and 102 mm of trail, steering was quicker than the earlier 907. Latest-specification

Brembo brake calipers were also employed, with revised internal fluid passages and wider bolt spacing to increase rigidity. These brake calipers would find their way to other models during 1998.

Styled by Miguel Galluzzi (who was also responsible for the Monster) at Cagiva Morizzone, the ST2 incorporated many features expected of sport-touring motorcycles of the late 1990s. Notable features were the aspherical rear-view mirrors, and an instrument panel that incorporated a digital display for fuel consumption, fuel reserve, time, and water temperature. The entire layout of the cockpit, with the ignition key on the fuel tank and cast handlebars, gave the ST2 a look of integrated design that was new to Ducati in the sport-touring segment. Complementing its status as a long-distance machine, the ST2 came with matching panniers from Nonfango, and exhaust pipes that could be adjusted for increased ground clearance. During 1997 the ST2 came in red, silver and black.

In the engine department the ST2 took over where the 907IE had left off. The basic six-speed, two-valve, water-cooled engine was inherited from the 907, but a 2 mm bore increase to 94 mm took the displacement out to 944 cc. Compression, too, was increased on air-cooled 900s to 10.2:1. The ST2 also received new camshafts, not only with different timing, but also increased valve lift. The inlet valve opened 26° before top dead centre, closing 72° after bottom dead centre, with 11.8 mm of valve lift. The exhaust valve opened 61° before bottom dead centre, closing 34° after top dead centre, with 11.4 mm of maximum valve lift. The six-speed gearbox was carried over, but the ST2 had the revised primary gears of the Corsa and SPS (32/59). The Weber Marelli electronic fuel injection used a 40 mm throttle body and the '1.6' CPU of other single-injector Ducatis.

Although no lightweight at a claimed 212 kg (467 lb), the measured wet weight was closer to 234 kg (515 lb) as tested by *Cycle World* in December 1997. However, the ST2 was a surprisingly strong performer for this type of motorcycle. Although power was only 83 bhp at 8,500 rpm, *Cycle World* achieved a standing quarter mile in 11.81 seconds at 113.10 mph (182 km/h). Top speed was 136 mph (219 km/h). These were very similar figures to the significantly lighter 900 Supersport, indicating that the ST2 was not only more powerful, but possessed excellent aerodynamics.

Undoubtedly a highly competent long-distance motorcycle in the best European tradition, there is still a question mark over how successful Ducati will be with this new attempt at the Sport Touring market. History tells us that it is an area where the company has always struggled. This was vinidicated by 2005 as sales of the ST range plummeted by 55% compared with those of the previous year.

1998

The affect of the TPG buy-out really became noticeable during 1998. The workforce increased to 714 employees, 434 in production and the remaining 280 in sales, research and administration. During 1997 the personnel had numbered 550, with 280 in production. Increased investment (30 billion lire by 1998) had seen new CNC machines installed and 30 CAD stations in the engineering department, as production moved from labour-intensive to capital-intensive. More components were sourced outside, leaving heat-treatment, finishing and engine assembly the primary processes now undertaken within the factory. While the existing motorcycles continued with only minor developments, there was a new emphasis on marketing and expanding the customer base. Thus not only were there more variations on the four themes, but TPG wanted to create a sport performance experience for Ducati owners in a manner similar to that of the Harley-Davidson lifestyle. Reflecting the increase in production was a huge increase in turnover, from 200 billion lire in 1996 to an estimated (by early 1998) 400 billion lire in 1997.

Central to TPG's plan was also a new logo and corporate identity. The previous logo had come with Cagiva in 1986 and TPG needed to create a fresh image. Ducati approached Massimo Vignelli, a leading American graphic designer responsible for corporate logos for Bloomingdales and American Airlines. Vignelli delved into the past to create a new logo that recalled the clean lines of the graphics on the 1972 Imola racers. A new symbol was also created alongside the logo; suggesting a spinning bike wheel, this came directly from the classic eagle logo of the overhead camshaft singles of the early 1960s. This interest in an association with past success would play an important role in TPG's vision for the future of Ducati, and to celebrate this further, the last-surviving Ducati brother, Bruno Cavalieri, was made honorary chairman of the company.

While other great Italian marques, notably MV Agusta and Moto Guzzi, were well known for their museums and maintaining their history, Ducati itself did not have a museum, and until Cagiva bought the company in 1985 all important racing machines had either been sold or destroyed. Thus the factory had lost the racing heritage of the 1950s, '60s and '70s. Many of the most significant bikes had survived in private hands, but many more were lost. Part of TPG's plan was to create a 10,000 sq ft museum on the first floor of the factory at Borgo Panigale, but the difficulty was in reclaiming some of the earlier bikes. It was not only racing machines either – there were also few examples of street bikes from the pre-Cagiva era. Fortunately most of the prototypes that had not made the production line had not been destroyed.

Charged with creating primarily a racing museum, Marco Montemaggi worked hard at persuading collectors in Italy to lend significant racing machines to the museum for its opening in June 1998. Noted restorer Primo Forasassi was also employed to restore some of the important exhibits. The museum was eventually to be linked with the Ferrari museum at nearby Maranello, emphasizing not only an underlying connection with Ferrari, but also the strong Emilia Romagna engineering tradition. Coinciding with the opening of the museum was the first World Ducati Weekend, held from 12–14 June 1998 at Misano, Rimini and Bologna.

It was obvious that TPG was now committed to raising the profile of Ducati beyond its previous boundaries. One way of doing this was by creating a special-edition silver 748L (with carbon-fibre front mudguard and chainguard) to be sold through the prestigious Neiman Marcus catalogue for men in the United States. Only 100 were available, and with a Donna Karan New York leather jacket and Dainese gloves provided, this became the first mail-order Ducati. Complementing this new marketing move was the opening of monofranchised flagship Ducati Stores, the first, along 'Gasoline Alley' in Manhattan, opening in March 1998. These 300 sq m superstores were designed by the US-based architectural studio Gensler in conjunction with Bologna architect Michele Zacchiroli. Offering accessories and an Internet site, they certainly represented a totally new direction for Ducati, and one that was not entirely welcomed by the traditional enthusiast. Other stores soon opened in various Italian cities – Bologna, Florence, Rome, Milan, Genoa, Savona, Treviso and Turin – followed by an Australian flagship store in Sydney.

One of the strongest product lines in the new Ducati Store was Ducati Performance. Formed in December 1996 as a joint venture between Gio.Ca.Moto. and Ducati Motor, it was established by September 1997. With the intention of developing new performance products with Ducati and using the same suppliers as that of original equipment, Ducati now hoped to also capture a large slice of the lucrative performance market. The Ducati Performance catalogues covered all models in the line-up, and included chassis as well as engine parts. Another new product line was that of official apparel; an agreement with the Vicenza-based Dainese company provided a range of high-quality leather racing clothing, and also available was a limited range of other lifestyle sportswear. Future developments in the accessory and performance sphere lay in specialized performance shops where customers could have their motorcycles modified with factory back-up.

Having lost the World Superbike Championship in 1997, a concerted effort was made in 1998 to win again. While out to make a profitable company, TPG realized the importance of racing, not only for product development, but also as a means of promotion. At the end of 1997 there had been some upheaval within the factory teams for World Superbike. Carl Fogarty wanted his own team and initially organized a one-rider team with a factory bike through Alstare with Corona sponsorship. In the meantime Troy Corser was welcomed back by Ducati after a disappointing year in the 500 cc Grands Prix. After two poor seasons, Neil Hodgson lost his place in the Virginio Ferrari team, Pierfrancesco Chili inheriting that berth. When Fogarty's team failed to materialize, Ducati was left with a difficult situation. Both Corser and Fogarty were past World Champions, and to have them both in the same team would be undesirable. Another team needed to be formed for one of them. Fortunately a solution was found with the formation of Ducati Performance with Gio.Ca.Moto. Having just won the Supersport World Cup, Daniele Casolari's team was expanded to run a one-rider World Superbike factory bike alongside the Supersport 748SPS. With Davide Tardozzi as team manager, it was expected that Troy Corser would go with Gio.Ca.Moto., but surprisingly Carl Fogarty left the Virginio Ferrari camp to a team where he was to be the sole rider.

Carl Fogarty was the only rider in
the Ducati Performance team,
and he won the 1998 World
Superbike Championship.

There were some considerable changes to the factory racers for 1998. Ducati Corse produced 18 machines this year with a new frame homologated through the SPS. There were upgraded forks, brakes and rear suspension, and a completely revised Weber Marelli engine management system developed for Formula 3 car racing. This MF3 type was reputed to operate 20 times faster than previously, with full connection to the telemetry system on the motorcycle. All the modifications were done to address the criticisms of the previous year, particularly in throttle response and handling. These developments resulted in Ducati again triumphing in the World Superbike Championship, Carl Fogarty taking his third World Superbike crown. Ducati once again won the Manufacturers' Championship with ten race victories (Chili five, Fogarty three and Corser two).

As an American company, TPG was determined to win the AMA Series for 1998. Thus two teams of two riders were supplied with World Superbike-specification factory bikes. The Fast by Ferracci team fielded Mike Hale and Tom Kipp, while the West Coast-based Vance & Hines had wild Australian Anthony Gobert joining Thomas Stevens. Although Gobert won three races, success in this series still eluded Ducati. After winning

THE DUCATI STORY

Below: The third and final 916
Senna of 1998 was most
distinctive.

the Supersport World Cup three years running, Ducati again supported Paolo Casoli on the Ducati Performance 748R, managed by Stefano Caracchi. Casoli could not repeat his success, finishing fourth in the 1998 World Supersport Championship.

Many of the detail improvements of the 1997 factory bikes made their way to the 916 Racing for 1998. Only 24 were built, the most significant changes being a new frame (shared with the 1998 factory bikes) and a magnesium swing-arm that lengthened the wheelbase 10 mm to 1,430 mm. The frame was TIG-welded in 25CrMo4, and while it looked identical externally, the tubes were thinner at 1.5 mm. There was also a new, lighter rear sub-frame. The front forks were similar to the 1997 factory bike and had the same axle lugs, and there was hydraulic adjustment for the preload for the rear Öhlins shock absorber. The shape of the carbon-fibre fuel tank was altered to mirror the factory racers and capacity increased by 1 litre to 24 litres. While the thicker 320 mm front brake discs were still fitted, alternative 290 mm discs of the type used on

the factory racers during 1997 were also supplied.

Only detail improvements were made to the engine, primarily in the use of 60 mm throttle bodies and new intake manifolds. Lighter pistons and con-rods, a new crankshaft, and changes to the primary drive spline couplings also featured on the 916R for 1998. There was a new gearshift selector drum to smooth out the gearshift, a new crankshaft inlet oil seal, and timing belt rollers with bigger rims. Completing the alterations was a bigger water radiator and a waterproof cover for the 'P8' injection control unit. With all 916Rs allocated to various distributors, and so many new developments featured, it indicated that the factory was very serious about winning the many domestic Superbike Championships around the world. While the factory bikes had been supremely victorious on the world stage, Ducati was still waiting for those wins in England, Australia and the United States.

New for 1998 was the 748R, primarily constructed for the Supersport World Cup. The tight regulations forbade any alteration to pistons, camshafts, valve sizes

196

before bottom dead centre, closing 28° after top dead centre. Valve lift was slightly different, and the same as the ST2, the inlet opening 11.8 mm and the exhaust 11.4 mm. While peak power was only marginally increased to 80 bhp at 7,500 rpm, the engine ran more cleanly, particularly at under 3,000 rpm. The new camshafts and injection system meant that there was no need for a high inertia flywheel and a lighter flywheel could be used. The Weber Marelli fuel injection ECU, the '1.5', was the third generation to be used by Ducati, and the first Marelli processor designed specifically for a motorcycle application. Not only was it cheaper and smaller than earlier units, but it could also be adapted for multi-point systems and would eventually be used on those models with twin injectors. Incorporating the absolute air pressure sensor inside the ECU, it also promised better reliability. With the injection system was a new 10-litre airbox.

Other engine changes for 1998 were new cylinders (Tecnol), pistons (Asso), and piston rings (NPR). There were also new intake manifolds and the ST2 520-watt alternator. Finally the troublesome 31/62 primary drive became the 32/59 (1.84:1) of the ST2 and 916SPS.

Many observers were surprised to see the new Supersport retain a similar frame and the cantilever swing-arm of the earlier bike. However, factory testers believed that for 90% of road use the cantilever rear suspension was a good compromise. It was lighter and simpler than linkage suspension, which was not seen as so critical on a sports bike that would see its use on the street rather than the track. The stroke on the Showa GD132-007-00 shock absorber was increased to 71 mm (up from 65 mm). Also, by retaining the cantilever swing-arm the historical link with the TT2 was retained.

Although his design came in for some criticism, Pierre Terblanche had tried to incorporate many of the features that had made the Supermono an outstanding design in 1992. As he said to me in early 1998, 'It is much more difficult designing a Supersport than a Hypersport because there are many compromises in the style. It cannot be a total racing look with a low front and high rear. A Supersport is by definition a less extreme motorcycle than a 916, more like a Honda CBR600. Though I found this a challenging project I am very pleased with it.'

One of the problems faced by the new Supersport in the marketplace was the typical reaction to something different, and with the Supersport customer being traditional and conservative, this effect was exaggerated. There was a similar reaction to the new logo at the end of 1997. However, with the new bike offering undoubted advantages in the areas of power delivery and handling, it was certain to gain acceptance over time. The new Supersport had no seat cover, but a single-seat version was planned for a later date using a redesigned seat unit. Beginning in March, production was scheduled for 4,403 units for 1998.

Following on from the success of the 'Ducati Monster Cup' held during 1997, the 1998 Supersport took to the Italian circuits in the 'Supersport Cup'. As with the Monsters, these were prepared by Techna Racing in Rome, the solo-seat Supersports being allocated by lot over a six-race series.

The 916 was still successful, but thought had to be given to its replacement. By 1998 Ducati was still working on the layout, but the trademark desmodromic 90° V twin in a tubular steel frame would undoubtedly be retained. The intention was to develop the engine and frame together to create a unified structure. Other plans looked at combining Massimo Bordi's 1975-thesis four-valve desmodromic cylinder head rocker layout with fuel injection to narrow the included valve angle. In the meantime, all Monsters would become fuel injected.

1999

On 31 July 1998, the Texas Pacific Group (TPG) and Deutsche Morgan Grenfell announced they had purchased the remaining 49% of Ducati Motor S.p.A. from Claudio and Gianfranco Castiglioni. This was also the most successful year to date for the company, with net sales of 465.1 billion lire and production up to 28,011 motorcycles. This success would pave the way for a global public offering of shares in March 1999.

1998 again saw Ducati triumph in World Superbike with Carl Fogarty taking his third World Superbike crown. Ducati once again won the Constructors' Championship with 10 race victories (Chili 5; Fogarty 3; and Corser 2). During the season there had been some problems with Virginio Ferrari, and after five years his contract was not renewed. In 2005, Ferrari sued Ducati Motor for damages of €6,714,000, for the alleged loss of income for three years of sponsorship as originally agreed. So for 1999, there was only one officially supported factory team, that of Ducati Performance, managed by Davide Tardozzi. The racing

department was reorganized with the formation of a separate company, Ducati Corse headed by Claudio Domenicali, supplying teams for four different championships: World Superbike, AMA, Supersport, and the Italian Championship. The two riders for World Superbike were Fogarty and Corser, with the 996 racer little changed from the previous year. Thus it incorporated the revised injection system with three injectors, and the new frame and airbox that had been introduced at Kyalami, mid-way through the 1998 season. There were a few changes to the brakes and suspension, most notably the use of smaller diameter (42mm) Öhlins front forks and Grand Prix-style radial brake calipers.

Thicker cylinder head castings provided increased rigidity, along with improved porting and re-angled valves. There was a new airbox and intake tracts, and the same triple injector MF3-S injection system with differential mapping between the cylinders. During the season the stainless-steel exhaust system was increased to 57 mm. With 168 bhp at 11,500 rpm the greatest improvements for 1999 were less power drop off throughout the range and a noticeable increase in engine reliability.

Fogarty still wanted to replicate the balance of the 1995 955 racer and to improve front tyre feel there were two smaller, 42 mm, diameter Öhlins front forks. While not as stiff they reduced unsprung weight and provided mounts for the new generation of Brembo radial four-piston brake calipers. These improved braking action as the calipers were more rigidly located

on the fork slider. The smaller, 290 mm discs also contributed to improved steering response. There was also a new Öhlins TT44 shock absorber and a revised rear suspension linkage.

Right from the outset, the combination of Fogarty and the 996 dominated the 1999 World Superbike Championship. Finally, the fine balance of the 1995 version was replicated and Fogarty won eleven races during the season. Corser's three race wins and victories at Laguna Seca by Anthony Gobert and Ben Bostrom further emphasized the superiority of the 996 this year. Undoubtedly much of this was due to the continual evolution of the design. Paolo Casoli was the official Ducati Corse testing and development rider, and on the 996 Factory Evolution racer he won every round of the Italian Superbike Championship. As a test bed for World Superbike continual improvements filtered through, although the single injector fuel-injection system, with the throttle butterfly even closer to the valves, was held over for 2000.

After finishing fourth in the World Supersport Championship of 1998, once again Paolo Casoli also rode the Ducati Performance 748 SPS in the World Supersport Championship. Casoli was also the chief development and test rider for Ducati Corse in the five-round Italian Superbike Championship. Here new developments were tested on an Evoluzione 996 before they made their way to the World Superbike machines. Though dominant in World Superbike, Ducati still failed to win any of the other national championships during 1998. Thus factory support continued,

Left: One of the most successful
racing Ducatis was the 1999
Superbike. Fogarty dominated
the World Superbike
Championship this year.

Below: The ST4 continued the
style of the ST2, but with the
Desmoquattro motor. This is the
author testing the new ST4 in
Italy.

particularly in the U.S. For the AMA Superbike
Championship two teams received factory 996s for
1999. Anthony Gobert and Ben Bostrom for the Vance
& Hines Team, and Matt Wait for Fast by Ferracci.
Bostrom performed well, only narrowly losing the
championship. Additionally, several teams received
support with the new customer 996 Racing Special.
These included Lucio Pedercini and Doriano Romboni
in World Superbike, and Neil Hodgson and Troy
Bayliss for the GSE Racing team in British Superbike.
Other 996 RSs went to Sean Emmett and John
Reynolds of the Reve Red Bull team for the British
Championship, Craig Connell and Steve Martin for the
Australian Superbike Championship, and Andreas
Meklau in the German Superbike Championship. As it
featured 60 mm throttles inside the airbox, 39 and
32 mm valves, and a 13 mm lift inlet camshaft, the
996RS was considerably more competitive than early
Corsas. Bayliss won the British Championship and
Steve Martin the Australian title.

The 996SPS continued as for 1998 but for minor
changes. These included a three-phase 520-watt
alternator, five-spoke black Marchesini wheels, and 320
x 5 mm semi-floating stainless steel front discs on
aluminium carriers. Production of the 1999 model
996SPS was only 808. There were more changes to the
916. Now nearly five years old, this was updated for
1999 by growing to 996 cc, the stronger crankcases
and 98 mm pistons shared with the SPS. The 996 now
featured twin injectors, although still with the Marelli
1.6 CPU. Thus the two injectors operated
simultaneously and not sequentially as with the P8
system of the 996SPS. The 996 also featured the 36 and
30 mm valves of the SPS, but retained the 916
camshafts. For the 996 the exhaust system was a larger
diameter (45 mm), with a 120 x 420 mm silencer.
Other features shared with the 996SPS were the three-
phase alternator, 32/59-tooth primary drive gears,
revised brake calipers with wider lug spacing, and the
new front discs. The wheels of the 996 were as before,
but were now lighter, being constructed of a higher
silicon alloy (GA/Si7). Many of these features were
shared with the 748 for 1999, although the front discs
were 320 x 4 mm and the 31/62-tooth primary gears
were retained. The 748SPS became more of a
homologation model for World Supersport racing, now
the only model to retain the lighter 350-watt alternator.

Released in October 1998, the ST4 was the most
significant new model for 1999. Basically the 916

engine of before was installed in an ST2 rolling chassis,
creating one of the best performing sport touring
motorcycles available. To retain the same weight
distribution as the ST2, the cylinder heads were shorter,
with the exhaust camshaft moved 10 mm closer to the
centre of the engine. Other improvements were shared
with the ST2, noticeably the revised sidestand, and
34 mm rear brake caliper. Both models now had lighter
wheels, and the three-phase alternator.

As the main new model of 1998, the 900 Supersport
continued unchanged, but was joined by a 750 and
half-faired varieties. The 750 Supersport used the five-
speed 750 Monster engine, but with Weber Marelli
electronic fuel injection with a 1.5 CPU. If anything
characterized 1999, it was the proliferation of
Monsters. This included the expansion of the highly
successful 600 Dark to 750 and 900 cc, along with the
creation of the City. As before there were two types of
900 engine, both with Mikuni 38 mm carburettors.
The Monster 900, 900 Dark, 900S, 900 Cromo, and

The top-of-the-line Monster for 1999: the M900S.

900 California received the 74 bhp version, while the Monster 900 City and 900 City Dark used the small valve 71 bhp engine. The 900S was the highest specification Monster, with an Öhlins shock absorber, steering damper, and numerous carbon fibre parts. The Dark represented the austere Monster with its black frame and matt black tank and guards. In between were the Cromo with a chrome-plated fuel tank, and the City with its windshield, more comfortable seat, higher handlebars and Mandarina Duck bags. Along the lines of the 900 was the Monster 750 Dark, 750 City, and 750 City Dark. These were also supplemented by the Monster 600 City and 600 City Dark. Along with the regular 600 and 750 Monster there were now 15 Monsters in the line-up.

Future production Ducatis would undoubtedly follow the pattern set by Pierre Terblanche's Mike Hailwood Evoluzione, first shown at the Munich Intermot in September 1998. Terblanche went to AKA design in Hitchin, north of London, where he developed this project in a mere 11 weeks, working with a three-dimensional computer model. Terblanche always had an affinity for the NCR Ducatis of the late 1970s. He admired their elemental simplicity. Thus he used an air-cooled 904 cc two-valve fuel injected 900 Supersport engine as the basis. 'I have a horror for all those ugly wires and tubes everywhere,' says Terblanche, 'that's why I have created sump covers to hide the oil cooler and lines, and placed the ignition coils on the camshaft bearing supports on the cylinder heads. It was my intention to visually clean up the engine.' Special components abounded on the bike including the lightweight diaphragm clutch, 305 mm Selcom (carbon-silesium) front disc, nylon polymer integrated fairing and fuel tank, 80 mm Valeo headlight, television rear view mirror and voice recognition locking system. The frame was specially constructed by the Dutch company Troll, placing the engine as far forward in the frame as possible, with a 23½° steering head angle, and 1,420 mm wheelbase.

On 4 March 1999, an initial public offering of 90,200,000 shares of common stock was issued in the form of shares or American Depository Shares, each representing ten shares. The initial price was 2.90 Euros or US$31.67 per ADS, with the public ownership expected to be 66.1%. There were 900,000 shares reserved for Ducati employees. This public offering coincided with an overall increase in production and sales, with motorcycle production totalling 8,110 units through until September 30, an increase of 16.6% over 1998. Twelve new Ducati stores were opened, bringing the total to 32 outlets worldwide.

As for the future of Ducati, much has changed at Ducati since the TPG buy out. Most of the management was replaced almost immediately, and there was considerable expansion of the marketing and communications divisions. Worldwide marketing was

coordinated through joint venture distribution in major markets, particularly Germany, France, Japan, and the UK. Ducati Motor also increased its stake in performance accessory company Gio.Ca.Moto to 99.9%. No longer will Ducati be only for the cognoscenti, and more investment and increased profitability will only add to the quality and competitiveness of the product. With exciting

developments on the horizon Ducati should be able to stay at the forefront of motorcycle technological supremacy. After four changes of ownership since 1926, and several more managerial upheavals, this new era for the company offered a promising scenario for the future. With many more innovative projects under consideration Ducati looked to the future with confident anticipation.

Carl Fogarty rode only briefly in the 2000 World Superbike Championship before a crash ended his racing career.

15 A NEW AGE

By the year 2000 it was evident a lot had happened at Ducati since TPG had acquired an interest in the company back in 1996. Although still a small manufacturer in world terms, Ducati was now known as a premier producer of high-quality sporting motorcycles, with a high international profile. Investment in plant and machinery resulted in motorcycle production increasing from 12,509 in 1996 to 34,657 in 1999. While racing continued as an essential element, the marketing programme was much broader than in the past. Ducati was taken beyond the closeted realm of the motorcycle enthusiast into the wider community. As the Western world became more affluent and there was increased demand for leisure products, emulating the success of the Harley-Davidson 'lifestyle' experience was working for Ducati.

2000

The new millennium began dramatically in Bologna when, on 1 January 2000, at 00.01 GMT, Ducati began selling the production MH900 Evoluzione on the Internet. This was the first motorcycle sold through E-commerce, with the same pricing (€15,000) throughout the world. The production version of the MH900e was similar to Terblanche's 1998 concept version, and remained based on the two-valve fuel-injected 900 Supersport. Production was initially scheduled to be undertaken at the Bimota factory in Rimini, but with the collapse of Bimota, the MH900e was delayed. The first three production machines were delivered at the World Ducati Weekend in June 2000, and only 21 were produced during 2000.

In the World Superbike Championship Ducati replaced Troy Corser with former AMA champion, 25-year-old Ben Bostrom, to ride alongside Carl Fogarty in the official Team Ducati Infostrada. However, Fogarty crashed at Phillip Island, the injuries ending his career. After test rider Luca Cadalora failed, Troy Bayliss took Fogarty's position. Bostrom had difficulty adapting to the factory machine and its Michelin tyres, and was soon relegated to the satellite NCR team on Corser's 1999 racer. Juan Borja replaced Bostrom in the Infostrada line-up.

The factory 996 received new cylinder heads, with more material around the studs and ports, and new

The final limited-edition 996SPS
was the 'Pista', or 'Circuit', of
2000.

camshafts with less overlap. The titanium valves were
still 39 and 32 mm. The compression ratio was now
over 13:1, and the Marelli MF3-S injection system,
while retaining 60 mm throttle bodies included a single
injector positioned above the throttle valve. Shorter or
longer bell mouths altered the power requirements for
individual tracks and there were 50–60 mm shorter
intakes, with the throttle bodies closer to the cylinder
head. The power was 173 bhp at 12,000 rpm, Ducati's
evolutionary development yielding an increase of
15 bhp over the previous three years. The chassis and
Pierobon frame were similar to the 1999 version, but
there were revisions to the internal cartridge of the
42 mm Öhlins fork. The weight was right on the
minimum 162 kg. Pre-season testing also saw
experimentation with a double-sided swingarm, with
high exiting exhausts similar to the earlier 888. These
experiments proved inconclusive, but the twin-sided
swingarm would reappear in 2002 on the next-
generation 999.

The 996 factory racer was still a formidable
machine, but the team was ill-prepared for Fogarty's
withdrawal from the championship. Bayliss went on to
win two races, Neil Hodgson two, and John Reynolds
one. Apart from the official factory machines a further
ten 996 Racing Specials were produced for selected
teams in World Superbike and national championships.
The specification included the revised single-injector
MF3-S Marelli injection system and a 57 mm stainless-
steel exhaust system with the engine producing 162
bhp. Niall McKenzie joined Hodgson in the INS/GSE
team, with James Haydon teaming with Reynolds on
the Reve Red Bull 996RS. The Ducatis dominated,
Hodgson winning the British Superbike Championship.

Bayliss was originally signed alongside Steve Rapp in
the Vance & Hines team for the AMA Superbike
Championship, and was replaced by veteran John
Kocinski when Bayliss moved to World Superbike.
Larry Pegram rode a 996RS for Competition
Accessories, but Ducati's results were again
disappointing.

For the 2000 World Supersport season Ducati Corse
produced a considerably higher specification 748RS
(Racing Special). Based on the new production 748R,
this featured a newly homologated frame and airbox,
and an injection system similar to that of the 996
Factory racer. A single Marelli injector was placed
above the throttle valve, with the throttle body inside
the airbox and very short intake ducts. The injection
system was the production Marelli 1.6M, but with
54 mm throttle bodies. There were also a number of
engine developments, including new camshafts, a 12:1
compression ratio, 36 mm and 30 mm valves, a closer
ratio gearbox, and lighter flywheel. There were also
wider, 19 mm, exposed cam belts and with a 54 mm
racing titanium exhaust system the power was an
impressive 124 bhp at 12,000 rpm. The chassis was
ostensibly the same as the 748R, and Team Ducati
Infostrada ran two 748RSs, prepared by veteran tuner
Pietro di Gianesin. Paolo Casoli was joined by Ruben
Xaus, and Casoli finished a close second in the
championship with two victories.

The Production 996SPS was upgraded yet again for
2000. The engine specifications were as before, but the
chassis received some development. Most significant
was the Öhlins front fork with TiN-coated fork legs.
The final series of 996SPS Factory Replicas was also
produced for 2000, the 996 Factory Replica 2, or
'Pista' (circuit), while for the USA the 996S was

Sport Touring became more
performance orientated with the
996 cc ST4S of 2001.

compact 5.9M Marelli electronic ignition and injection control unit. Unlike the P8 system that used a separate rpm sensor and injection timing sensor, the 5.9M was similar in design to the 1.6M with a single inductive pick-up. The throttle bodies were increased to 54 mm, with a single spray-type injector per cylinder. The power was 135 bhp at 10,200 rpm, and each 996R came with an optional power kit that included Termignoni mufflers and ECU remapping, providing an additional six bhp.

The 996R frame was a modified Fogarty-type, constructed of 2 mm diameter chrome-molybdenum tubing, with an aluminium rear subframe and larger, 12 mm engine mounting bolts as were all Superbike models that year. While the Öhlins suspension and Marchesini wheels were similar to those of the 996SPS, the front brakes included thinner discs, and four-pad Brembo front brake calipers with four 34 mm pistons. The carbon-fibre fairing no longer incorporated side vents, while the weight was down to 185 kg.

Built as a limited production of 500 units, 350 996Rs were sold immediately over the Internet on its

release on 12 September 2000. The other 150 were retained for racing homologation, but these did not feature an individually numbered plaque. Also, because of difficulties regarding street homologation, all US examples came without lights and stands, although the wiring remained in place.

With the 996R a limited-edition model, the previous 123 bhp 996SPS engine powered the 996S, filling the line-up between the 996R and basic 996. While the engine specifications were similar to the SPS, the con-rods were not titanium, and the electronic injection system was the 1.6M instead of the P8. The Monoposto or Biposto chassis included an Öhlins shock absorber, and a Showa front fork. The 996 also received an Öhlins shock, but retained the earlier 112 bhp engine. There was also a specific US 996S, with an Öhlins front fork and Ducati Corse decals. All US examples retained the lower bhp motor.

As for 2000, there were three versions of the 748, with the 748R receiving several updates. Inside the engine was a lighter flywheel, tungsten inserts to

Below: The first limited-edition
retro model was the MH900e,
but it was more a styling than a
functional exercise.

balance the crankshaft, titanium valve cotters, and a
vacuum precision-cast gear selector drum. The power
was unchanged at 106 bhp. The chassis included a
1.5 mm thick chrome-moly tubular steel frame, lighter
996R-type Brembo braking system, an Öhlins TiN-
coated 43 mm upside-down fork, and Öhlins racing
rear shock absorber. Apart from small updates shared
with all Supersport models (such as the sealed-for-life
battery), the 748 and 748S were as before.

The ST4S joined the Sport Touring line-up alongside
the ST2 and ST4. Powered by a 117 bhp (at 8,750 rpm)
Desmoquattro 996 motor, this featured similar cylinder
heads to the 916 cc ST4, with a lowered exhaust
camshaft. The intake valves were 36 mm with 8.74 mm
lift, and the exhaust valves 30 mm with 9.7 mm lift. The
injection system was the new 5.9M, while the gearbox
ratios were the same as the other STs. Also new for the
ST4S was Asahi-Denso switchgear, an Öhlins rear shock
absorber, aluminium swingarm, and Brembo five-spoke
wheels. The ST4 now had a Sachs rear shock absorber,
while the ST2 included new timing belt rollers with
stepless hub adjustment for more accurate valve timing.
These were used with all two-valve models this year, as
were the gunmetal grey frame and wheels.

As only a few examples of the limited-edition
MH900e were produced during 2000, general
production commenced the following year. Powered by
the 75 bhp fuel-injected 900 cc engine of the 900

Supersport, several components were changed from the
prototype in the transition to production. The 43 mm
Showa front fork was now the non-adjustable type of
the 750 SS, and the round headlight was more
conventional. The tubular steel trellis frame was
specific to the MH900e, as was the 60 mm steel single-
sided swingarm. Like the earlier prototype, the engine
featured styled sump covers, and the graphics were the
earlier Giugiaro style. Not only was the MH900e
technical specification disappointing, it was not the rare
limited-edition model that was originally envisaged.
Total MH900e production was 2,010, with most
produced after September 2001, as 2002 models.

The Supersport range was expanded to include three
models for 2001, an entry-level 750 Sport joining the
750 and 900 Supersports. There was also a 34 bhp 750
for European age-related licence restrictions. The matt
black 750 Sport came with a single front disc brake,
and all Supersports featured a Sachs rear shock
absorber. Updates included an improved lubrication
system, allowing the 900 to use air-cooled cylinders as
on the 750 instead of the previous air-oil cooling
system. Oil jets at the base of the cylinder cooled the
piston and con-rod small-end. Brembo five-spoke
wheels set the 900 apart from the 750 this year.

While there were only limited updates to the
Supersport, the Monster range was expanded to include
the long-awaited Desmoquattro Monster S4. This was
not a variant of the existing two-valve versions, but an
adaptation of the ST4, sharing its basic engine and
frame architecture with the sport-touring model. From
the ST4, came the 916 cc Desmoquattro engine with
lowered exhaust camshafts, enabling the engine to be
positioned further forward for optimum weight
distribution. There was a new Weber Marelli 5.9M
electronic engine management system, with a single
injector positioned inside the 50 mm throttle bodies.
The only different engine specification from the ST4
was the inlet camshaft, closing the inlet valve earlier
(61° degrees after bottom-dead-centre). With an 11:1
compression ratio the power of the Monster S4 was
lower than that of other 916s, at 101 bhp at 8,750 rpm.
To improve the engine aesthetics the battery was moved
to behind the airbox and above the rear cylinder, and
there was a new water pump housing and engine cover.
The Desmoquattro engine was still not exactly
beautiful, but these changes were an improvement.

Although the Monster S4 styling followed that of the
two-valve Monsters, the frame was based on that of the

The S4 Monster Foggy, which was
only available over the Internet,
was very much an expensive
Monster S4. *Ducati Motor*

ST4, with thicker, 28 x 2 mm, tubing and a 24° steering
head angle. The engine was positioned 20 mm higher
than the 900 IE Monster, and the wheelbase lengthened
to 1,440 mm. The 43 mm Showa front forks and
Brembo brakes were similar to those on the ST4, and
there was a Sachs rear shock absorber. With a dry
weight of 193 kg Monster S4 promised exciting and
lively performance.

In honour of their most successful ever racer, Carl
Fogarty, Ducati offered the limited-edition Monster S4
Fogarty for sale over the Internet in June 2001.
Ostensibly a standard Monster S4, there were a number
of updates to justify the €18,000 price. The impetus
came from Daniele Casolari of Ducati Performance in
October 2000. Casolari asked the stylist, Aldo Drudi,
to create new colour-coded bodywork, reshaping the
fuel tank and incorporating additional carbon-fibre
body parts. The Foggy S4 received upgraded Showa 43
mm forks with TiN-coated fork legs, and the weight
was reduced to
189 kg. The optional high level exhaust system with
oval carbon-fibre Termignoni mufflers, saw the power
climb to 110 bhp at 9,750 rpm. Within the first 24
hours of release 142 of the 300 Fogarty S4s offered

were sold over the Internet on 20 June 2001.

After the restyle of the Monster range for 2000 there
were only minor updates to the air-cooled Monsters for
2001. The engine sizes were unchanged, at 400 cc
(exclusively for the Japanese market), 600, 750 and
900 cc. All but the 900 featured carburettors. There
were four versions of the Monster 900 and three of the
Monster 600 and 750, including the Dark; Metallic (a
Dark variant with metallic paint), the Cromo, and the
900 Special. For America there was a Monster 600
USA, with a 35 mm lower seat. All versions now
included a tachometer.

Motorcycle sales increased by 2% in 2001, and were
noticeably stronger in Japan (up 51%) and the UK (up
10%) with total motorcycle production being 40,016.
While it was a significant year for new designs, the year
also marked the end of two earlier eras. On 14 May,
the sole-surviving Ducati brother, Bruno, died at the
age of 96, and on 19 July the great engineer Fabio
Taglioni died at the age of 80. But already a new age
had begun when Ducati announced in May, that
Ducati Corse was developing a four-stroke
Grand Prix motorcycle to compete in the forthcoming
MotoGP class.

Below: Bayliss only narrowly failed to retain the World Superbike Championship in 2002 on the Infostrada F02.

Right: Gérard Rancinan produced a series of 'Genesis Speed Art' for Ducati Corse to celebrate the creation of Desmosedici. The riders are Troy Bayliss (left) and Loris Capirossi, with the main proponents of the project looking on: Preziosi, Domenicali and Cecchinelli. *Ducati Corse*

2002

Alongside the development of the MotoGP racer, Ducati Corse continued to update the Factory Superbike. The 998 was to be an interim model until the advent of the new 999, but received a second-generation Testastretta engine. Chief Engineer Filippo Preziosi enlarged the engine slightly to 999 cc, with a 104 mm bore and 58.8 mm stroke. All the engine castings were new, the throttle bodies were non-cylindrical (still with a single injector per cylinder), and with a revised exhaust system the output of the 998F02 went up to 188 bhp at 12,500 rpm. Braking updates saw metallic brake pads, allowing 290 mm front discs to be used all season. During the year other improvements included the installation of a cooling duct from the right side of the radiator to the rear cam belt and pulley.

There were new minimum weight regulations this year. The 1,000 cc twin's weight was now 164 kg with the 750 cc fours at 159 kg, a reversal of the original regulations that were drafted when fours were dominant. The change reflected the success of Ducati's process of on-going evolution that had seen them continue to dominate the World Superbike Championship.

There was no change to the official factory Superbike team line-up for 2002, and this year Ducati narrowly failed in their quest for another World Superbike Championship. In one of the most exciting racing seasons ever Bayliss set the stage with 14 victories, before Colin Edwards countered on the Honda SP-2 to win the final eight races, and the championship by nine points. The HM Plant Team with riders Hodgson and James Toseland ran the 2001-spec 998F01s, with a claimed 179 bhp at 12,000 rpm, and weighing in at 165 kg. The customer 998RS was powered by a Testastretta this year, and this was also competitive in the hands of Lucio Pedercini and Juan Borja.

Ducati was also back in force contesting the British and AMA Superbike championships. This year Steve Hislop, riding for Paul Bird's MonsterMob, was equipped with a customer 998 Testastretta, as were the Renegade duo of Michael Rutter and Shane Byrne. The British Championship was also one of the most exciting seasons to date, the Ducatis totally dominating with Hislop winning the title. The season was again less satisfactory in the USA, however HMC was the only sponsored team, and began the season at Daytona with Canadian rider Pascal Picotte. Political machinations saw Picotte fired, replaced by ex-Kawasaki veteran

Left: The 999R Fila was released during 2003 to celebrate 200 Ducati World Superbike victories. *Ducati Motor*

Below: The 1000DS motor also made it to the Supersport for 2003, bringing a new lease of life to this traditional family.

Bottom: More sporting than the standard Monster, the S4R featured a number of technical innovations, as well as a 996 cc motor.

a new airbox housing the 50 mm throttle bodies, and a wider ratio gearbox. Several styling and technical features differed from the S4. The exhaust was a high-rise two-into-one-into-two, and the tubular aluminium swingarm single sided. The handlebar was a variable section aluminium type, and new footpegs allowed for an increase in ground clearance. Quality suspension included a Showa fork with TiN-coated tubes, and a Showa rear shock absorber. The Multistrada also made it into production during the year, and was immediately successful, sales numbering 6,025 in 2003. In March, Carlo Di Biagio resigned as CEO, his position taken by Federico Minoli, and in May, Ducati announced it was teaming up with Warner Brothers to promote the movie *The Matrix Reloaded* that featured a road chase on a Ducati 998 Superbike. In October, three new concept bikes, the SportClassics were unveiled in Tokyo. Headed by the Paul Smart 1000, these replicated the famous 'round-case' 750 twins of 1971–74; the 750 Super Sport, 750 Sport, and 750GT. The PS1000 was inspired by Paul Smart's 1972 Imola race winner.

Below: The D16GP4 was almost
all new, but the performance was
disappointing. *Ducati Corse*

Despite the release of the 999 and Multistrada, motorcycle sales decreased in 2003, down 3.5%, to 38,128. Total motorcycle production was down 2.8%, to 38,417. Hardest hit were the Sport Touring (down 34.6% to 2,275) and the Superbike and Supersport (down 26.3% to 12,126).

2004

After surprising everyone with the Desmosedici in 2003, Ducati Corse produced an updated D16GP4 for the 2004 MotoGP season. Of the 915 individual components, 60% were new on this evolutionary model. Although the bodywork was outwardly similar, it was built of four parts to simplify maintenance, and was designed to improve cooling. Overheating had been a problem during 2003.

A new titanium exhaust was produced by Termignoni, with the vertical cylinders exiting under the tail and the horizontal cylinders on the right. This allowed the fuel tank to be redesigned, extending under the seat to improve mass centralization. The tubular steel frame was similar in design, with different engine mounts to allow easier engine removal, and the redesigned pressed-aluminium swingarm was lighter. The front fork went back to 42 mm, while the airbox was larger. Inside the engine was a new combustion chamber and new components to reduce weight and internal friction. This resulted in a 10 bhp increase, to 230 bhp at 16,500 rpm, and allowed the D16 to achieve a top speed of 347.4 km/h in pre-season testing (again the fastest MotoGP bike).

Unfortunately, the D16GP4 did not fulfil initial expectations. Power was not a problem, but alterations to the chassis affected stability and from the outset the riders struggled. Ballast was added to the front to improve the weight balance and 2003 models were built out of spares for a test comparison. After Cataluyna there was a new traction control. Eventually there was a new 'twin-pulse' engine, but with the cylinders decoupled by around 45°, staggering the power impulses to avoid the earlier reliability problems. After Phillip Island a new chassis and swingarm was tested, and there was an improved Öhlins TT25 fork. By the end of the season the bike was better, with some rostrum finishes, but the GP4 was a disappointment after 2003. Capirossi finished a lowly ninth in the World Championship, while Bayliss's frequent crashing saw him finish 14th, and lose his ride for 2005. The 2003 D16s were ridden by Hodgson and Xaus for the d'Antin team, occasionally beating the factory Marlboro team.

For the 2004 World Superbike Championship, Ducati signed 23-year-old James Toseland and Régis Laconi to ride the Fila 999F04s. The only official factory squad in the series, the 999s managed first and second in the championship, Toseland becoming the youngest ever champion. This year was much more hard fought as the Fila team no longer had the advantage of special tyres, all teams using Pirelli, while new regulations allowed the four-cylinder machines to displace 1,000 cc. Updates to the F04 racers included new two-ring Omega pistons and longer titanium Pankl connecting rods designed to reduce weight and friction. Valve sizes were 43.5 mm inlet and 34 mm exhaust. To improve reliability the rev limit was set 500 rpm lower

Below: James Toseland narrowly won the 2004 World Superbike Championship from Regis Laconi. *Ducati Corse*

Right: Compact and powerful, the V-four 990 cc Desmosedici motor. *Ducati Corse*

than in 2003, at 13,200 rpm. The compression ratio was up to 15.8:1, and with a titanium 2-1-2-1 63.5 mm exhaust system output was 189 bhp at 12,500 rpm. The carbon-fibre airbox and intake ducts were designed by Alan Jenkins, and the Verlicchi frame was as before. The 999 continued to be very sensitive to set up, and Toseland only narrowly won the championship from Laconi. The Fila bikes won ten races.

The factory also supplied customer teams (DFX, Renegade, NCR, and PGS-1) with close replicas of the F03 999. These RS04 racers were close in specification to the F04, except for the latest pressurized 42 mm Öhlins front fork, but didn't share the factory machines' reliability. On the track they were as fast, Haga winning six races and McCoy one. They also proved fickle to set up, and Chili openly criticized his 999, switching back to the older 998. Handling

The 749R was the highest specification production Ducati available in 2004, and was raced with some success in the World Supersport Championship by Lorenzo Lanzi. *Ducati Corse*

Right: The ST3 replaced the ST2 for 2004, all STs receiving a new headlight and fairing this year. *Ducati Motor*

problems were also evident in the British Superbike Championship, with Sean Emmett struggling on the pre-season favourite MonsterMob Ducati. Emmett could only manage two race wins, to finish fifth overall. In the AMA Superbike Championship Eric Bostrom was the sole Ducati factory entry on the Ducati Austin 999. Shod with Michelin tyres, Bostrom had a disappointing season but took one victory, at Pikes Peak.

After an absence of three years, Ducati Corse re-entered the World Supersport Championship. It was a tentative entry, with only one rider, Lorenzo Lanzi on the new 749R. The short-stroke 749R (detailed in the next section) was already the most advanced production bike offered by Ducati, and racing developments included a Magneti Marelli MR600 ECU, 57 mm Termignoni exhaust system, ported cylinder heads, and racing air filters. The power was an impressive 140 bhp at 13,000 rpm, and Lanzi was timed at an astonishing 292 km/h at Monza. Lorenzo Lanzi proved very competitive on the Breil 749R,

finishing the World Supersport Championship in fifth place. In other championships, David Muscat took the French Supersport Championship on a 749R, and Michael Laverty won one race in the British series on the MonsterMob 749 and ended second overall.

By 2004, the 999 and 749 range was firmly established and two final versions of the 998 were released, the 998 FE (Final Edition), and 998 Matrix. The 998 FE was similar to the earlier 998S, with an Öhlins front fork, while the 998 Matrix was a 998, painted dark green, as in the *Matrix Reloaded* film. This year there were three versions of the 999 and 749, standard, 'S' and 'R', with most updates centred on the 749. The 749S motor was uprated, the power increasing from 103 to 110 bhp, and the 749R was released for Supersport racing. There were only a few updates to the top-of-the-range 999R. All the bodywork was now carbon-fibre, including the heat dissipation partition, which was previously aluminium alloy. The headlight support was magnesium. As World Superbike Championship rules did not allow the

Below: For 2006 the 695 Monster
became the base model in the
line-up. *Ducati Motor*

was aluminium. The S4R was as before, but with the additional colours of red and black, both with white stripes. The power for the 2005 S4R was quoted at 117 bhp at 8,750 rpm.

While the importance of the Supersport and Sport Touring families waned during 2005, further emphasis was placed on expanding the Multistrada. This went in two directions; towards the more sporting with the Multistrada 1000S, and the budget, with the 620 and 620 Dark. This demonstrated the Multistrada idea of combining enduro and sports in a street-orientated motorcycle was one on which Ducati placed considerable emphasis, and it was well rewarded. Multistrada sales rose 111% in the first nine months of 2005, making this Ducati's second-most popular family after the Monster.

It was not difficult to see why the Multistrada was the new sales success story. In the wake of an ageing motorcycle clientele and increasing speed restrictions there was a general move away from racetrack-orientated sports bikes to real-world usable machines.

For many, including the author, the Multistrada was arguably the ideal street bike. For 2005, Multistrada updates included redesigned seats with a new anti-slide system for the passenger, a taller screen, new rear-vision mirrors, and more stable side stand. Options included panniers, rack, GPS navigator, and a racing exhaust.

Heading the Multistrada line-up was the 1000S DS, with variable section aluminium handlebars, carbon-fibre front mudguard and timing belt cover, and Öhlins suspension front and rear. The 43 mm front fork included TiN-coated fork tubes. The Multistrada 1000DS was similar to before, but there were two new entry-level 620 versions, the Multistrada 620 and 620 Dark. The 63 bhp 620 engine included the APTC clutch. While ostensibly identical to the 1,000 cc version, the 620s featured a smaller, 15-litre fuel tank, a Monster-style double-sided swingarm, and simplified instrument panel. The wheels were three-spoke, and suspension was a Marzocchi 43 mm front fork and a Sachs rear monoshock with adjustable preload and

rebound. The front brakes were two 300 mm front discs with floating piston calipers, as on the S2R. The Dark featured a matt black colour scheme and a single front 320 mm disc brake.

As the public response to the SportClassic was extremely favourable, with the first series sold out by July 2004, it was announced this new retro family would go into production. The first Paul Smart 1000 would be available in November 2005 as a 2006 model, with the Sport 1000 and GT1000 to follow.

2006

The year 2006 was a significant one for Ducati, marking the 80th anniversary of the foundation of the company, the 60th anniversary of the start of motorcycle production and the 50th anniversary of Taglioni's desmodromic valve system.

At the end of 2005 it was announced that Sete Gibernau would join Loris Capirossi in the Ducati Marlboro team on the D16 GP6. The Desmosedici GP6 was an evolution of the GP5, developments including more power, a broader powerband, and increased fuel efficiency due to a reduction in internal friction and a revised engine management system. The cooling system within the cylinder block was also changed and the fully-computerised throttle arrangement now included the potentiometer in the twistgrip. This eliminated the previous complex system where all four throttle cables were operated electronically by a computer-controlled potentiometer. A new frame, wheels and front fork also enabled the GP6 to be lighter and stiffer. Although 13% lighter, the new frame included additional tubes between the downtubes and steering head while the 42 mm front fork featured carbon-fibre outer tubes and an Öhlins TTX20 damping system. Welded stiffening swingarm supports replaced the outrigger supports of 2005. The electronics were relocated into a carbon-fibre subframe around the nose and a reshaped fuel tank

allowed the riders to tuck in better. Weight was 148 kg and the claimed power in excess of 235 horsepower at 16,500 rpm, with maximum torque of approximately 100Nm/10.2 kg at 14,000 rpm.

Livio Suppo remained team manager but the team's exploits were constantly monitored by Ducati Corse boss Claudio Domenicali and president Federico Minoli. Capirossi's engineer Roberto Bonazzi left, to be replaced by Cristhian Pupulin, while one of the key figures in the Desmosedici project from its inception, Corrado Cecchinelli, also departed. Alongside the official Marlboro team was the d'Antin Ducati satellite team. This included two riders for 2006 – Alex Hofmann and Jose Luis Cardoso. Their 2006 bikes were termed the GP6-Sat, for satellite team, and were a mixture of the factory GP5 and GP6.

The season started brilliantly for Capirossi, with a victory in the opening race at Jerez, and at Mugello the bikes were raced in special livery to celebrate the three anniversaries for Ducati. By mid-season Capirossi was leading the championship and in May 2006 test rider Vittoriano Guareschi tested the 800 cc D16 GP7 at Ducati's home circuit Mugello in preparation

for the change of regulations in 2007. But disaster struck in round 7 at Catalunya when both Ducatis were eliminated in a crash on the first corner, dealing Capirossi's title hopes a fatal blow. Despite victories in the Czech Republic and Japan he only managed third in the World Championship. Gibernau's season was extremely disappointing, injuries sustained at Portugal hastening his retirement and allowing World Superbike Champion Troy Bayliss to ride the Desmosedici 990 in its final race. Bayliss was magnificent, leading from start to finish, and becoming the tenth rider to win races in Superbike and the premier GP class.

After a season on the Camel Honda in MotoGP, Troy Bayliss made a return to the factory Xerox Ducati in the World Superbike Championship. Lorenzo Lanzi partnered him on the Xerox 999F06. During 2005 Ducati also announced they would no longer provide a customer 999RS, citing the increasing cost of electronic systems. They would continue to supply engines, matched to standard electronic management systems, but for the first time in fifteen years the World Superbike grid wouldn't be filled with customer Ducati racers. This was of no concern for the factory Xerox

One of the most exciting models
ever offered by Ducati: the 998 cc
S4RS of 2006. *Ducati Motor*

team as Bayliss soon stamped his mark, winning eight
races in succession in the first half of the season.

A triumph of evolution over revolution, the 104 x
58.8 mm V-twin utilized Magneti Marelli Marvel 4
electronics with a single IWF1 injector per cylinder.
The power of the 999F06 was 194 horsepower at
12,500 rpm and there was considerable crossover
between the 999F06 and GP6. This included
electronic traction control, the Öhlins TTX20 42 mm
pressurizsed front fork and Öhlins TTX36 rear shock
absorber. This featured smaller springs, saving 600 gs.
The brakes were the usual Brembo, 320 mm on the
front and 290 mm on the rear. Although the second
half of the season wasn't as profitable for Bayliss,
ultimately he won the World Superbike Championship
with ease, with twelve victories.

After such a successful season in 2005, it was no
surprise to see Lavilla again on the Airwaves F06 in the
British Superbike Championship. Leon Haslam rode
the second machine. Both were provided with official
Ducati Corse 999F06 bikes and Lavilla soon stamped
his mark with a string of wins and podium finishes.
Haslam also impressed, with wins at Croft, Cadwell
Park, and Brands Hatch, but narrowly missed taking

the championship. Ducati Corse was also officially
involved in the AMA Championship for a second
year, providing factory 999s to the Parts Unlimited
Ducati Austin team. Neil Hodgson was partnered
this year by Ben Bostrom, who replaced his brother
Eric, and returned to Ducati after a three-year break.
Unfortunately it was a miserable season for Hodgson,
and with only a handful of podiums he finished fifth in
the championship.

With so many developments to the 999 and 749
occurring for 2005, there were only minor updates to
this series for 2006. Heading the Superbike line-up was
the 999R Xerox, with the colours and graphics of the
World Superbike team. Also distinguishing the Xerox
from the regular 999R were a black anodized steering
head and footrests, plus the red Brembo Racing logo on
the radial brake calipers and mounts. The rear Öhlins
shock absorber was a racing type, with adjustable
compression damping for high and low speed, an
aluminium body, hydraulic adjustment of spring
preload, and a top-out spring.

The 999R, 999S, and 999 were much as before,
the 999R engine still with specific cylinder heads,
semi-cone valve adjusters, and stiffer con rods and

The first production MotoGP replica
motorcycle was the Desmosedici RR, available
in limited numbers during 2007. This promised
to be the most exotic and best performing
production motorcycle available. *Ducati Motor*

Rosso GP with a white number plate on the tail section
and a white Ducati logo on the fairing, and the 'Team
Version' painted like factory Corse bikes, with a white
stripe on the fairing. A team sponsor decal kit was
provided with each bike. They also came with a new
lightweight multi-function dashboard, with LCD graph
tachometer, trip/odometer, anti-theft immobilizer, lap
time measurement, and readings for oil pressure, fuel
reserve, clock and air temperature. This was the same
as fitted to the 2007 Desmosedici GP7.

As the most expensive and exotic production
motorcycle available, the Desmosedici RR created
a huge impression and was soon sold out. Racing
success is supposed to generate sales, but despite their
success in MotoGP and World Superbike this wasn't
happening. Ducati desperately needed an exotic
range-leading motorcycle to ensure their status as
Italy's premier manufacturer of sporting motorcycles.
Such a technologically advanced limited-edition
motorcycle would surely spearhead a sales revival
further down the range. But if the RR heralded a new
era of limited-production, high-profit motorcycles, it
remained to be seen if this change in direction would
save the company.

Ducati's 2007 MotoGP winning team. Casey Stoner is on the right and Loris Capirossi on the left.

Stoner carried the number 1 plate during 2008, and finished second in the MotoGP World Championship.

associated increase in revenue of 20%. The Milan show in November 2007 saw the release of the new Monster 696, with the Superbike range completed by the 848 and 1098R. But the most exciting motorcycle in the production range was the Desmosedici RR, first announced in 2006 and finally available during 2008. This year also represented the 30th anniversary of Mike Hailwood's spectacular victory in the Isle of Man TTF1 race, and also the 50th anniversary of Ducati's first appearance at the famous circuit. To celebrate, Ducati sent a selection of seven historic racing machines to the Island and sponsored a parade of vintage Ducatis, with many past champions present.

MotoGP

After five years spearheading the MotoGP assault, Loris Capirossi's failure to conquer the GP7 saw Marco Melandri drafted into the team alongside World Champion Casey Stoner. Livio Suppo was again team manager and most of the team personnel remained unchanged.

As Ducati had finished the 2007 season as MotoGP World Champion there were minimal updates to the 800 cc GP8. Ducati's philosophy of extracting as much power as possible from the 800 cc V4 continued, but with more mid-range power than before. The 21-litre

Below: The F08 World
Superbike was based on
the 1098R.

Bottom right: Bayliss's F08
would be the final successful
factory Superbike.

Right: Troy Bayliss went out in
style, easily winning the 2008
World Superbike Championship.

fuel capacity restriction encouraged even more sophisticated electronics, and to improve performance with the least possible use of fuel a variable-length intake system was tried early in the season. This was problematic and most of Stoner's early performances were disappointing. Apart from a win at the opening round at Qatar, Stoner struggled and Ducati reverted to the earlier throttle system.

By round 7 the new set-up was working and Stoner won the British, Dutch and German Grands Prix before losing out to Rossi at Laguna Seca. Stoner's championship hopes began to suffer when he fell while in the lead in the Czech Republic and at San Marino. Although he bounced back to win two of the last three races (Australia and Valencia) hopes of a second World Championship were already dashed. In Australia the GP7 had a new, nimbler fairing to suit the high-speed nature of the circuit. Stoner finished second overall, again with little assistance from his team-mate. Melandri had more difficulty than Capirossi in coming to terms with the 800 cc Desmosedici, and following only one top-six finish his contract was terminated.

Again Pramac d'Antin ran Ducati's satellite MotoGP team, this year with riders Toni Elias and Sylvain Guintoli. With Alice sponsorship they worked closely with the Ducati factory, but their riders could do little to dispel the notion that the GP8 was only suited to Casey Stoner. Although Elias managed a second at Brno, and came third at Misano, he finished twelfth overall in the championship. The team also struggled

with internal instability and Spanish figurehead Luis d'Antin suddenly departed mid-season.

WORLD SUPERBIKE

This was to be Troy Bayliss's final season and he was determined to win World Championships on three successive incarnations of the Ducati twin (996, 999 and 1098). The 1098F08 was based on the homologated 1098R and fewer engine changes were allowed under the new regulations. The engine now measured 106 x 67.9 mm, providing a capacity of 1,198 cc, and featured Omega RR58 two-ring pistons, stock Pankl forged titanium con rods, and a revised combustion chamber to the 1098. The four chrome nitride-coated titanium valves (44.3 mm inlet and 36.2 mm exhaust) were set at an included angle of 24.3°. The racing camshafts provided the same lift, but with different duration, and the 63.9 mm throttle bodies included an FIM-sanctioned 50 mm restrictor. The new engine and larger torque pulses required updates to the Magneti Marelli Marvel 4 EFI that now vaporized fuel through two differently sized injectors. Other internal updates included a full-race six-speed gearbox with the pinions shot-peened for extra strength. The dry clutch was the usual ramp-type design, but with two springs removed to locate the trolley starter pins. With a Termignoni 52 mm–57 mm stainless steel exhaust system (0.8 mm thick) the power was a claimed 198 horsepower at 11,000 rpm.

The 9 kg tubular steel chassis was identical to that of the 1098, but included a different single-sided fabricated aluminium swingarm to allow for a 16.5-inch rear wheel. This was slightly stronger than the standard swingarm, approximating the rigidity of the 999's double-sided swingarm and provided a wheelbase of 1,435 mm. Weight distribution was 51/49% front and rear. The front suspension was a 43 mm Öhlins TTX20 racing fork, with a TTX36 rear shock absorber, and the forged Marchesini wheels carried smaller 320 mm front discs and a 218 mm rear disc. While the suspension was basically the same as fitted to the production 1098R, and not the newer electronic Öhlins, electronic traction control was an essential component. The minimum weight for twins this year was 168 kg (compared to the 162 kg of the fours) so there was little need for extremely exotic components. Even the electric start was retained.

Team manager Tardozzi and technical director Marinelli again headed the Xerox Ducati team, and this

year 23-year-old Michel Fabrizio earned the second factory bike. Lanzi rode the RG 1098RS, surprising many with a win at Valencia, while Sterilgarda (Max Biaggi and Ruben Xaus), and Guandalini Racing (Jakub Smrž) entered other 1098RS machines. For the first time in several years these were all real privateer Ducatis rather than year-old factory bikes. But, as usual, it was the factory Xerox bikes that predominated, Bayliss immediately stamping his authority with five race wins in the first four rounds. After a mid-season slump he came back to take a further six victories, easily winning his third World Superbike Championship before hanging up his leathers. Bayliss retired as one of Ducati's most successful riders, his career with them spanning from 2000, when he was first drafted in to replace the injured Carl Fogarty, to his title in 2008.

The 1098RS was also successful in the British Superbike Championship, veteran Shane Byrne winning the title on the Airwaves Ducati (formerly GSE Racing). Rising star Leon Camier joined him in Colin Wright's team while Michael Rutter lined up on a 1098RS for

North West Ducati. Ultimately Byrne took his first BSB Championship since 2003 with ten victories. Camier also won three races and Rutter one.

Below: The Desmosedici
finally went into
production in 2008.

Right: The 1098R was produced
as the World Superbike
homologation version.

DESMOSEDICI RR

When the D16RR finally appeared during 2008 the production numbers were increased significantly from 400 to 1,500. Only one series was produced, and most of the specifications were unchanged from the 2006 prototype as described in chapter 15. Alan Jenkins supplied the design of the aerodynamic carbon-fibre bodywork.

The V4 engine followed the specification of the GP6, with an 86 mm bore and 42.56 mm stroke and a displacement of 989 cc. The positions of the desmodromic valve operating system (camshaft rotation axis, rocker arm centre, and valve centre distance), valve angle and twin pulse timing were also as for the GP6. The pistons had a double-ribbed undercrown and 13.5:1 compression, while the one-piece machined crankshaft rotated on brass bearing shells with the pins offset by 70°. This generated soft timing pulses at 0°, 90°, 290° and 380° to provide useable power. The cone-shaped end of the crank maximized the use of space below the pistons and optimized balance during assembly. The intake and exhaust valves were titanium with a chromium nitride coating, while the camshafts were drilled to reduce weight. The throttle bodies, while serving two opposing cylinder heads, lay on the same plane, resulting in a straight intake port.

Further attention to detail extended to lightening of the timing gears through finite-element simulation (FEM). A racing-style six-speed cassette gearbox was also employed, with a hydraulic dry multi-plate slipper clutch. The crankcases included integral Nicasil-lined cylinder bores, the trochiodal (Gerotor) oil pump also controlling the water pump. The D16RR engine dimensions were extremely compact, only 567.4 mm long, 567.7 mm high and 427.3 mm wide. Completing the specification was a specifically developed 4-2-1 exhaust system of AISI 309 42 mm diameter tubing

Left: The 1198S replaced the 1098S for 2009.

Right: A special-edition 1098R Bayliss was produced for 2009.

Below right: Xavier Siméon won the 2009 Superstock 1000 World Cup on the 1198S.

Left: The 1198S replaced the 1098S for 2009.

Right: A special-edition 1098R Bayliss was produced for 2009.

Below right: Xavier Siméon won the 2009 Superstock 1000 World Cup on the 1198S.

Although the 1198 was unsuccessful in the World Superbike Championship, the Belgian rider Xavier Siméon won the Superstock 1000 FIM Cup on the Ducati Xerox Junior Team 1198S. Two factory bikes were entered in the championship, the other ridden by Daniele Beretta. Siméon won five of the ten races, finishing second in the remaining five to take the championship comfortably.

STREETFIGHTER AND STREETFIGHTER S

Another new family joined the Ducati line-up for 2009, the Streetfighter. This was ostensibly a naked 1098 Superbike, effectively replacing the Monster S4RS, and the product of 33-year-old French in-house designer Damien Basset. Monster team leader Giulio Malagoli headed the project. The Streetfighter culture was born on the back streets of northern Europe during the late 1970s and 1980s. Unlike the Café racer movement that was about transforming traditional bikes into race replicas, Streetfighters converted sport bikes into a naked style. They evolved by removing the fairings and fitting higher bars to create high-performance naked Superbikes. Like the Hypermotard, Ducati's Streetfighter was another factory custom interpretation of a popular concept and it was Malagoli's intention to produce the quickest naked bike in the world.

Although it looked very much like an unclothed 1098, nearly all the Streetfighter parts were new, even the engine, which was a blend of the 1098 and 1198. The Testastretta engine combined the cylinder heads of the 1098 with the 3 kg lighter vacuum die-cast 1198 crankcases. Also from the 1098 came the same Marelli ECU with single top-spray injector and elliptical throttle body equivalent to a 60 mm circular throat. The 2-1-2 exhaust system was 58 mm to 63.5 mm diameter 1 mm thick with two lambda probes to ensure precise fuel mapping for optimum performance and an electronic valve in the mid-section to achieve a wide spread of power. Two cannon-style vertically stacked brushed steel mufflers on the right were similar in style to the Monster S4R. Shorter air intake ducts, revised ECU mapping and a 12.5:1 compression ratio saw the Streetfighter engine produce 155 horsepower, 25 more than the Monster S4RS. Other distinguishing engine features were a magnesium clutch cover, black engine covers, and carbon grey crankcases. As the 1098

radiator was too wide for the naked look the Streetfighter's curved radiator was split in two, the upper radiator assisted by electric fans with the lower sitting in the front of the belly pan. As there was no longer room for an oil cooler this also housed a water-cooled oil heat exchanger.

Although the Streetfighter was developed in tandem with the 1098, the chassis differed in a number of areas. The purpose-built trellis frame had 25.6° of rake compared to the Superbike's 24.5°, and the black anodized single-sided aluminium swingarm was 35 mm longer (providing a longer 1,475 mm wheelbase). The Streetfighter had an adjustable 43 mm Showa fork up front and an adjustable Showa monoshock at the rear, the Streetfighter S receiving a 43 mm Öhlins fork with low-friction TiN fork tubes. The 'S' also received an adjustable Öhlins rear shock absorber unit fitted with a top-out spring to maintain rear tyre contact under extreme conditions. Both the Streetfighter and Streetfighter S had rear ride-height adjusters that allowed adjustment independent of spring preload.

New-style cast aluminium Enkei ten-spoke wheels graced the Streefighter, while the Streetfighter S had

Another new family, the
Streetfighter, was created
for 2009.

even lighter Y-shaped, five-spoke Marchesini forged wheels. The front brakes on both were radial Brembo, the twin monobloc calipers with four 34 mm pistons and bodies machined from a single piece of alloy. These gripped 330 mm discs with narrow, racing-style braking surfaces.

As style was an important component in the design, myriad special components adorned the Streetfighter. From the multi-reflector headlight with LED positioning lights to minimal passenger seat cover, rear wheel hugger and licence plate holder, the detailing was outstanding. Even the switchgear was revised to represent minimalism, with new slim bodies and easier to use buttons. Small, low, symmetrically mounted remote brake and clutch reservoirs were connected to slim Brembo radial master cylinders. The Streetfighter riding position differed considerably from the Superbike 1198 and the more relaxed Monster. A tall 840 mm seat and one-piece pulled-back tapered aluminium handlebar mounted on risers provided an aggressive upright riding position.

The dry weight of 169 kg provided the Streetfighter with an impressive power to weight ratio, the 'S'

slightly lighter at 167 kg. The 'S' also received a carbon-fibre front mudguard and cam belt covers, with Ducati Traction Control (DTC) and Ducati Data Analysis (DDA) as standard issue. Combining the best new-generation technology in a real-world style, the Streetfighter was an outstandingly well-conceived bike. It was fun to ride and provided performance able to satisfy the most demanding customer.

MONSTER 1100, 1100S AND 696

Another significant model release for 2009 was the new Monster 1100. The Monster family had been pivotal to Ducati since 1993, but the traditional line-up was showing its age. The release of the new-generation 696 in 2008 indicated a larger evolution Monster was imminent and this appeared in the guise of the 1100 and 1100S. With the Monster 1100 the Monster line-up was now reduced to only two capacities, the 696 and 1100.

Like the 696, the Monster 1100 was a product of

Following on from the 696
for 2009 was a new
Monster 1100.

Bart Janssen Groesbeek, and both models were developed in tandem from mid-2005. The 1100 project manager was Giulio Malagoli and central to the design was a new version of the 1,100 cc air-cooled dual-spark Desmodue twin. Although the basic engine specifications were unchanged from the engine already powering the Multistrada and Hypermotard (98 mm bore and 71.5 mm stroke), the lighter crankcases were cast using the same Vacural® technology as the 848. This saved 3 kg compared to the previous 1,100 cc engines. Black cylinders and carbon grey cam covers distinguished the new 1,100 cc engines and a new Siemens engine management system combined Alfa-n (throttle) and speed-density strategy for carburation adjustment. A new dry clutch was fitted, and the exhaust system featured an electronically controlled exhaust valve that enabled the use of silencers similar to those of the 696. Like the 696, the exhaust system included one lambda probe for each cylinder. The power was 95 horsepower at 7,500 rpm with 10.5 kg of torque at 6,000 rpm.

The Monster 1100 steel trellis frame was developed in conjunction with Ducati Corse and shared the

Desmosedici short-frame concept and the same tube diameter and thickness as the 1098R. The cast aluminium rear subframe was also derived from the Desmosedici RR and was combined with aluminium footpeg assemblies and a gravity cast and heat-treated aluminium single-sided swingarm. The front fork was a 43 mm fully adjustable Showa and the rear suspension a cantilever Sachs, with adjustable spring preload and rebound damping. The steeply angled rear unit was similar to the 696 set-up, but the ride height was 40 mm higher for increased ground clearance. Aluminium alloy Y-spoke wheels were the usual 3.50 x 17-inch front, with a 120/70ZR tyre, and 5.50 x 17-inch rear, with a 180/55ZR tyre. The Brembo braking system was state of the art, the front brakes including 320 mm discs with four-piston radial calipers and a radial master cylinder with an adjustable lever. The rear brake was the usual two-piston caliper and 245 mm disc.

The general style of the Monster 1100 followed that of the 696, with the distinctive triple-parabola headlight, fuel tank and airbox cover, and digital instrumentation. Setting the 1100 apart were new tapered aluminium handlebars. The Monster 1100

Below right: Stoner struggled to overcome the GP10's front-end problems throughout the season.

Right: The GP10 was an evolution of the GP9.

weighed only 169 kg, making it the lightest of all other 750 cc naked motorcycles, 8 kg less than the outgoing S2R1000. Also available was a higher specification Monster 1100S, arguably the ultimate air-cooled naked motorcycle available. Ostensibly similar to the Monster 1100, the 1100S featured fully adjustable 43 mm titanium nitride-coated Öhlins forks and rising rate linkage Öhlins rear shock absorber with adjustable preload and return damping. Front brake disc carriers were aluminium, while carbon-fibre cam belt covers, silencer guards and front mudguard reduced weight by a further 1 kg. The wheels were the same as the Monster 1100, but painted gold.

HYPERMOTARD, MULTISTRADA AND SPORTCLASSIC

Apart from colours, there were no changes to the Hypermotard 1100 or Multistrada 1100 for 2009, but the Hypermotard 1100S was updated with a Kayaba fork, DDA kit as standard, and black colour option. The Multistrada 1100S was now available in the additional colour of pearl white. Both these families were due for an update that would appear in 2010, but a Hypermotard 1100S still won the 1,200 cc category at the Pike's Peak International Hill Climb, in Colorado, in November 2009. The SportClassic family now included the Sport 1000S, with a classically shaped half-fairing with central round headlamp in keeping with the 1970s styling, the GT 1000 and the new GT 1000 Touring, in black with a white stripe. The Touring version also had chrome front and rear mudguards, a protective screen and a chrome luggage rack. A two-tone scheme of silver and smoke grey was a new colour for the GT 1000.

2010

2010 was a difficult year for the motorcycle industry, but Ducati managed to withstand the worst. During the first six months of 2010 the world market declined 10%, but Ducati was able to improve its sales by 0.3%. In the US the situation was particularly grim, with sales declining by almost 17%, and Ducati's by 14%. Yet Ducati's overall global market share doubled between 2007-2010, from 4.3% to 8.6%, and by the end of

2010 they anticipated sales growth of 6% compared to 2009. At the end of June 2010, Ducati announced €66 million EBIDTA (Earnings Before Interest, Taxes, Depreciation and Amortization). Ducati was also rated the best motorcycle make in Europe, with warranty costs that have declined by 70%.

Despite a difficult time for the motorcycle industry in general, Ducati continued to release new and updated models. There were now sixteen models in six families: five Superbikes, two Streetfighters, two Multistradas, three Monsters and now only one SportClassic. The Hypermotard gained an entry-level model, the 796, while the 'S' became an even more exclusive SP. But the most important new release this year was the Multistrada 1200, a motorcycle that expanded many parameters of design in the sport/touring sector.

MotoGP

After a disappointing 2009 season Ducati was still determined to win the 2010 World Championship, but circumstances were against them this year. Following Livio Suppo's departure to Honda, Alessandro Cicognani became MotoGP project director, Vittoriano Guareschi team manager and Cristhian Pupulin team technical coordinator. Cristian Gabarrini continued as Stoner's race engineer with Juan Martinez working for Hayden.

Since 2007 Casey Stoner had proven to be the only rider to come to terms with the difficult Desmosedici, responsible for 23 of its 24 victories, but during the season the Australian felt unsettled and was looking for an alternative ride. Although Nicky Hayden still struggled to adapt to the D16, changes in riding position and electronics saw an improvement in his performance.

At the end of 2009 Ducati debuted a new 799 cc D16 90° V4 engine with 180° crankshaft instead of the 360° 'Screamer'. This 'big-bang' design allowed earlier mid-corner throttle application. Engine restrictions were also much stricter for 2010, with only six engines allowed during the season. The chassis rear section was also made more rigid, with six mounting points instead of four, and experimentation continued with at least three different carbon-fibre swingarms to reduce the rear suspension pumping during aggressive corner exiting. Other chassis differences included the headrace

support and the suspension linkage design. New this year was a larger diameter (48 mm) Öhlins TTXTR (through-rod) front fork with 61 mm outer fork tubes, but the D16 still suffered front-end problems. Stoner crashed out while in the lead at the opening race at Qatar and it wasn't until mid-season that he finished on the podium. The lack of front-end feel saw him revert

to the earlier 42 mm TTX fork (without the newer through valve) and after testing at Brno Stoner decided to try the newer 48 mm TRSP25 Öhlins fork. Öhlins also had a new steel-bodied TRSP44 shock absorber for the Brno test.

Although Stoner had already signed for Honda for 2011, and the Rossi deal with Ducati was finalized by August 2010, Stoner's form improved towards the end of the season. A 12 mm shorter swingarm, the riding position moved forward 10 mm and the 42 mm front fork provided the improvement that saw him win at Aragón. Hayden completed Ducati's best Grand Prix weekend of the season there with third. Stoner followed this with victories in Japan and at Phillip Island (for the fourth consecutive year) and finished fourth overall in the championship, with Hayden seventh.

After some impressive riding during 2009, Kallio was re-signed on the Pramac Ducati, this year partnered by Aleix Espargaro. A third satellite Ducati D16 was also entered this year, Hector Barbera riding for Paginas Amarillas Aspar. Barbera was the most successful of the satellite riders, finishing twelfth overall.

WORLD SUPERBIKE

Without the experienced Tardozzi overseeing its World Superbike operation, Ducati had a torrid 2010 season. The riders, Noriyuki Haga and Michel Fabrizio, were unchanged, but, under the management of Ernesto Marinelli and the technical direction of Marco Lozej, the 1198F10 struggled. Penalized by FIM regulations, the twin cylinder Ducati was limited to an air restrictor between 46 and 52 mm, depending on race results, and weight between 162 kg and 171 kg. There were few changes to the 1,198 cc desmodromic twin: engine management was still by Magneti Marelli Marvel 4 and the fuel injection by IWP 162 and IWP 189, twin injectors each cylinder. The elliptical throttle bodies included an air restrictor below the butterfly, and the power was 200 horsepower at 11,000 rpm at the crankshaft. The suspension included a 42 mm pressurized TRVP25/TTX25 upside-down Öhlins fork, with Öhlins RSP40 shock absorber, while the Marchesini magnesium forged wheels were 3.50 x 16.5 on the front and 6.25 x 16.5 on the rear. The Brembo brakes were also unchanged, radial P4X34–38 calipers and 320 mm floating discs on the front, and a radial P2X34 caliper and 218 mm disc on the rear. The wheelbase was 1,435 mm, and the 1198F10 began the season weighing 168 kg. Disappointing results saw the Ducatis receive a weight reduction to 162 kg, the same as the fours, from Silverstone onwards.

Left: Haga had a difficult 2010 season on the F10 1198; this year handicapped by the regulations.

Below left: Carlos Checa rode the Althea 1198R during 2010, and was more successful than the factory riders, finishing third in the World Superbike Championship.

Below: A special-edition 1198S Corse with an aluminium fuel tank was available during 2010.

With only three victories and Haga managing a fairly lowly sixth overall, however, 2010 was the least successful season ever for the factory team in the World Superbike Championship, a series Ducati had dominated since 1990. This prompted Ducati to withdraw their factory team from the World Superbike Championship for 2011, with a plan to return at some stage in the future with a new-generation Superbike.

Supporting the Xerox Ducati team was the Althea Racing team with 2010 model Ducati 1198Rs. Team manager Genesio Bevilacqua enjoyed a close relationship with the factory, and Massimo Tulli proved an excellent mechanic. In the hands of former MotoGP rider Carlos Checa and Shane Byrne the Althea bikes often outperformed the factory machines. Checa won at Phillip Island, following this with a double victory at Imola later in the season, and he finished the season with an impressive third in the championship. The other satellite World Superbike teams were the DFX Corse team with Lorenzo Lanzi, PATA B&G Racing with Jakub Smrž, and Luca Scassa on the Supersonic Racing team 1198R, which was basically an 1198F09.

Ducati was again represented in the British

Superbike Championship for 2010, Michael Rutter chalking up his first British Superbike race win since 2008 when he took the Ridersmotorcycles.com Ducati to victory in the first race at Knockhill in July. Rutter also won a wet Silverstone round in September to finish fifth overall. Rutter's team-mate, team owner Phil Jessopp's son Martin, missed most of the season after breaking a leg at Mallory Park. In the AMA Pro Superbike Championship Larry Pegram again rode the semi-factory 1098R, taking his Foremost Insurance Pegram Ducati to a thrilling victory at Fontana and fourth overall in the championship.

848, 1198, 1198S, 1198R AND CORSE SPECIAL EDITIONS

To celebrate winning the 2009 World Superbike and Superstock manufacturers' titles, Ducati presented two Corse special editions, both also marking the introduction of a new Ducati Corse logo. The 1198S Corse special edition and 1198R Corse special edition both featured factory team-style aluminium fuel tanks,

275

An early release 2010 model
specifically for the US was the
Nicky Hayden 848.

848 NICKY HAYDEN EDITION

Released as an early 2010 Model Year example at the
United States Grand Prix at Laguna Seca on 4 July
2009, the Nicky Hayden 848 was exclusively
produced for the US market and was distinguished by
a personally autographed fuel tank and American-
inspired colour scheme. The basic specifications were
as for the standard 2010 model 848, including the
updated LED dashboard, aluminium cam belt
tensioners and mirror extensions.

In an effort to promote the 848, still overshadowed
by the 1198, Ducati supported the AMA Pro Racing
Sportbike class in the US and the fifteen-race 848
Challenge in the UK. At Daytona Steve Rapp led
home a group of five 848s which finished in the top
twenty, while the eight-round 848 Challenge included
six rounds in the UK plus races at Assen and Misano.
All competitors used the same model (848/848 Dark)
that was predominantly standard.

MULTISTRADA 1200

When it was released in 2003 the Multistrada
established a new motorcycle concept, one that
combined sports performance, trail blazing and
unrivalled versatility. After beginning life with the air-
cooled 1,000 cc dual-spark engine, and receiving the
1,100 cc version in 2006, for 2010 the Multistrada
was completely redesigned. Hailed as four bikes in
one, this established new technological boundaries for
an all-round motorcycle and was a tribute to Ducati's
advanced engineering and development.

Instead of the air-cooled Desmodue DS engine,
powering the Multistrada 1200 was a version of the
1198 Testastretta Evoluzione. The valve overlap
(when both the intake and exhaust valves were open
simultaneously) was reduced from 41° on the 1198 to
11°, resulting in a reduction in unburnt hydrocarbon
emissions (pre-catalyser) of 65% and an increase in
specific fuel consumption (and consequent CO_2
emissions) of 15% (Euro3). The injector bodies were
new, with smaller oval Mikuni throttle bodies with
the injectors under the butterfly, and flywheel mass
was increased. For the first time on a Ducati the
electronic injection system was Mitsubishi. The
compression ratio was reduced slightly, to 11.5:1, but

Ducati Traction Control (DTC) and new Ducati Corse
livery, while the 848 was now available in a 'Dark'
colour scheme. Also setting the 1198S and 1198R apart
was a red-painted frame, and while the 1198 and
1198S swingarms were finished in black, the 1198S
Corse and 1198R Corse swingarms were natural
aluminium to match the aluminium fuel tank. The
special-edition 1198S also weighed 1 kg less than the
1198S (at 168 kg) thanks to the larger (18 litre) 2 mm
thick brush-finished clear-coated aluminium fuel tank.
The 1198R Corse was also 1 kg lighter at 164 kg and
was supplied with a 186 horsepower race kit that
included a full racing exhaust system with 102dB
Termignoni carbon-fibre mufflers, dedicated ECU, bike
cover designed by Aldo Drudi and official cased
authentication plaque. Other than colours, the
technical specifications of the rest of the Superbike
range were unchanged for 2010, although the 848 now
received the 1198 LED dashboard with improved
illumination, a 30 mm mirror extension kit, and
aluminium cam belt tensioner pulleys, reducing weight
and rotating mass.

Lorenzo Zanetti rode for the SS Lazio Motorsport
team in the Superstock 1000 FIM Cup, but the Ducati
1198S was totally outclassed by the BMW S1000RR
this year. Scott Smart and Leon Hunt also campaigned
the 1198S in the British Metzeler National Superstock
1000 series, riding for Moto Rapido Ducati. As the
1198R was disallowed in this class, the Ducatis were
handicapped by the lack of power and a slipper clutch.

With its advanced electronic suspension, the Multistrada 1200S was one of the most versatile motorcycles available.

the power was still an impressive 150 horsepower at 9,250 rpm, with a better engine response under 7,000 rpm than the Superbike 1198. The gearbox and final drive ratios were changed to include a higher ratio sixth gear and the wet clutch was a slipper type. The new Testastretta engine also had major service intervals stretched to 24,000 km.

The trellis frame was signature Ducati, with large diameter, light gauge tubing with two central cast aluminium sections and a trellis rear subframe. The frame had 19% more torsional rigidity than the Multistrada 1100, with a high-pressure, die-cast, magnesium front subframe reducing high frontal weight. The rear subframe was a polymer material, doubling as bodywork, and the gravity die-cast aluminium rear engine mount and swingarm pivot were

similar to those on the Monster 1100. The single-sided aluminium swingarm was a single piece casting, with fabricated and welded sections. The chassis was designed to achieve lean angles of up to 45° and provided generous steering lock of 76° (38° left and right).

The standard Multistrada 1200 was fitted with an adjustable 50 mm Marzocchi front fork, with a forged fork bottom, and the rear suspension was a fully adjustable Sachs monoshock. Both the front and rear had a generous 170 mm of travel to suit occasional off-road forays. The 'S' versions were equipped with the latest generation 48 mm Öhlins suspension featuring Ducati Electronic Suspension (DES) developed in conjunction with Öhlins. This enabled spring preload and rebound and compression damping adjustment to

The Hypermotard 1100EVO SP
was the most radical version yet
of the Hypermotard family.

be electronically controlled via the instrument panel. Spring preload, rebound and compression damping for the Öhlins rear monoshock could be adjusted electronically, the electronic suspension adjustment either being pre-set or set manually. Adjustments made via the instrumentation sent a signal to electronic actuators mounted on the suspension units.

The front brakes were twin radial Brembo four-piston, two-pad calipers with 320 mm discs, with a single 245 mm disc on the rear and twin piston Brembo caliper. A Bosch-Brembo ABS system was optional on the standard version and fitted as original equipment on the 'S'. The Marchesini wheels were cast aluminium on both the standard and 'S' versions, and Ducati worked with Pirelli to develop a special Scorpion Trail tyre, the rear a massive 190/55. This dual compound tyre included a harder compound central section but still delivered racing performance on the road in terms of grip and lean angle.

Considerable effort was expended on ergonomics, particularly the 'ergonomic triangle' of wide tapered steel handlebar, seat and footpegs that were designed to optimize comfort while providing an upright riding position. The screen provided 60 mm of vertical adjustment, the 20-litre fuel tank a range of more than 300 km, and a special connection provided for optional Garmin satellite navigation.

Undoubtedly the most revolutionary aspect of the Multistrada 1200 was the choice of four riding modes: Sport, Touring, Urban and Enduro. The Sport riding mode provided 150 horsepower, a sports-oriented suspension set-up, and reduced Ducati Traction Control (DTC) intervention. While the Touring riding mode still produced 150 horsepower, the torque delivery was smoother, the DTC system was set to level 5 (intermediate intervention), and the suspension was set up for comfort. Selecting the Urban riding mode instantly reduced the power to 100 horsepower, the suspension was softened, and the traction control level set to 7, providing high system intervention. The final Enduro riding mode also provided 100 horsepower, higher suspension, and the option to disable the ABS. Traction control was reduced to the minimum level 1 for almost no intervention. The electronic ride-by-wire system (without a throttle cable) administered three different engine mappings to change the character of the engine, while DTC incorporated eight levels of system interaction. On the Multistrada 1200S the Ducati Electronic Suspension

(DES) instantly configured the suspension set-up to suit 'rider only', 'rider with luggage', 'rider and passenger' or 'rider and passenger with luggage'.

Many other new features also distinguished the Multistrada 1200. The frontal air intakes, carbon fibre on the 'S' version, acted as airflow conveyors to the oil coolers and the airbox, while the symmetrical headlight used four halogen lamps, two for low and two for high beam. The ignition no longer actuated with a normal key, but by an electronic key operating within a distance of two metres. An on-board computer system included a large LCD displaying multiple functions.

Weight reduction was an important design consideration, the 189 kg Multistrada 1200 being lighter than any other road enduro, touring or sport touring bike currently available. Three versions were offered: the 1200S Sport, the 1200S Touring, and the 1200 (without optional ABS). The 'S' featured ABS and the DES system in two equipment options, Sport edition and Touring edition. A number of carbon-fibre components distinguished the Sport edition while the Touring edition included heated handgrips and a centre stand. A wide range of accessories was available, including 57- and 77-litre panniers, and a 25 mm lower seat.

HYPERMOTARD 796, 1100EVO AND 1100EVO SP

Ever since it was first shown as a concept at the Milan show, at the end of 2005, the Hypermotard had proved the value of market research, with 15,000 completing an internet survey favouring production of the concept bike. While many at the factory had reservations about implementing production, the Hypermotard had become one of the most popular families in the range. For 2010 the 'less weight and more power' philosophy was expanded and the range extended to include the entry-level 796 and higher specification 1100EVO SP.

Powering the Hypermotard 796 was a new engine, not simply a stroked 696. The crankshaft featured a lighter 848-type flywheel, and with a 66 mm stroke and 88 mm 11:1 pistons displaced 803 cc. The crankcases were the lighter vacuum die-cast type, now featuring across the range, and the engine weight was 1.9 kg less than the 2009 696. Like the 696 the

Below: The 848EVO was particularly suited to track use.

Below: The Monster 796 was an early release for the 2011 Model Year.

efficiency and increase the compression ratio to 13.2:1. New camshafts provided 13 mm of valve lift (compared with 11.5 mm) on the inlet and 11.6 mm on the exhaust (against 10.7 mm). The inlet duration increased from 253° to 257° and the rev limiter raised 500 rpm to 11,300 rpm. The trademark under-seat exhaust system was unchanged except for the addition of a second oxygen sensor.

The basic chassis was unchanged for the 848EVO, with a lightweight magnesium front subframe, Showa suspension and five-spoke Enkei wheels. New was a cross-mounted steering damper and Brembo monobloc brake calipers (with 34 mm pistons) for the 320 mm front discs. Three colours were available for the 848EVO, with arctic white silk and 'Dark Stealth' joining the traditional red. In March, an 848EVO ended Ducati's legendary Daytona, FL, drought, with privateer Jason DiSalvo riding the Team Latus Motors Racing 848EVO to victory in the Daytona 200.

MONSTER 1100EVO, 1100S, 1100, 796 AND 696

The Monster range was expanded for 2011 with the early release 796 and Monster 1100EVO. A further range of colour choice was available, with Monster Art extended from three standard colours to thirteen with the new collection, 'Logomania'. These were a tribute to historic Ducati logos and colour schemes spanning more than fifty years.

For the Monster 1100EVO the power was increased to 100 horsepower and the under-seat exhaust system replaced by a curving side-mounted system similar to the Diavel. The riding position was more relaxed, with a new seat and 20 mm bar-riser, while electronic additions included the Ducati Safety Pack (DSP) consisting of ABS and new four-level adjustable Ducati Traction Control (DTC). With a new Marzocchi front fork the 1100EVO weighed 169 kg. The Monster 1100 and 1100S were ostensibly unchanged. Updates for 2011 on the Monster 1100 and 1100S included a new aluminium rear subframe suitable for accepting an accessory grab-rail. ABS was optional on both versions, and alongside the standard colours a choice of ten additional colour schemes was also available from Monster Art.

An early release model for 2011 was the Monster 796. Available from early 2010, the new 796 Desmodue engine featured redesigned crankcases that were 1.2 kg lighter than the 696 castings. The 796 engine was 1.9 kg

lighter than the 696 unit. The stroke was increased from 57.2 mm to 66 mm, and a light, 848-type flywheel fitted. Displacing 803 cc, the compression ratio was 11:1, and, with Siemens electronics and a 2-1-2 catalytic exhaust system with twin lambda probes and regulating valve, the power was 87 horsepower at 8,250 rpm. The clutch was the wet APTC 'slipper' type of the 696, while the 796 received an oil cooler, and the clutch and alternator outer casings were finished in carbon grey.

The Monster 796's style was slightly different from both the larger 1100 and smaller 696. A black single-sided swingarm came from the 1100, but the riding position was revised with a lower seat height (800 mm) and 20 mm higher tapered section aluminium handlebars. Suspension was by a 43 mm Showa fork and single Sachs shock absorber. The front brakes were twin 320 mm semi-floating discs gripped by radially mounted four-piston Brembo calipers, and ABS was optional. The five Y-spoke 17-inch wheels were differentiated by a pin stripe for 60 degrees of the circumference of the rim which created a full circle of

red when in motion. The tyres sizes (180/55 rear and 120/70 front) were the same as the 1100, and the weight was only 167 kg.

Although the 796 was already released as an early 2011 model, after six months it received an updated 43 mm Marzocchi front fork, replacing the Showa. The 696 also received the Marzocchi fork, along with the new rear subframe, a 20 mm handlebar-riser, optional ABS, and new 'Dark Stealth' and stone white colour schemes. Also available this year was the Monster 696+, a factory custom featuring a single seat cover and micro-bikini fairing.

STREETFIGHTER, MULTISTRADA AND HYPERMOTARD

Still relatively new, the Streetfighter received only cosmetic updates for 2011. Colours included arctic white for the Streetfighter, the 'S' receiving a matching

Left: Logomania was a range
of alternative paint schemes
honouring Ducati's past.

Below: New for 2011 was the
Monster 1100EVO, with a low
curved exhaust system on the right.

red frame for the red version and a racing black frame for the new diamond black examples. Both models now had black radiator covers and all versions of the 'S' had black wheels. Another recently released model was the 1200 Multistrada and this continued unchanged for 2011. Also unchanged was the Hypermotard range of the 796, Hypermotard 1100EVO and the Hypermotard 1100EVO SP.

In June, Carlin Dunne won the Pikes Peak International Hill Climb on a Multistrada 1200, setting an all-time motorcycle record, and providing Ducati its second consecutive victory at Pike's Peak.

So Ducati entered 2011 on the verge of a new racing era and releasing some ambitious and possibly risky new products in a difficult economic environment. While the marketing benefits of involvement with Valentino Rossi were undeniable, the move into the mega cruiser market could be considered questionable.

Throughout Ducati's history the legend has always been sustained by high-performance sporting motorcycles. These may also have been stylish but they always epitomized the finest functional attributes. Certainly the motorcycle market has changed considerably over the years, and Ducati has been at the forefront of adapting to shifts in the marketplace. The success of the Monster is a tribute to this. But models come and go, and the one constant throughout Ducati's history has been the importance of the high-performance sporting motorcycle. Whether it was the Marianna, 250 Mach 1, 750 and 900SS, 916, D16RR or 1198, these were the bikes that created the Ducati legend. Ducati motorcycles are synonymous with performance, and that performance has always been inspired by racing. As Ducati's great engineer Fabio Taglioni told me in 1995, 'We are a racing company first and foremost, and only when we follow this path does Ducati prosper.'

Valentino Rossi struggled with the D16GP12, and would depart the team after a disappointing two years.

Below: A new GP14.1 was produced for 2014, shorter in the front and with a reshaped fuel tank. #35 is Crutchlow and #04 Dovizioso.

Bottom: The GP14.2 appeared at Aragón in September. This was slimmer, with a slightly relocated engine, Dovizioso scoring Ducati's first pole position in four years a few weeks later at Japan.

Below: The factory resumed control of the official World Superbike team for 2014; the Panigale benefited from further development.

class allowed seven additional engines and unlimited development, but with Dorna-controlled electronics. A compromise eventually saw Ducati stay in the Factory category with its own sophisticated electronics, but benefit from Open class concessions such as more engines, soft tyres and extra fuel. British rider Cal Crutchlow joined the factory team alongside Dovizioso.

Ducati started the season with a new bike: the GP14.1, shorter in the front and longer at the rear than the GP13. Engine development saw the power at around 270 horsepower, revving to 18,000 rpm, and during the season the engine received different external flywheels and dampers to reduce vibration. The bike became progressively shorter at the front and longer at the rear, with three different swingarms tried, along with a new linkage. New bodywork was also introduced to improve cooling and reduce drag. The final update appeared at Aragón – the narrower 14.2 version, with a relocated engine. By this stage, regulations allowed for larger diameter (340 mm) carbon-carbon Brembo front brakes.

The D16GP14 was an immediate improvement over its predecessor, and eleven top six finishes vindicated Dall'Inga's decision to persevere with in-season development. Dovizioso's consistent results (including a

third in Texas) saw him finish fifth overall. Although Crutchlow finished the season strongly (with a podium at Aragón), early crashes eroded his confidence and he wouldn't complete his two-year contract. After several years in the doldrums, the satellite Pramac Racing Team enjoyed full factory support during 2014, Andrea Iannone's steady results eventually earning him a factory ride for 2015.

WORLD SUPERBIKE

Ducati Corse resumed control of the World Superbike Team, with new riders Chaz Davies and Davide Giugliano. Under the control of Ernesto Marinelli, the Panigale 1199R enjoyed the lack of restrictors this year, the power climbing to beyond 217 horsepower at 11,500 rpm. Regulations also required the Ducati to retain more stock engine components than the fours. Ducati also now opted for the more modern T-type Brembo brakes. Set-up was still tricky, but the Panigale performed much more consistently during 2014. Davies achieved two second places, and Giugliano one, finishing sixth and eighth, respectively, in the World Superbike Championship. Several teams fielded EVO

Bottom: Leandro Mercado
provided Ducati its fifth victory in
the FIM Superstock 1000 Cup in
eight years on the Barni 1199
Panigale R.

Below: Welsh rider Chaz Davies
rewarded Ducati Corse with
significantly improved
performances over 2013.

class machines, the most successful being Canepa,
who finished 13th overall on the Althea Racing 1199
Panigale R EVO.

While the Panigale still had a way to go before it
threatened a repeat of Ducati's historical dominance of

the World Superbike Championship, in other
championships it was successful. Argentinian rider
Leandro 'Tati' Mercado rode his Barni Racing Team
1199 Panigale R to victory in the Superstock 1000 FIM
Cup, Ducati's fifth Superstock 1000 riders' title since
2007. Ducati also dominated the Italian Superbike
Championship, winning nine of the ten races in the
season, and Ivan Goi taking the title on the Barni
Racing 1199 Panigale R. Ducati also won its first
German IDM Superbike Championship this year, Xavi
Forés and Max Neukirchner taking the first two places
on the 3C Racing Team 1199 Panigale R.

1199 SUPERLEGGERA

Ducati continued its tradition of offering expensive
limited edition models with the release of the 1199
Superleggera during 2014. Produced in a limited
edition of 500, with its cocktail of titanium, magnesium
and carbon-fibre materials, the 200+ horsepower
Superleggera provided the highest claimed power-to-

Below: When released in 2014, the limited edition 1199 Superleggera was arguably the finest sporting motorcycle available.

Bottom: Central to the 1199 Superleggera was a magnesium monocoque frame.

weight ratio of any production motorcycle. Ducati's R&D team, headed by Eugenio Gherard, employed high level technology and exotic materials regardless of cost, developing more than 200 separate new components exclusively for the Superleggera.

Based on the 1199R, the Superquadro engine included, for the first time on a Ducati street engine, racing Superbike-style two-ring pistons. The redline was increased to 12,500 rpm, 500 rpm more than the 1199 Panigale R. The racing kit included a titanium Akrapovič exhaust, and provided a five horsepower increase and 2.5 kg weight loss.

More attention was paid to reducing chassis weight. Instead of the Panigale R's diecast hollow aluminium semi-monocoque 4.2 kg frame, the Superleggera employed a sandcast magnesium structure weighing only 3 kg. The rear subframe was now carbon-fibre, with forged carbon composite fastening bushes. Front suspension included individually-numbered billet-machined triple clamps, and a 43 mm Öhlins FL916 fork specifically developed for the Superleggera; this included machined axle carriers, TiN-coated stanchions, an aluminium piston shaft, and asymmetrically machined outer tubes. It was 1.4 kg lighter than the

1199 R's NIX30 front fork, but the process of weight saving also saw the elimination of the R's electronic damping. The Öhlins TTX36 rear shock absorber also lost the electronic damping, but was still adjustable for length, and thus ride height. The spring was now titanium. The wheels were forged magnesium, and the front brakes consisted of a pair of semi-floating 330 mm discs with radially-mounted monobloc Brembo M50 four-piston calipers, with a 19-21 MSC master cylinder and Bosch 9ME ABS.

Left: Ducati produced an improved all new Desmosedici for the 2015 MotoGP season. Pictured here is Dovizioso's bike.

Below: Andrea Iannone was Ducati's most successful MotoGP rider of 2015. During the season, the D16 GP15 gained small wide wings on the fairing to increase downforce. This is the final version at Valencia in November.

MOTOGP

MotoGP regulations for 2015 continued with two categories, Factory and Open. Both classes were restricted to Dorna-supplied Magnetti Marelli ECU and, while Ducati was classed as a factory team, it still enjoyed Open class concessions such as 12 engines (with free development), softer tyres and 24 initial litres of fuel. The riders this year were Andrea Dovizioso and Andrea Iannone, with test rider Michele Pirro filling in for an injured Iannone on occasion.

This was Dall'Inga's second full season as Ducati Corse General Manager, and the smaller, more tightly packaged GP15 was all-new. The engine was still a 90-degree Desmo V4, but was redesigned so it could be mounted further forward to improve turn into corners. The heavier V4 now rotated backwards (like the earlier bevel-drive twins), this helping to keep the front wheel down under acceleration. The output shaft was also moved to alter the bike's pitch under acceleration. The frame was similar to the previous version but was shorter and narrower, and stiffer at

the rear. Retained was a carbon-fibre swingarm. The new bike was not only vastly improved; it was the fastest bike on the track, and Iannone was timed at 350.8 km/h at Mugello. During the season, Ducati introduced aerodynamic wings attached to the fairing, with several different types tried before the end of the season.

With the chronic understeer that had plagued earlier Desmosedicis gone, Dovizioso set pole position at the opening round at Qatar. He went on to finish second, with Iannone third, Ducati's first double podium since 2006. Dovizioso followed this with two more second places, but his season then went downhill. Iannone was more consistent, eventually finishing fifth in the championship, with Dovizioso seventh.

Ducati also supplied a range of older Open class GP14 to GP14.2 bikes to Pramac (riders Danilo Petrucci and Yonny Hernandez) and Avintia Racing (Hector Barbera and Mike Di Meglio). Petrucci was the most successful, finishing an astonishing second in a wet British Grand Prix at Silverstone, and 10th overall in the World Championship.

WORLD SUPERBIKE

Intent on reducing costs, and the advantages enjoyed by factory bikes, Dorna introduced new regulations limiting engine and chassis modifications beyond the homologated model. Thus the factory racers were now based on the production Panigale R, with the usual RS customer racing model no longer available. No longer with air restrictors, the factory Panigale R produced around eight horsepower less than the previous model at the beginning of the season. This eventually climbed to 223 horsepower at 11,700 rpm. The Marelli MLE ECU was also cost-capped and, during the season, a longer, more convoluted Akrapovič exhaust introduced

to boost power. This also included an exhaust valve to slow the bike down into corners.

The unusual Monocoque chassis was continually developed, with more brackets attached to the engine and rear subframe. The suspension was an Öhlins 42 mm RSP25 front fork and RSP40 rear shock, while the front brakes included T-type Brembo 336 mm discs with four-piston, four-pad differential piston monobloc EVO calipers. The rear brake was a 230 mm disc with twin-piston radially-mounted caliper. The minimum weight was increased to 168 kg this year.

Marinelli was again technical director, the factory Aruba.it Racing team retaining riders Davies and Giugliano. Troy Bayliss was a stand-in for Giugliano at Phillip Island and Buriram, with Xavi Forés, Luca Scassa and Michele Pirro filling in later in the season. Althea Racing also fielded two Panigale Rs, initially with Nicolas Terol and Matteo Baiocco, with Barni Racing providing a Panigale R for Superstock 1000 champion Leandro Mercado. Mercado ended up the top privateer, his consistency earning him eighth overall.

The Panigale R was immediately more competitive and, at Aragón, Chaz Davies provided Ducati its first Superbike win since 2012. He followed this with a double at Laguna Seca, and wins in Malaysia and Jerez, ultimately ending second in the championship.

Left: New regulations favoured the Panigale 1199R and it was improved for 2015.

Below left: Chaz Davies provided Ducati with its first World Superbike victory in three years.

Below: The high specification Panigale R replaced the 1199 Panigale R as the factory homologation model for 2015.

PANIGALE R

As new World Superbike regulations limited engine, frame, and electronic modifications, Ducati offered a new limited edition homologation model for 2015, the Panigale R. Superbike regulations still limited twins to 1100 cc with a minimum of 1,000 offered for sale, the Panigale R replacing the 1199 Panigale R. As the Superbike engine needed to retain the stock pistons and crankshaft, the Panigale R had forged 13.2:1 two-ring 112 mm pistons with Superbike-spec crowns, Pankl titanium con-rods, and a lighter crankshaft with tungsten inserts. The 46.8 mm inlet and 38.2 mm exhaust valves were now titanium (replacing the previous steel exhaust), operated by DLC-coated rocker arms by new camshafts with increased lift and revised timing. An elliptical Marelli throttle body (effectively 67.5 mm) with dual Mitsubishi injectors fed the large intake valves. One of these was positioned directly above the inlet trumpet, and the other underneath the butterfly. With a 2.5 kg lighter, 60 mm titanium Akrapovič exhaust (replacing Termignoni this year and including an electronic valve) the Panigale R produced 205 horsepower at 11,500 rpm.

As on the 1199 Panigale R the chassis featured an adjustable swingarm pivot, but included sharper steering (24-degree rake and 96 mm of trail) and a 5 mm longer wheelbase (1,442 mm). With weight distribution of 53/47, front-end bias was a little more pronounced. Like the 1199 Superleggera, the Öhlins suspension was also the mechanical type, a 43 mm NIX30 fork, and a TTX36 Twin-tube shock absorber, but the wheels were 17-inch forged aluminium. Braking consisted of racing style Brembo 330 mm floating front discs with radially-mounted four-piston EVO M50 monobloc calipers. A new electronics package included a Bosch 9.1MP inertial measuring unit that provided cornering ABS.

At 184 kg (wet) the Panigale R weighed 6 kg less than the 1199R, and the new Panigale R paralleled the

Below: The production 1199
Panigale evolved into the 1299
Panigale for 2015. This is the 1299
Panigale S with Öhlins semi-active
suspension.

evolution of the 999R. First introduced in 2003, the 999R was also significantly upgraded two years later to suit then-current Superbike regulations.

1299 PANIGALE, S

The search for more midrange torque saw the 1199 Panigale evolve into the 1299 Panigale this year. Since the existing compact crankcases couldn't accommodate a longer stroke, chief engine designer Dr. Marco Sairu and his team opted for an even larger bore, the 116 mm pistons combined with the 60.8 mm stroke to provide 1,285 cc. The bore/stroke ratio of 1.91:1 was the most extreme ever in a production engine, up considerably on the 1199's 1.84:1 and the 1198's 1.56:1. The titanium 46.8 mm inlet and steel 38.2 mm exhaust valves were unchanged, and a secondary air system was employed to alleviate the need for twin spark plugs per cylinder. The desmodromic camshafts were long duration with 45 degrees of overlap and the crankshaft rebalanced, with new con-rods. The basic

engine architecture was unchanged from the 1199, notably the gear and chain camshaft drive and oil bath slipper clutch. The oval 67.5mm throttles were unchanged, and an all-new exhaust system underneath the engine was tuned to a different length than the 1199. With a slightly higher 12.6:1 compression ratio, the power was 205 horsepower at 10,500 rpm, making it the most powerful production twin cylinder streetbike ever offered for sale. Torque also jumped 10% to 144Nm, but more importantly increased 15% between 5-8000 rpm. Updated electronics included a Bosch Internal Measurement Unit, which measured acceleration in three planes, working with Wheelie Control and semi-active suspension.

The Panigale chassis was basically unchanged, but the single-sided 5.1 kg aluminium swingarm was 39 mm longer and the steering head steepened to 24 degrees with 96 mm of trail. The swingarm pivot was 4 mm lower than the 1199, providing less anti-squat under acceleration, this improving traction. The 1299 Panigale S featured semi-active Öhlins suspension.

Below: The seventh generation Multistrada 1200 continued the style of its predecessor but included a new fairing, lower seat, and more advanced electronics package.

Below: The Desmodromic Variable Timing system fitted to the 2015 Multistrada Testastretta included rotating phasers on each camshaft. Oil pressure and electronic valves moved these to the desired angle as requested by the ECU.

Styling updates extended to a wider fairing, with wider front air intakes, a more protective windshield, and a new tail unit. The twin headlamps were integrated as part of the front intake ports and, after years of complaints, beautiful machined aluminium footrests replaced the slippery cast type. Although there was no competition future for the 1299, it was arguably the finest sporting twin Ducati had ever built.

MULTISTRADA 1200, 1200S

An indication of the importance of the Multistrada in Ducati's range over the previous 12 years was the release of the seventh-generation version for 2015. While still claiming to represent four motorcycles in one, the Multistrada now featured Desmodromic Variable Timing (DVT), designed to smooth out the rough edges that had always defined the 1198 cc Testastretta. This included independent variable timing on both the inlet and exhaust camshafts, allowing reduced overlap at low rpm. Bosch injection, with 56 mm elliptical throttle bodies, replaced the Mitsubishi and the maximum power increased to 160 horsepower at 9,500 rpm.

The trellis frame was stiffened, with the engine raised to increase ground clearance. To compensate for the additional height, the seat was narrower, while the fairing was widened, the headlight and front beak styling more aggressive than before. Other equipment upgrades included new handlebar switches. Electronic updates included the new Bosch inertia measurement unit that measured roll and pitch angles in three axes, and electronic cruise control.

Two versions were available, the Multistrada 1200 and 1200S. Instead of the previous 50 mm Marzocchi fork the 1200 received a 48 mm upside down fork and a Sachs shock with remote preload adjustment. The S model featured a 48 mm Sachs front fork and Sachs shock absorber with semi-active electronic Skyhook suspension, upgraded to the DSS Evo. The S also received an upgraded braking system, with 330 mm front discs (up from the 1200's 320 mm) and Panigale-style Brembo EVO M50 monobloc calipers. Both received a 265 mm rear disc with twin-piston caliper and standard cornering ABS. Four different option packs were available; Touring, Sport, Urban and Enduro, each offering a range of specific equipment. Other innovations this year saw the introduction of D-Air on the 1200S, an integrated air bag system developed in conjunction with Dainese. With the new, sophisticated DVT Testastretta, the Multistrada continued as a standout in Ducati's range. Combining

Panigale sporting prowess, Hypermotard punch, Monster urban chic, ST4S touring capability, and a toss of BMW GS-style adventure, only the substantial size and wet weight of 232 kg (235 kg for the S) detracted from the Multistrada's appeal.

MONSTER 821

With over 290,000 Monsters sold since 1993, and comprising more than 50% of production over the previous 21 years, the Monster range was still pivotal for Ducati. Over that time the Monster had become an icon, and this year the Monster 821 was introduced, sitting underneath the new 1200 in much the same way as the 899 Panigale complemented the 1299. In many respects the Monster 821 mirrored the 899 Panigale. Both shared the larger models chassis platform, but with a double sided swingarm and lower specification hardware.

The engine was the same liquid-cooled 88 x 67.5 mm Testastretta 11-degree unit of the Hypermotard, but produced slightly more power (112 horsepower at 9,250 rpm). The pair of 53 mm circular Mikuni throttle bodies included a single injector, repositioned to spray fuel at the rear of the intake valves to enhance atomisation. The Marelli ECU also operated a secondary air system.

Modelled on the Monster 1200, the trademark trellis frame was new. Made from 34 mm steel tubing, as on the 1200, the frame bolted directly to the cylinder heads. This provided a claimed 99% greater torsional stiffness than the air-cooled 796 frame while weighing 1.23 kg less. The dual-sided diecast aluminium swingarm was shorter than the 1200, but the 1,480 mm wheelbase was 30 mm longer than the 796. This delivered a 47.5/52.5% rearward weight bias. Suspension included a budget-spec, non-adjustable 43 mm Kayaba fork and Sachs cantilever shock (adjustable for spring pre-load only). Braking consisted of semi-floating 320 mm discs with Brembo M4-32 monobloc calipers and a 245 mm rear disc, with Bosch ABS. Other budget components included a black and grey LCD instrument panel rather than the 1200's dazzling TFT colour unit.

New styling by Giandrea Fabbro took the Monster 821 back to the minimalism of Galluzi's original, the fuel tank no longer with air intakes. The compact Monster 821 emphasised ergonomics, with a higher and closer handlebar and low seat. An accessory 745 mm seat was Ducati's lowest ever. Also available were a black Monster 821 Dark, and a more exclusive Monster Stripe version (available as both 1200S and 821), including a small fairing, and double white stripes on the front mudguard, tank, and seat cover.

Left: The new mid-range Monster 821 was also available in bold white, with red wheels.

Below: The 1970s advertising that featured Ducati employees Franco and Elvira inspired the new Scrambler marketing material.

Bottom: Retro features of the Scrambler included a traditional round headlight, but with modern LED power. Instrumentation was minimal. The Scrambler Icon here had special cast aluminium wheels.

SCRAMBLER

While the Multistrada 1200 and Monster 821 built on existing successful platforms, the Scrambler took Ducati in a different direction. A contemporary take on the popular Scrambler that ran from 1962 to 1975, the new Scrambler was aimed beyond the traditional Ducati buyer, and at the lifestyle market. Inspiration for the new Scrambler's marketing campaign came from the original 1973 Scrambler advertising material that was built around two Ducati employees at the time, Franco and Elvira – Franco was a test rider, and Elvira worked in administration. The new Scrambler was intentionally styled by designer Julien Clement to replicate the earlier model.

Under Project Manager Antonio Zandi, the Scrambler evolved as a mild dual-purpose motorcycle, with some off-road capability. Unlike some other retro models, the Scrambler was very much a modern motorcycle, much as it would have been if production had continued. Powered by a development of the Monster 796 unit, the air-cooled 803 cc (88 x 66 mm) two-valve twin featured an 11:1 compression ratio and camshafts with an 11-degree valve overlap. A heavier flywheel smoothed power delivery, and a single 50 mm throttle body inside the airbox replaced the Monster's dual external type. Each cylinder received a single injector, the new airbox and throttle arrangement necessary to obtain a long, slim tank in the style of the original. Although not tuned for peak power, the Scrambler still produced 75 horsepower at 8,250 rpm.

The frame was a new, compact, steel trellis type, tightly packaging the engine and airbox with an offset direct-mount cantilever single shock Kayaba. After testing a steel swingarm, the final production version received an aluminium swingarm. Front suspension included a Kayaba 41 mm inverted front fork, and front braking was by a Hypermotard-spec single Brembo 330 mm disc with a four-piston monobloc caliper. At the rear was a 245 mm disc with single piston caliper, and Bosch ABS was standard. The wheels were 18 x 3.0-inches front and 17 x 5.50-inches rear (cast or wire-spoked), shod with specially developed dual sport Pirelli MT60RS tyres. The standard seat height was 790 mm, with optional seats going as low as 760 mm to suit a range of riders. Rolling on a compact 1,445 mm wheelbase, and weighing a claimed 170 kg dry, the Scrambler was a moderately sized machine designed to appeal to a wide range of riders.

Below: Along with a number of titanium and carbon-fibre components, the exclusive limited edition Diavel Titanium featured a special finish on the wheels, exhaust, and frame.

Four versions were initially available; the standard Icon, Urban Enduro, Full Throttle and Classic. The 'Wild Green' Urban Enduro was designed for dual purpose, the Full Throttle as homage to flat-track, and the Classic for nostalgic 1970s devotees. Both the Urban Enduro and Classic featured wire-spoked wheels. Retro features included a 'born in 1962' inscription on the fuel filler cap, an ignition key that inserted into the headlamp as on the original, and a classic round headlamp.

While many retro bikes have struggled to match classic style with modern function, Ducati found the right formula with the Scrambler: light and compact, with excellent detailing. It was no surprise that the Scrambler was such an immediate success. During 2015, the Scrambler was the tenth best selling streetbike in the world – the first time Ducati had entered the top ten.

DIAVEL TITANIUM

While the Diavel and Diavel Carbon continued much as before, an exclusive Diavel Titanium was also available this year, in a limited edition of 500. This edition included a number of distinctive cosmetic features, including satin-etched titanium tank and headlight covers. The passenger seat cover was redesigned and widened, with the titanium combined with carbon fibre. The wider air intakes were also carbon fibre, as were the radiator covers, front and rear mudguards, front sprocket cover, and filler cap cover. The hand-stitched Alcantara seat was embellished with leather inserts, while the frame finish was dark chrome with matt black ceramic coated exhaust pipes. The machine-finished forged wheels were exposed aluminium, and an individually numbered, tank-mounted plaque (XXX/500) ensured exclusivity.

Left: The XDiavel was arguably Ducati's most radical design yet. With the water pump moved between the cylinders, the left side of the engine was considerably cleaner looking.

Below: The higher performance Monster 1200R was also released for 2016.

Bottom: Joining the Multistrada line-up for 2016 was the Multistrada Enduro. The optional Touring pack included aluminium Touratech panniers.

from a higher (13:1) compression ratio, larger (56 mm) elliptical throttle bodies, and a two-litre larger exhaust that required two new pentagonal shaped mufflers. Along with noise suppressing material added to the engine cases the new engine was more powerful (160 horsepower at 9,250 rpm) and quieter.

Weight saving measures included forged aluminium Panigale-style Marchesini wheels (saving 1.5 kg), and to improve sporting capability the Öhlins suspension was lengthened to raise the bike 15 mm front and rear. The longer shock absorber also increased ride height and allowed a 3 mm shorter wheelbase (to 1,509 mm). Completing the updated sporting package were new milled footpegs, a larger 200/55 mm rear tyre, a small fairing, and a narrower tail section and rear subframe. Electronic aids included the usual riding modes and traction control. The claimed dry weight was 180 kg, and the 1200R was the highest performing Monster yet.

MULTISTRADA 1200 ENDURO

Although the Multistrada was already suitably competent off-road a more serious Enduro version was released for 2016. Developed in parallel with the standard Multistrada from the beginning, 266 model-specific components transformed the Multistrada into a true adventure tourer. And for naysayers who believed Ducatis had no place on the dirt, the Multistrada Enduro harked back to the days of the Dakar-winning Cagiva Elefant of the early 1990s. New Multistrada Product Manager, Canadian Federico Valentini, formerly with Husqvarna, oversaw the 1200 Enduro's development.

At the Multistrada Enduro's heart was the Multistrada's 1198 cc Testastretta with Desmodromic Variable Timing, identical but for a lower first gear. The overall gearing was also lowered substantially to assist off road ability. The silencer was designed with a high exit, to increase wading height through water. The steel trellis frame was longer, stronger, and stiffer, with a new longer, double-sided aluminium swingarm. Suspension was the latest EVO version of the semi-active electronic Skyhook, the 48 mm Sachs upside down fork a leading axle type. The shallower 25-degree steering head angle, and 16 mm of fork offset, contributed to a 65 mm longer wheelbase of 1,594 mm. Suspension travel front and rear was 200 mm, up from 170 mm. Tubeless 19 and 17-inch wire spoked wheels, a redesigned rear hub and brake, and slightly smaller (320 mm) front discs completed the chassis specification. Electronic aids included four riding modes and cruise control.

Along with a 30-litre plastic fuel tank, giving a range of 450 km, the Enduro was offered with four optional packs; Touring, Sport, Urban, and Enduro. The Touring pack included Touratech-made aluminium panniers. The Multistrada Enduro was undoubtedly an impressive offering in the competitive world of large capacity adventure motorcycles, but with a non-adjustable 870 mm seat height (850 and 890 mm optional), and a wet weight of 254 kg, it wasn't a bike for novices.

This year also saw a return of the high specification Multistrada Pikes Peak. Along with special white, red and black colours, suspension was by Öhlins: a 50 mm front fork and TTX36 shock absorber. The three-spoke black wheels had red trim, the seat included red stitching, and the front mudguard was carbon fibre.

Below: The Hypermotard became
the 939 for 2016; the SP version
still with Öhlins suspension.

Bottom: With its small fairing and
luggage the Hyperstrada 939 was
a more versatile model than the
Hypermotard, but destined to last
only one year.

HYPERMOTARD 939, HYPERMOTARD 939SP, HYPERSTRADA 939

In order to pass new Euro 4 regulations, a third generation Hypermotard was released for 2016. All three versions, the Hypermotard, SP, and Hyperstrada, were powered by the new Testastretta 11-degree engine. Still with the 67.2 mm stroke, the bore went up to 94 mm, creating 937 cc. The crankshaft received a 42 mm crankpin, and the engine new pistons, cylinders and cylinder heads with improved cooling passages. The compression ratio was increased to 13.1:1, while the 52 mm diameter throttle bodies, controlled by a ride-by-wire system were unchanged. With a new 50 mm two-in-one exhaust system, the power was 113 horsepower at 9,000 rpm. The engine was also equipped with an oil-bath APTC clutch with a progressive self-servo system and an oil cooler.

The frame was a 34 mm diameter tubular steel trellis type with 25.5 degrees of rake and 104 mm of trail, the rear diecast subframe incorporating a techno-polymer mid-section. The Hypermotard and Hyperstrada 939 suspension was a 43 mm upside-down Kayaba fork and Sachs shock absorber, with adjustable rebound damping. Dry weight was 181 kg for the Hypermotard and 187 kg for the Hyperstrada. With MotoGP-inspired livery the Hypermotard 939SP included a fully adjustable, 50 mm diameter, upside-down Öhlins fork, and fully adjustable Öhlins shock absorber. The raised

ride height allowed for a 47.5 degree lean angle, and the dry weight was slightly lower than the standard Hypermotard at 178 kg. The Hyperstrada 939 came equipped with 50 litre semi-rigid removable bags and a centre stand. The handlebars were raised 20 mm and a touring windshield and wider seat increased rider comfort. The three-model range was equipped with the Ducati Safety Pack that included three-level ABS, eight levels of Ducati Traction Control, and three Riding Modes.

The front brakes featured twin radially-mounted Brembo, four piston, monobloc M4-32 calipers actuated by a master cylinder with a four-point adjustable lever on the Hypermotard 939 and Hyperstrada 939 and five-point on the high performance radial master cylinder of the SP. The front discs were 320 mm, with a single 245 mm disc on the rear, and Bosch-Brembo ABS was standard. With the 939, the Hypermotard moved further on from the hard-edged, air-cooled original, this more refined version appealing to a wider market.

DUCATI SCRAMBLER FLAT TRACK PRO AND SIXTY2

Joining the highly successful existing four-model Scrambler range were the Flat Track Pro, and Sixty2. Based on the Scrambler Full Throttle, and inspired by

the American AMA Pro Flat Track 2015 Championship bikes of Troy Bayliss and Johnny Lewis, the Flat Track Pro featured a new racing yellow fuel tank, with two-tone painted side panels and racing logo. Other unique features included a special seat, side-mounted plate holder, nose fairing, short front mudguard, machined-from-solid rear-view mirrors, and special handgrips.

The Sixty2, named after the year of the original Scrambler, was launched as a nostalgic pop-icon and aimed at a younger, entry-level, clientele. The 399 cc engine had a bore and stroke of 72 x 49 mm, and with a 10.7:1 compression ratio produced 41 horsepower at 8,750 rpm. The chassis included a 41 mm Showa fork and steel dual-sided swingarm, this stretching the wheelbase slightly to 1,460 mm. Other changes from the standard Scrambler included a smaller 320 mm front disc with two-piston floating caliper, and a 4.50 x 17-inch rear wheel with a 160/60R17 tyre. The teardrop 14-litre fuel tank was slightly slimmer, and the Sixty2 was offered with dedicated colours and graphics.

Collaboration between Ducati and Italia Independent, a company blending fashion and design, tradition, and innovation, resulted in a limited edition Ducati Scrambler Italia Independent. Produced as a limited, numbered edition of only 1,077 bikes, features included a black engine with machined cylinder head fins, Termignoni exhaust with black pipes and silencer covers, low tapered bars, and low-slung aluminium rear view mirrors. A short front mudguard, 'café racer' nose fairing and leather seat with Night Copper stitching further emphasised its unique style.

Below: Jorge Lorenzo moved to Ducati for the 2017 season, and continued to carry the number 99.

2017

Eight new models were released for 2017: the 1299 Panigale S Anniversario, 1299 Superleggera, SuperSport, Multistrada 950, Monster 797, Monster 1200, and two new versions of the Scrambler: Scrambler Café Racer and Scrambler Desert Sled. Additionally, a limited edition Diavel Diesel was available. Engine rationalisation saw the Testastretta now predominately produced as a 1262, 1198, and 937, and the Desmodue as 803 and 399. The Superquadro was, as before, in 1285, 1198 and 955 cc. The only surviving 821 Testastretta was the Monster 821, the Hyperstrada discontinued. Motorcycle sales totalled 55,871 during 2017, the Scrambler the most popular with 14,061 sales. Again, the US led the way with 8,898 sales, but the Italian market was close behind, climbing 12%, with 8,806 motorcycles delivered. In Europe, sales totalled 31,123, the Spanish market, growing 28.3%.

MOTOGP

Early in the 2016 season, reigning MotoGP World Champion Jorge Lorenzo signed a two-year deal with Ducati for 2017 and 2018. Seeking to emulate the few that had won the world title on different makes, the motivation for this change came from Lorenzo's association with Dall'Inga that went back to his 250 cc World Championships with Aprilia. Cristian Gabarrini headed Lorenzo's team, Gabarrini guiding Stoner to his 2007 World Championship, and subsequently following him to Honda. Stoner continued as an occasional test rider, but former Moto2 winner Michel Pirro undertook most testing.

The Desmosedici GP17 was a development of the promising GP16. Now without external winglets, the 2017 fairing was initially similar to the previous year, with the nose narrowed. Internal ducted loops provided additional downforce, while the electronics were moved to a box under the seat, freeing up space in the nose. As

Left: The GP17 was extremely competitive during 2017: Lorenzo here leading Dovizioso and Petrucci.

Below: Midway through the 2017 season a controversial new fairing was introduced. Dovizioso used it occasionally and finished second in the MotoGP World Championship.

it was similar to earlier systems it had used, the Magneti Marelli control software was also familiar to Ducati, providing an advantage. A change to a harder construction front Michelin tyre also seemed to suit the GP17. But although Dovizioso won in Mugello and Barcelona, the GP17's mid-corner turning initially troubled both him and Lorenzo.

Unlike some other teams Ducati kept its homologated fairing options open, and at Brno, following the mid-season break, a new, controversial, innovative hammerhead aerodynamic fairing appeared. Tested earlier in the year, this featured squared off hoops added on either side. Dovizioso used the new fairing to win in Austria, claiming, 'Ducati's engineers managed to get close to the effect of the previous years' winglets'. Despite this vote of confidence, Dovizioso won the next race at Silverstone with the earlier fairing, and continued with it until his spectacular victory in

the wet at Motegi. As the additional downforce generated by the new fairing made the bike heavier to turn, Dovizioso preferred the earlier fairing on faster tracks with multiple changes of direction. Lorenzo favoured the improved front wheel contact generated by the new fairing.

During the season the Ducati team concentrated on expanding technological development, anticipating this would provide an edge within ever-restricting regulations. As a result, and unlike other teams, Ducati embraced the new Öhlins front fork with carbon fibre tubes. These were not only lighter, but could be produced in alternate weaves to increase longitudinal stiffness for improved braking or lateral flex to improve full lean performance. Ultimately, the 2017 season was Ducati's most successful in a decade, Dovizioso winning six races and ending second in the World Championship.

After usually receiving year-old factory equipment, this year OCTO Pramac received one GP17. Danilo Petrucci won the ride after he beat Redding in an in-team competition in the later part of the 2016 season. With several podium finishes, including seconds at Assen and Misano, Petrucci certainly did justice to the GP17. Other satellite Ducati teams for 2017 were the Pull&Bear Aspar team of Karel Abraham and Alvaro Bautista (on GP15s), and Reale Avintia Racing with Hector Barbera (GP16) and Loris Baz.

Below: For 2017 the factory
Panigale R benefited from five
seasons of development.

Bottom: Davies' Panigale R
was decked in final edition
livery for the Laguna Seca
World Superbike round.

WORLD SUPERBIKE

All bikes were required to have stock intake butterflies
and generators this year, disadvantaging the four-
cylinder bikes that previously used split throttle
bodies. Four-cylinder bikes were also required to retain
production balance shafts, so the Ducati Panigale
started the season without any disadvantage. In the
Aruba.it Racing team, former MotoGP rider Marco
Melandri joined Chaz Davies, with the Barni Racing
entry the only privateer Panigale this year, with Forés
in the saddle. Ernesto Marinelli oversaw the team,
but, after 22 years with Ducati, this was to be his final
season in World Superbike. The 1198 cc Panigale R
Superbike specifications were little changed from 2016.
The Marelli MLE electronic injection system included
independent motorised elliptical throttle bodies, with
twin Mitsubishi SF2204 injectors per cylinder. With an
Akrapovič titanium 2-1-2 exhaust system, horsepower
was more than 215 at 12000 rpm at the crankshaft.
The suspension included a 42 mm pressurised
RVP25 upside down Öhlins fork, and Öhlins RSP40
shock absorber. The wheels were Marchesini forged

aluminium: 3.5 x 17-inch on the front and 6 x 17-
inch on the rear. Front braking was by Brembo radial
P4X30-34 calipers with two 336 mm floating discs,
while the rear brake was a Brembo radial P2X34
caliper and 230 mm disc. As in 2016, the single-sided
swingarm was initially a lengthened stock item, but
early in the season a special racing version replaced
it. The factory Panigale R was very competitive this
season, Davies winning seven races and Melandri one,

Left: Michael Ruben Rinaldi won the 2017 FIM Superstock 1000 series on the Aruba.it Panigale R.

Below: The limited edition 1299 Panigale S Anniversario included a new generation electronics package.

1299 PANIGALE S ANNIVERSARIO

Unveiled by Casey Stoner at the 2016 World Ducati Week, the 1299 Panigale S Anniversario was an early release 2017 model, created to celebrate the company's 90th anniversary. Inspiration for the white, black, and red bodywork, and gold wheels, came from Ducati's racing bikes. The top triple clamp and steering head inserts were machined-from-solid aluminium alloy, the top triple clamp laser-etched with the bike's production number of 500. The steering head inserts shifted the front wheel forward 5 mm, providing the same geometry as the Panigale R. A lighter lithium battery, along with carbon fibre heel guards, rear mudguard, and shock absorber cover reduced the weight by 2.5 kg.

The electronics included all-new traction and wheelie control, the evolutionary Ducati Traction Control (DTC) and Ducati Wheelie Control (DWC) termed EVO. In addition to the new DTC and DWC EVO, the 1299 Panigale S Anniversario also featured Bosch Cornering ABS, Ducati Quick Shift (DQS), Ducati Electronic Suspension (DES), and Öhlins Smart EC. The twin-cylinder, 1285 cc, 205 horsepower Superquadro engine

but they weren't consistent enough to win the World Championship. Davies finished second overall, and Melandri fourth.

The Panigale R continued its success in the UK. Northern Ireland rider Glenn Irwin provided Ducati its first ever win in the North West 200. His race average on the Be Wiser/PBM Panigale R was 121.649 mph. Veteran British Superbike rider Shane Byrne also pulled off a surprising victory in the BSB Championship on a similar machine, unexpectedly winning by three points after Leon Haslam crashed out of the final race at Brands Hatch. The Panigale R was also victorious in the FIM Superstock 1000 Championship, Michael Ruben Rinaldi securing the title in the final round in Spain. Rinaldi took four victories during the season on his Aruba.it Racing-Junior Team Pangale R.

featured Engine Brake Control (EBC), which optimised vehicle stability under extreme turn-in conditions.

Further emphasising the sports performance, each bike came with a racing kit consisting of an Akrapovič Racing exhaust in titanium, billet aluminium mirror plates, and a cover for the hole created by removing the license-plate holder for track days.

1299 SUPERLEGGERA

Continuing on from the spectacular 1199 Superleggera, the 1299 Superleggera took the world of street legal twin-cylinder Superbike to an new level. The first production bike to be equipped with a carbon fibre frame, swingarm, subframe, and wheels, the 1299 Superleggera was also the most powerful production Ducati yet.

Updates to the 1,285 cc Superquadro engine included sand-cast crankcases and a 'silent' camchain. The lightened crankshaft now featured a larger crankpin,

and tungsten balancing pads. The titanium con-rods were new, as were the 13:1, 116 mm two-ring pistons. Aluminium cylinder liners replaced the 1299 Panigale's steel type, and a lighter flywheel resulted in an engine weight saving of 2.1 kg over the 1299 Panigale. The cylinder heads were 0.4 kg lighter, and received larger titanium valves (48 and 38.2 mm), and new higher-lift camshafts. The clutch featured a new slipper and self-servo system, while the intake system now included an SBK-style, high-permeability, larger-surface P08 Sprint Air Filter. The throttle body featured new aerodynamic throttle openings with a profile designed to improve airflow, while intake horn heights were optimised for each cylinder head, unlike the 1299 Panigale which had equal length horns. The 1299 Superleggera also had an all-titanium Akrapovič exhaust with a high dual silencer, similar to official factory WSBK Panigale. Euro 4 compliant, the power was 215 horsepower at 11,000 rpm. The 1299 Superleggera also came with a track kit, with a 4 kg lighter Akrapovič titanium

exhaust system, which also boosted power by five horsepower.

Design of the carbon fibre frame and swingarm was handled internally, with component structural quality ensured by three different NDI (Non Destructive Inspection) methods used in the aerospace industry. These included Active Transient Thermography along complex shapes and edges, Ultrasonic Phased Array, based on Pulse Echo technique, and Computed Axial Tomography, consisting of X-ray 3D inspection.

Resistant to high temperatures, the high-strength carbon fibre monocoque frame and single-sided swingarm also included laminated 7075 aluminium alloy inserts. This resulted in a 1.7 kg monocoque frame, a 40% saving on the 1299 Panigale, and 0.9 kg swingarm, saving 18%. The 1299 Superleggera also featured a carbon fibre rear subframe, fairing, front mudguard, rear mudguard, and exhaust heat guard. The wheels were high-strength carbon fibre, with aluminium hubs screwed into the composite structure, saving a further 1.4 kg.

Completing the advanced chassis specification were racing-quality Öhlins suspension and Brembo brakes. The 43 mm Öhlins FL936 upside-down fork weighed 1.35 kg less than the Öhlins NIX30 Panigale R fork, while the rear Öhlins TTX36 shock absorber had a titanium spring, shaving off another 0.5 kg. Front braking consisted of two 330 mm Brembo discs with Brembo M50 monobloc calipers and a Brembo MCS 19.21 radial pump. The calipers featured new

TT29OP1 brake pads, and braking included a newly calibrated Bosch Cornering ABS system.

A new electronics package included a six-axis Inertial Measurement Unit (6D IMU), this improving the Ducati Traction Control EVO (DTC EVO) and allowing the introduction of Ducati Slide Control (DSC). The 1299 Superleggera was also the first Ducati Superbike to be equipped with Ducati Power Launch (DPL). Each bike came with a track kit and, like the earlier 1199 Superleggera, only 500 were available.

SUPERSPORT

Resurrecting a great name from Ducati's past, the SuperSport, evolving from Super Sport (1973-82) and Supersport (1989-2006), continued in the style of the 1991-97 version. With its lower 810 mm seat and higher handlebars, this was less hard edged than the Panigale, and designed to be more suited to everyday street use. A redesigned fairing included a height-adjustable Plexiglas screen that could be set to two different positions over 50 mm of travel.

Powering the new SuperSport was an adapted Hypermotard twin-cylinder 937 cc Testastretta 11-degree. With a secondary air system, a 12.6:1 compression ratio, and Continental electronic fuel injection with 53 mm Mikuni throttle bodies, the power was 113 horsepower at 9,000 rpm. To meet Euro 4 emissions, the 2-1-2, 54 mm exhaust system included a large belly silencer with two stacked end cans. The

engine was a fully stressed frame component, and the crankcase and cylinder heads were redesigned externally, further modifications including re-routing of the water through the heads, and a specifically designed alternator cover to allow installation of the new gear sensor. This enabled the fitting of the Ducati Quick Shift (DQS) unit. The clutch was an oil-bath slipper type and three Riding Modes (Sport, Touring, and Urban) were offered.

The steel trellis frame was based on the Monster 821, the engine a fully stressed chassis component. The trellis frame connected to the front cylinder head, the rear steel subframe to the rear cylinder head, and the single-sided diecast aluminium swingarm to the crankcase. This structure helped keep the wet weight around 210 kg. Steering rake of 24-degrees, with 91 mm trail, and a 1,478 mm wheelbase, afforded the SuperSport light handling and excellent stability.

Two versions of the SuperSport were available, the standard version with a 43 mm Marzocchi fork and Sachs monoshock. The SuperSport S included Öhlins suspension; a 48 mm TiN coated front fork and fully adjustable rear shock absorber with integrated gas cartridge. On both versions, the wheels were Y-spoked aluminium at 3.50 x 17-inches and 5.50 x 17-inches; the front brakes, radial monobloc Brembo M4-32 calipers,

with a Brembo PR18/1 radial pump and two 320 mm discs. A two-piston Brembo caliper gripped the rear 245 mm disc, and the braking system was controlled by the Bosch 9MP ABS system with three mappings. Three option packages were also available, Sport, Touring, and Urban. Blending real world sportsbike performance with track day ability, rather than filling a void in the range, the new SuperSport created a new market segment.

MULTISTRADA 950 AND 1200 ENDURO PRO

With 50,000 sales since its introduction in 2010, until the release of the Scrambler in 2015, the Multistrada 1200 had consistently been Ducati's best-selling model. Because of this success, it was inevitable a mid-sized version would appear, this lacking since the short-lived 620 cc Multistrada of 2005-06. Already adapted for the SuperSport the new Hypermotard 937 cc Testastretta 11-degree engine proved an ideal power plant for downsized Multistrada. As with the 1200 Enduro, the Product Manager was Federico Valentini, with Project Leader MotoGP engineer Davide Previtera.

For the Multistrada 950, the Euro 4-rated engine received a redesigned oil system, new desmodromic

Left: The SuperSport S included
Öhlins suspension, and was
available in white. Since it was
intended as a sports tourer,
designated luggage was optional.

Bottom: The Multistrada 1200
Enduro Pro was more off-road
focused than the 1200 Enduro.

Below: Combining features of the
Multistrada 1200 and Multistrada
1200 Enduro, the Multistrada 950
offered similar versatility in a more
economical package.

cylinder heads with revised porting and secondary air intake ducts, a 12.6:1 compression ratio, 53 mm cylindrical throttle bodies with a Bosch ECU, and revised fuelling for each of the four riding modes. Maximum power of 113 horsepower at 9,000 rpm was unchanged.

Combining the style of the Multistrada 1200 and 1200 Enduro, the 950 frame included a large-diameter thin tube Trellis with two lateral aluminium sub-frames to ensure maximum torsional rigidity. The fork rake was stretched out more than the 1200, at 25.5-degrees (as opposed to 24-degrees). As on the 1200 Enduro the swingarm was double-sided shell-cast aluminium, the front fork a 48 mm upside down Kayaba, with an adjustable Sachs rear shock absorber connecting the swingarm to the left sub-frame. The wheels were cast aluminium: a 3.00 x 19-inch on the front, and 4.50 x 17-inch on the rear.

Braking was also similar to the 1200 Enduro, with twin 320 mm front discs and Brembo M4.32 monobloc twin pad radial calipers with four 32 mm diameter pistons. The rear brake featured a 265 mm disc,

Brembo floating caliper, and Ducati Safety Pack, and included three-level Bosch 9.1MP ABS, and eight-level Ducati Traction Control.

Taking styling cues from the two larger Multistradas, the 950 fairing with adjustable screen was similar to the

Multistrada 1200 while the narrow seat and high exit single silencer was comparable to the 1200 Enduro. Four optional packages were also available; Touring (with panniers), Sport, Urban, and Enduro. But rolling on an even longer (1,594 mm) wheelbase than the 1200 and weighing a similar 204 kg dry, the Multistrada 950 wasn't really a downsized version of the larger Multistrada. More of a budget version, it still offered acceptable performance without the sophisticated new generation electronic aids of its larger brother. Offering versatility with long 15,000 km service intervals the Multistrada 950 was certain to expand a successful formula.

Joining the Multistrada line-up during 2017 was the Multistrada 1200 Enduro Pro. Even more off-road focused than the 1200 Enduro, the 1200 Enduro Pro Testastretta DVT, with Bosch electronic fuel injection and elliptical 56 mm throttle bodies, produced 152 horsepower at 9500 rpm. Specific features included a rough-finished, sand-coloured front end and tank cover, two-tone seat, and a black sub-frame and clutch/alternator covers. Other Pro features included Touratech bull bars with LED lights, a low screen, and Termignoni titanium exhaust. The electronic package was shared with the Multistrada 1200 Enduro, and the dry weight was increased to 232 kg.

MONSTER 1200, 1200S

A more-powerful updated and restyled Monster 1200 and 1200S were introduced this year. Inspired by the elemental style of Galluzzi's original 1993 version, under the direction of project engineer Giuseppe Caprara the new 1200 featured a sleeker fuel tank and redesigned tail. As on the original Monster, the steel tank was fitted with an anodised aluminium attachment clip. The Testastretta 11-degree DS engine was retuned to deliver 150 horsepower at 9,250 rpm (15 horsepower more than the previous Monster 1200, and 5 horsepower more than the previous Monster 1200S). Attached to the engine was a new single-sided swingarm and die-cast aluminium footpegs. The new swingarm provided a shorter (1,485 mm) wheelbase. The Monster 1200 featured an adjustable 43 mm Kayaba front fork and Sachs shock absorber, with 320 mm front brake discs and Brembo M4.32 calipers. The higher specification Monster 1200S included a 48 mm Öhlins fork and Öhlins monoshock with two 330 mm Brembo front discs and M50 monobloc calipers. The Monster 1200S also featured the Ducati Quick Shift (DQS) system, wheels with three Y-spokes, and a carbon fibre front mudguard.

Both versions included a comprehensive electronics

Left: The Ducati MotoGP team of Jorge Lorenzo and Andrea Dovizioso was unchanged for 2018. Setting the GP18 apart from the previous year were new colours and livery.

Bottom left: Jorge Lorenzo was looking for a more successful season on the Desmosedici GP18.

Bottom: The final version of the factory Panigale R. This was Chaz Davies' fifth season on the 1200 cc twin.

2018

Despite uncertainty regarding Ducati's future ownership, a swathe of new models were released for 2018. This year also saw a forty-seven year tradition of Ducati factory racing 90-degree V-twins come to an end. Although the factory Panigale R continued for one more year in World Superbike, its four-cylinder replacement, the Panigale V4, appeared this year. To celebrate the end of the V-twin's reign, Ducati released the 1299 Panigale R Final Edition.

MOTOGP

The Ducati MotoGP team continued with Dovizioso and Lorenzo as riders. As the 2017 season was very successful, the GP18 was evolutionary, the engine more powerful and developed to improve rideability. Other updates included a new Öhlins front fork, and new aerodynamics. Aerodynamic developments were introduced during the season, the final version appearing after the first few races. Petrucci's excellent results during 2017 also saw him earn a ride on the GP18, with Jack Miller replacing Scott Redding in

the OCTO Pramac team on the GP17. The Pull&Bear Aspar team continued with Karel Abraham and Alvaro Bautista, while new riders for Real Avintia were Tito Rabat and Xavier Simeon.

WORLD SUPERBIKE

Marco Melandri continued alongside Chaz Davies on the Aruba.it Racing Panigale R. 2017 European Superstock 1000 winner Michael Ruben Rinaldi also rode a third bike at the European rounds. Following the retirement of Ernesto Marinelli, Marco Zambenedetti assumed the position of Ducati Corse On-track technical coordinator. This was to be the final year for the Panigale R in World Superbike, new technical regulations seeing a reduction in maximum rpm to 12,400. This replaced the previous air restrictor system. A concession system was also introduced to restrict the engine development of the most competitive teams. While the claimed maximum power was reduced slightly, to more than 210 horsepower at 12,400 rpm, a number of engine and chassis updates were introduced to make the Panigale twin more competitive against the four cylinder Superbikes.

Below: Marco Melandri showed an immediate improvement for his second season on the Panigale R, winning both races at the opening round in Australia.

Bottom: The 1299 Panigale R Final Edition was released to celebrate the end of the larger displacement Panigale.

1299 PANIGALE R FINAL EDITION

With Ducati's tradition of factory racing twins coming to an end, the 1299 Panigale R Final Edition was released as a commemorative model. Available as a numbered (but not limited) series, the 1299 Panigale R Final Edition was Euro 4 compliant and based on the 1299 Superleggera and Panigale R. The Final Edition Superquadro engine featured a lightened crankshaft with a larger crank pin and tungsten balancing pads, and titanium con-rods. As on the racing engines, the two-ring 116 mm pistons, ran on steel cylinder liners. The titanium intake valves were 48 mm (up from 46.8 mm on the 1299 Panigale) and the titanium exhaust valves 39.5 mm (from 38.2 mm). Remodelled intake and exhaust ducts were combined with new higher

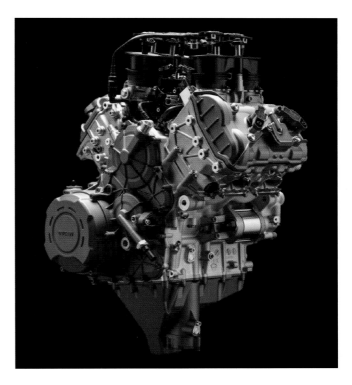

Right: Inspired by the MotoGP engine, the Desmosedici Stradale was a compact 90-degree V4.

lift camshafts. The clutch featured a new slipper and self-servo system, and a new forged aluminium clutch basket.

The air intake system included a high-permeability filter, with the throttle body featuring aerodynamic throttle openings. The intake horn heights were optimised for each cylinder head, unlike the equal length horns on the 1299 Panigale. Also new was the titanium Akrapovič exhaust with racing style a high dual silencer. The engine produced 209 horsepower at 11,000 rpm.

The electronics package included the Bosch Inertial Measurement Unit (IMU) and ABS Cornering, Ducati Wheelie Control EVO (DWC EVO), Ducati Traction Control EVO (DTC EVO), and Engine Brake Control (EBC). All these systems were set according to the selected Riding Mode (Race, Sport, and Wet) and could be individually customised by the rider.

The chassis was similar to the Panigale R, with a die-cast aluminium monocoque structure that included the engine as a stressed member. Attached to the cylinder heads, the forward protruding monocoque housed the steering head bearings in two aluminium bushes. The rake was 24-degrees, and the monocoque also incorporated the airbox with air filter, throttle bodies, and injectors. The underneath of the aluminium fuel tank sealed it. Also shared with the Panigale R was Öhlins mechanical suspension, including a 43 mm fully adjustable NIX 30 TiN-coated upside down front fork, TTX36 monoshock with a titanium spring, and adjustable Öhlins steering damper. Front braking was by a pair of Brembo M50 monobloc calipers, with four 30 mm pistons, and 330 mm discs. Rolling on a 1,443 mm wheelbase, the dry weight was only 168 kg.

Representing the end of the V-twin as Ducati's premier sporting model, the 1299 Panigale R Final Edition was historically significant and undoubtedly destined to be a future collectable.

DESMOSEDICI STRADALE

Evolving from the experience gained in fifteen years of MotoGP competition the Desmosedici Stradale was a new 90-degree V4 engine designed to power future top-of-the-range sporting models. The Desmosedici Stradale project began in 2014, under the direction of project leader Stefano Strappazzon, with the MotoGP engine as a basis. As with the other Ducati engines, the 90-degree V layout was chosen, as the perfect primary balance negated the need for heavy power-sapping

countershaft balancers. Compared to a classic in-line four, the compact V arrangement allowed for improved mass centralisation and narrower front cross-section. The shorter crankshaft also reduced the gyroscopic effect, these combining to provide lighter and faster direction changes. Inside the V was ample space for a gear-driven water pump and large (12.8 litre) airbox. The compact Desmosedici Stradale shared the cylinder heads, dimensions, and geometry with the Desmosedici GP. As on the MotoGP unit, the 90-degree V4 was rotated rearward by 42-degrees, optimising weight distribution, allowing for larger radiators, and bringing the swingarm pivot as far forward as possible. Like the Superquadro twin, the engine was designed as a structural chassis element, with frame attachment points at the front of the upper crankcase and the rear cylinder head. The crankcase also acted as a rear suspension and swingarm attachment point.

As in MotoGP, the engine was designed with an 81 mm cylinder bore, the maximum limit allowed by MotoGP rules. Thus the Stradale and MotoGP Desmosedici shared engine fluid dynamics, valves, intake ducts, and throttle bodies. The gravity die-cast aluminium crankcases were horizontally split, the upper crankcase half incorporating the four Nikasil-coated aluminium cylinder liners. Inside the liners were 14:1 moulded aluminium pistons, with two low-attrition compression rings and an oil ring. The pistons featured 'box in box' construction, reducing skirt height and below-chamber thickness, in turn reducing wear and inertia, while maintaining strength and stiffness. The

Left: The Desmodromic system
was also more compact.

The Desmodromic system was redesigned, with smaller, lighter, components inside a more compact four-valve cylinder head. The inlet valves were 34 mm, and the exhaust 27.5 mm, with sintered steel valve seats. Emphasizing the compact design were smaller, centrally-mounted spark plugs.

Instead of the racing engine's gear driven camshaft drive, the camshaft drive for the Stradale was similar to the two-cylinder Superquadro. Featuring a combination of chain and gears, a 'silent' timing chain on the right side of the engine drove the front intake camshaft, this transmitting drive to the exhaust camshaft by a pair of gears. On the rear a chain on the left drove the exhaust camshaft, this transmitting drive to the intake camshaft by gears. Each cylinder head incorporated an anti-knock sensor.

The combination of 70-degree crank pin offset and a 90-degree V-layout generated a 'Twin Pulse' firing order, the engine reproducing a firing sequence similar to a twin-cylinder. The two left cylinders fired 90-degree apart, followed by a 200-degree interval, then the two right cylinders again at 90-degrees apart. The firing order of 0, 90, 290, and 380-degrees replicated the MotoGP Desmosedici and provided optimal power delivery.

The four oval throttle bodies (52 mm diameter equivalent) connected to variable-height air intake horns, the first time on a production Ducati engine. As rpm and load varied, the air intake horns ducts were lengthened or shortened as required, optimising the ducts' pressure wave fluid dynamics. The ECU controlled the system, which consisted of two stages: a fixed horn on the throttle body, and a mobile horn, moved along steel guides by an electric motor. When the latter was lowered, it came into contact with the short horn, geometrically lengthening the duct. When raised, the fluid dynamics involved only the fixed lower horn, and the engine configuration became that of a very short duct.

Each throttle body had two injectors: a sub-butterfly for low-load use, and another above for maximum engine performance. The throttle bodies for each cylinder bank were moved by a dedicated electric motor. A full ride-by-wire system allowed complex electronic control and modulation of engine 'feel' according to the selected riding mode.

As on the MotoGP Desmosedici, the lubrication system was semi-dry sump, with separate delivery and return stages. The oil circulation system involved four

stroke was 53.5 mm, and the forged steel con-rods 101.8 mm eye-to-eye. The 1103 cc displacement was more than allowed for MotoGP or World Superbike but was designed to provide more low speed torque for a street engine.

Mounted on brass bushings, the three main bearing nitrided steel crankshaft was offset at 70-degrees, as on the MotoGP Desmosedici engines. This allowed for a 'Twin Pulse' ignition sequence. As on the MotoGP Desmosedici (and the original bevel-drive 90-degree V-twin), the crankshaft was counter-rotating. This counter-rotating crank offset some of the gyroscopic effect generated by the wheels, improving handling and direction changing. Another benefit was the inertia-linked torque produced in the opposite direction during acceleration that reduced wheelie effects. Similarly, during hard braking the decelerating crank produced inertial torque that reduced rear wheel lift.

Unlike the earlier bevel-drive V-twin, which featured a direct drive gearbox with the layshaft above the mainshaft to reduce engine length, the Stradale incorporated a jackshaft to transfer crankshaft drive through the indirect gearbox to the rear wheel, this reversing the drive direction.

pumps: one delivery lobe pump, and three recovery pumps. A gear recovery pump drew oil from the heads via two ducts, while the other two lobe pumps ensured efficient oil recovery. This kept the crankcase zone under the pistons in a controlled, constant low-pressure state, reducing airing losses (power absorption caused by the aerodynamic resistance of the air and oil splashing). The oil tank, also a filter housing, was a magnesium sump mounted underneath the crankcase and connected to the gearbox separately from the crankcase. An oil cooler was attached below the water radiator.

The six-speed gearbox was specially designed for the Desmosedici Stradale engine, and featured a rotary gear sensor to ensure optimal operation with Ducati Quick Shift (DQS). The sensor accurately assessed the position of the gear shift drum and the gear shift forks, ensuring precise gear selection. With torque transmission restored only after the gear change has been completed, undue gear mesh stress was prevented. The hydraulically-controlled wet clutch had 11 driving plates, and featured a progressive self-servo mechanism, compressing the friction plates under drive. While enhancing frictional efficiency, this also resulted in a lighter clutch action. In sport riding conditions, the same mechanism reduced friction plate pressure,

enabling a racing 'slipper' action, and reducing rear end destabilisation during aggressive down-shifting.

To reduce weight, the cam covers, oil sump, alternator cover, and two-piece clutch cover were die-cast magnesium. The resulting Desmosedici Stradale engine weighed 64.9 kg, just 2.2 kg heavier than the 1,285 cc Superquadro twin. With a 14,000 rpm rev ceiling, the power of the Euro 4 compliant engine was 214 horsepower at 13,000 rpm, with maximum torque of 124 Nm at 10,000 rpm.

PANIGALE V4, V4 S, V4 SPECIALE

The Desmosedici Stradale engine was installed in the Panigale V4, Ducati's first production four-cylinder since the 2008 D16RR. Replacing the Panigale 1299 as Ducati's premium sporting model, the Panigale V4 also established a new blueprint for the production race-derived Ducati. The philosophy followed that of the MotoGP Desmosedici, and involved the integration of the engine, chassis, and rider as a complete unit. Three versions were initially offered; the Panigale V4, Panigale V4 S, with higher specification suspension, and the limited-edition, single-seat Panigale V4 Speciale.

Below: There was a strong family continuance with the Panigale V4 S's styling.

Right: The Panigale V4 Speciale was a Tricolore limited edition version.

To achieve an impressive power to weight ratio of 1.1 hp/kg, the traditional perimeter aluminium frame, as on the MotoGP Desmosedici, was eschewed for a 'front frame' type. The Desmosedici Stradale engine acted as a load-bearing component. Developed from experience in MotoGP, the frame was an evolution of the previous Panigale's monocoque design. Compared to the monocoque design, the front frame allowed the separation of torsional and lateral rigidity, allowing the frame to better absorb road surface roughness during cornering.

Weighing only 4 kg, the compact front frame attached directly to the front and rear cylinder heads, with the engine also acting as a fixing point for the rear suspension and a fulcrum point for the swingarm. This allowed the engine to contribute to overall rigidity, reducing the frame's size and weight, and providing a better rigidity-to-weight ratio. The shorter pillars resulted in a more compact design, particularly around the rider's seat. A magnesium sub-frame attached at the front, while a shell-cast aluminium seat rear sub-frame attached to the front frame and the rear cylinder head. The rising rate linkage rear suspension attached to the

engine via a forged aluminium element, while the cast aluminium single-sided swingarm was a long 600 mm. The rake was 24.5-degrees with 100 mm of trail.

The front suspension was by a 43 mm front fork, an adjustable Showa Big Piston Fork (BPF) on the Panigale V4, and Öhlins NIX-30 on the Panigale V4 S and Panigale V4 Speciale. The Panigale V4 featured a Sachs rear shock absorber, the Panigale V4 S and Panigale V4 Speciale employing an Öhlins TTX36 rear shock. Unlike the Panigale 1299, the shock absorber was positioned more conventionally. On the two higher spec versions, an Öhlins steering damper replaced the Sachs, the suspension and the steering damper controlled by the second-generation Öhlins Smart EC 2.0 control system with a new Objective Based Tuning Interface (OBTi). While the Panigale V4 was fitted with five-spoke cast aluminium wheels, the Panigale V4 S and Speciale featured five-spoke forged aluminium alloy wheels. The sizes for both were 3.50 x 17-inch and 6.00 x 17-inch; these shod with the latest racing-inspired Pirelli Diablo Supercorsa SP tyres. The slightly higher profile 200/60 ZR 17 rear tyre was designed to maximise the contact patch at extreme lean angles, and

included bi-compound technology, with an SC2 compound for the shoulder area.

Front braking for the Panigale V4 was by new Brembo Stylema monobloc calipers, these an evolution of the M50. Machined from an alloy block, the Stylema featured lighter fixing bushings, and were more compact than the M50. Weight was reduced by 70 grams per caliper, without compromising rigidity. Internal ventilation ensured higher efficiency, while the enhanced rigidity improved hydraulic feel, with shorter brake lever travel. The front calipers each had four 30 mm pistons and gripped 330 mm discs, while the rear brake was the usual a single 245 mm disc with a two-piston caliper. The braking system included the ABS Cornering EVO system, with a lightweight 9.1MP Bosch control unit.

Designed by the Ducati Design Centre under the direction of Julien Clement, the Panigale V4 evolved from the existing 1299 Panigale. The styling development involved combining design minimalism, component integration, and aerodynamic efficiency. This led to a dual-layer fairing design, with a less stretched-out main fairing, and another layer acting as an air outlet. Inspired by racing Ducatis, the 'dual layer' was also more compact. As on the racing models, the aluminium 16-litre fuel tank relocated some fuel storage below the rider, allowing the electronics and battery to be placed at the front of the tank. The kerb weight was 198 kg for the Panigale V4 and only 195 kg for the V4 S and Speciale.

The latest-generation electronics package featured new dynamic vehicle controls, including controlled drift during braking, ABS cornering on the front wheel only, and Quickshift taking lean angles into account. All these controls were incorporated in the three new Riding Modes (Race, Sport, and Street), and could be adjusted via the TFT panel.

While the Panigale V4 and V4 S were only available in red, with a grey frame and black wheels, the Speciale was a Tricolore, also with grey frame and black wheels. Limited to 1500 examples, also included with the Speciale were carbon fibre mudguards, machined top triple clamp with identification number, Alcantara seat, adjustable footpegs, racing levers, carbon fibre swingarm cover, and GPS data logging. It was also supplied with a racing titanium Akrapovič exhaust system, which boosted the power to 226 horsepower, and dropped the dry weight to only 164 kg.

In moving away from its traditional V-twin format the Panigale V4 represented a significant change for Ducati. Acknowledging the radical Panigale V-twin hadn't fulfilled racing expectations, the Panigale V4 was more conservative in execution, and drew heavily on the existing racing Desmosedici. In the process, Ducati moved away from the pursuit of chassis perfection, balance, and minimal weight that had characterised its Superbikes for 45 years. But while the format was new, with its instantly recognisable styling and trademark single-sided swingarm, the Panigale V4's execution was familiar. One thing was certain. By combining brutal power with the latest electronics, the Panigale V4 was the most advanced production Ducati yet.

Below: Also setting apart the 959 Panigale Corse was the Öhlins suspension. The non-Euro version had an under-engine muffler.

Right: Colours for the 959 Panigale Corse were inspired by the MotoGP Desmosedici. The Euro 4 version had a titanium Akrapovič muffler.

959 PANIGALE CORSE

As there was no longer a higher specification Panigale in the line-up following the demise of the 1299 Panigale S, Ducati introduced the 959 Panigale Corse for 2018. As with the previous 959, two versions were available, the Euro 4, approved for Europe, and the non-Euro 4 for the US. The Euro 4 version featured a twin titanium muffler by Akrapovič, the 955 cc engine producing 150 horsepower at 10,500 rpm with the maximum torque of 102 Nm at 9,000 rpm. While the new exhaust saved 2.5 kg, the power was a little less than the previous 959. US versions retained the under engine muffler. The standard 959 Panigale now also shared the 150 horsepower engine, but was otherwise unchanged.

The 959 Panigale Corse's chassis retained the compact die-cast aluminium monocoque structure, with the Superquadro engine incorporated as a structural element. Attached directly to the cylinder heads, it housed two aluminium bushes at the front containing the steering head bearings. The monocoque also acted as an air-box, containing the air filter, throttle bodies and injectors while being sealed by the aluminium fuel tank. Also carried over from the 959, rather than 1299, was the double-sided swingarm. Setting the 959 Panigale Corse apart was a 43 mm adjustable titanium-nitride treated Öhlins NIX30 fork, an adjustable Öhlins TTX36 shock absorber, and Öhlins adjustable steering damper. Front brakes were from the standard model, with 320 mm Brembo discs and four-piston M4.32 calipers. The electronics package included ABS, Ducati Traction Control (DTC), Ducati Quick Shift (DQS), Engine Brake Control (EBC), and ride-by-wire (RbW)

with three riding modes: Race, Sport, and Wet. With a lighter lithium-ion battery replacing the lead acid unit, the 959 Panigale Corse weighed 197.5 kg, 2.5 kg less than the 959 Panigale.

For many long-time Ducati observers, the Panigale is seen as the pinnacle of the 90-degree Ducati twin. This is an opinion I tend to agree with; with its sophisticated camshaft drive system, and horizontally split crankcase design, the Panigale offered the optimal combination of power with reliability and minimal maintenance. A testament to its strength was the result of a *Motorrad* 50,000 km test and strip down of a 1199 Panigale. Although the engine is required to be a main structural element as well as produce extraordinary horsepower, this showed minimal wear at the end of three years hard use. The analysis more than affirmed the excellence of the design. Although the Panigale is undoubtedly more expensive to manufacture than the long-running Testastretta, it will be interesting to see if it gradually usurps it as a powerplant for other models. The Superquadro engine is certainly too good to remain on the sidelines, powering only one mid-range sporting motorcycle.

The Multistrada received an update for 2018, now forged Y-spoke wheels and a longer swingarm. The Multistrada 1260 S here also featured Sachs semi-active Ducati Skyhook Suspension.

MULTISTRADA 1260, 1260 S, 1260 S D-AIR, 1260 PIKES PEAK

For 2018, the Multistrada was updated with a new Ducati Testastretta DVT (Desmodromic Variable Timing) 1262 cc engine, new chassis, more advanced electronics, and an aesthetic update. This included new fairing panels and lighter, sportier looking wheels. Similar to the engine powering the X-Diavel, the 1262 cc displacement came through increasing the stroke from 67.9 to 71.5 mm, while retaining a 106 mm bore. This required new connecting rods, crankshaft and cylinders. The DVT system was recalibrated to maximise low-to-mid range torque delivery, the maximum power now 158 horsepower at 9,750 rpm, and maximum torque now 13.2 kg/m at 7,500 rpm. 85% of the torque was available at 3,500 rpm, and torque at 5,500 rpm was 18% higher than before. The air intake, exhaust tubing, and pre-silencer were redesigned. Also new were the timing belt covers, while the updated generator cover accommodated a more advanced gear sensor, a core component of the DQS (Ducati Quick Shift). Both

generator and clutch covers were painted in 'Mercury Grey', while the clutch slave cylinder was now a more compact design.

The frame and swingarm were also refreshed. The tubular steel Trellis frame included two lateral subframes, closed off by a fibreglass-reinforced plastic rear load-bearing element, for maximum torsional rigidity. The 48 mm longer single-sided aluminium swingarm was die-cast, with fabricated and welded core sections. The steering head angle increased from 24-degrees to 25-degrees, and the wheelbase increased to 1,585 mm, 55 mm longer than before.

The Multistrada 1260 featured a fully adjustable Kayaba 48 mm upside-down fork, with a cast lower bracket, while the rear shock absorber was a fully adjustable Sachs monoshock. For the Multistrada 1260 S, and 1260 S D-Air, the suspension was the semi-active Ducati Skyhook Suspension (DSS) Evolution system, this featuring a 48 mm Sachs front fork (with ceramic grey tubes) and adjustable Sachs rear shock absorber. The suspension travel front and rear for all systems was 170 mm.

Also new were the five-spoke alloy wheels, in sizes of 3.50 x 17-inches and 6.00 x 17-inches. These were 340 grams lighter than those on the Multistrada 1200. The Multistrada 1260's front braking system included Brembo monobloc radially mounted Brembo four-piston calipers with 32 mm diameter pistons and two pads, a radial master cylinder with adjustable lever, and dual 320 mm discs. At the rear was a single 265 mm diameter disc and twin-piston floating caliper. For the Multistrada 1260 S, the discs were increased to 330 mm, coupled with Brembo M50 monobloc radial four-piston calipers. Electronic aids now included a Vehicle Hold Control (VHC) system, applying rear wheel braking if required on a hill. While continuing the style of the 1200, the 1260 Multistrada also included new side fairing panels, an aluminium rear subframe, redesigned number plate holder, LED turn signals, and higher resolution TFT instrument panel. The four riding modes were now assigned different colours. Also making a return for 2018 was the higher specification Multistrada 1260 Pikes Peak. Last seen in 2014, the Pikes Peak was based on the Multistrada 1260 S, and shared the 1262 cc Testastretta DVT engine, new front end geometry, and longer swingarm. Along with the racing-inspired colours and red frame, the Multistrada 1260 Pikes Peak came with new black forged aluminium wheels, even lighter than those of the

Multistrada 1260 S. The front fork was a 48 mm Öhlins, and the suspension by an Öhlins TTX36 shock. Adjustment on both was mechanical only, while the braking system was shared with the 1260 S.

Celebrating Ducati's success at the Pikes Peak International Hill Climb in Colorado was the Multistrada 1260 Pikes Peak. This top of the line Multistrada had Öhlins suspension and a Termignoni muffler.

In addition to a specific silencer and nose fairing, a carbon fibre Termignoni muffler and low racing-type carbon fibre screen are also available for the 1260 Pikes Peak. Further carbon fibre components included the front mudguard, hands-free cover and front side panels, and red-stitched seat. Also shared with the Multistrada 1260 S was the range of electronic aids. Undeniably competent, but with a seat adjustable between 825 and

Below: New for 2018 was the
Scrambler 1100. This is the classic
Special version, with wire spoked
wheels.

845 mm, and a wet weight around 235 kg (229 kg for the Pikes Peak), the Multistrada 1260 was still a very large, and for some, intimidating, motorcycle.

As they were more recent introductions, the Multistrada 950 and 1200 Enduro continued unchanged, but it was likely that the Enduro would be updated to 1260 in the future.

SCRAMBLER 1100, 1100 SPECIAL, 1100 SPORT, STREET CLASSIC AND MACH 2.0

As the original Scrambler evolved from a smaller capacity, initially 175 cc and ultimately 450 cc, the current Scrambler range followed suit with the addition of an 1100 for 2018. Now encompassing three different capacities (400, 800 and 1100 cc) and a range of variants, the Scrambler now offered something for everyone.

Powering the Scrambler 1100 was an updated version of the air/oil-cooled Monster 1100 engine. Last seen in 2013, this retained the 98 mm bore and 71.5 mm stroke, 1079 cc displacement and two-valve desmodromic cylinder head. Now Euro 4 compliant, the compression ratio was increased slightly, to 11:1, and the electronic injection included a single 55 mm full ride-by-wire throttle body with two sub-butterfly injectors. To ensure a wide powerband the cam timing featured 16-degrees of valve overlap. Unlike the previous Monster 1100, which had reverted to a single spark plug per cylinder, the new 1100 featured twin spark plugs per cylinder to ensure a smoother power delivery with minimal emissions. With a large airbox and a secondary air system, the maximum power was 86 horsepower at 7,500 rpm, with maximum torque of 88.4 Nm at 4,750 rpm. The clutch was a hydraulically-actuated wet multiplate type with a servo-assisted slipper function. Cosmetic engine updates saw machine-finished aluminium clutch, alternator and belt covers.

Left: The Scrambler 1100 Sport featured Öhlins suspension. All Scrambler 1100s had a distinctive round headlamp with aluminium rim.

Bottom: Joining the Scrambler range for 2018 was another variation on the Classic, the Street Classic.

Also new for the Scrambler 1100 was the twin upper spar steel Trellis frame with aluminium rear subframe. To provide agility in the city and mountain passes, the steering head angle was 24.5-degrees, with 111 mm of trail, achieved by a 110 mm offset on the aluminium triple clamps. Compared to the 800, the Scrambler 1100 was generally larger, rolling on a 1,514 mm wheelbase, with an 810 mm seat height. The riding position was also different, with a wider seat/footpeg relationship, and lower and further forward handlebars.

Three versions were initially available: the basic Scrambler 1100 fitted with an adjustable Marzocchi 45mm upside down fork, Kayaba rear shock absorber (with 150 mm of travel), and machine-finished ten-spoke alloy wheels. The front was a 3.50 x 18-inch with a 5.50 x 17-inch on the rear. Front braking was by a pair of semi-floating 320 mm discs and Brembo

Bottom: Created by renowned Californian designer Roland Sands, the Scrambler Mach 2.0 colours were inspired by the Bell Cross idol helmet from the 2017 Scrambler apparel collection.

Right: The Monster 821 received a face-lift for 2018 and now looked more like the Monster 1200.

monobloc M4.32B four-piston radial calipers, with Bosch cornering ABS. At the rear was a 245 mm disc with a single 34 mm piston floating caliper. The wet weight was a considerable 206 kg, and colour options were '62 Yellow' or 'Shining Black'.

A more classic interpretation, the Scrambler 1100 Special, featured a similar suspension and braking package to the Scrambler 1100, but included black-spoked wheels, gold anodised front fork sleeves, chrome exhausts and aluminium mudguards. A 'Custom Grey' colour was unique to the Special, as were the brushed-effect swingarm, low-slung tapered handlebars, and brown seat. The wet weight was also increased slightly, to 211 kg. The third variation was the Scrambler 1100 Sport. Inspired by various Scrambler customs, Scrambler 1100 Sport featured an adjustable 48 mm Öhlins fork and Öhlins shock. The wheels and brakes were shared with the Scrambler 1100 but specific features included 'Viper Black' paint with yellow accents, tapered handlebars, and a special seat. The Scrambler 1100 was the first in the Scrambler family to feature Ducati Traction Control (DTC) adjustable to four different levels. Three riding modes were also offered; Active (full power), Journey (everyday), and City (75 horsepower).

The Scrambler Icon, Full Throttle, Classic, Café Racer, Desert Sled, and Sixty2 continued unchanged for 2018, with a Street Classic and Mach 2.0 joining the range. The Street Classic was similar to the Classic, with wire-spoked wheels and a brown seat, but the engine featured black cylinder heads with brushed fins, derived from the Café Racer, and the bike had a 'Volcanic Grey' finish. Also sharing the black cylinder heads with brushed cooling fins was the Mach 2.0; created by Californian designer Roland Sands, the name was inspired by the 250 Mach 1 of 1964-66. The graphics and colours were intended to evoke a 1970s West Coast style, further conveyed by a low tapered aluminium handlebar, Flat Track Pro seat, and black exhaust.

DUCATI MONSTER 821

The mid-sized Monster 821 received a styling update for 2018, with a more streamlined tank and tail, new silencer, and headlight influenced by the Monster 1200. The Euro 4 compliant liquid-cooled Testastretta 11-degree engine delivered slightly less maximum power than before, 109 horsepower at 9250 rpm. Electronic aids included the usual Ducati Safety Pack, comprising Bosch ABS and Ducati Traction Control, and three riding modes. Also new was a colour TFT display with selected gear and fuel indicators, and accessories including the Ducati Quick Shift up/down system.

Returning to the naked sport bike concept of the

original Monster 25 years earlier, the fuel tank included the classic anodised aluminium attachment clip, and a round headlight (as on the Monster 1200). The engine acted as a load-bearing element, also akin to that of the the 1200, attaching directly to the cylinder heads. The redesigned rear subframe also attached directly to the engine and supported the new passenger footpeg mounts, these now separated from the rider's pegs. The wheels, brakes, and suspension were unchanged. Since the other models in the Monster line-up (797, 1200, 1200 S, 1200 R) were still recent introductions or updates, they all continued unchanged.

HYPERMOTARD 939, DIAVEL, XDIAVEL, SUPERSPORT

The Hypermotard 939 continued as before, but with the option of a 'Star White Silk' finish. The claimed power for the 937 cc Testastretta 11-degree engine was now 110 horsepower, with 95 Nm of torque. Also unchanged were the Diavel, XDiavel, and SuperSport.

As Ducati successfully negotiates a constantly changing marketplace, it continues to draw heavily on its history. Now a backbone in the line-up, the Scrambler has unapologetically emphasised nostalgia,

and even more technologically advanced models like the SuperSport continue a tradition by evoking a great name of the past. One tradition that hasn't survived is Ducati's adherence to the Desmodromic 90-degree V-twin. As in 1970, when Fabio Taglioni discovered his desmodromic single-cylinder racers to be outclassed, by 2017, Ducati's V-twin was no longer dominant in World Superbike. In 1970, Ducati's solution was to create a V-twin out of two singles, and in 2018 its answer was to build a V4 inspired by the MotoGP racer. It's unlikely that the Panigale V4 will lead to the creation of a new engine blueprint for all Ducati motorcycles, as the 750 twin did in 1971, but it will certainly establish a new order for racing and Superbike versions. Fabio Taglioni was a strong advocate for racing, believing that only through competition could designs be effectively proven. As Ducati is at the forefront of both the MotoGP and World Superbike Championships, Taglioni's philosophy continues, and while market trends see the current production line-up moving away from its previous concentration on high-performance Superbikes, the importance of racing in the development of new models will undoubtedly continue. Now approaching seventy-five years of motorcycle production, Ducati has come a long way since the humble clip-on 48 cc Cucciolo.

APPENDIX

DUCATI MOTORCYCLES 1952–2018

Model	Years	Engine	Bore (mm)	Stroke (mm)	Displ (cc)	Comp ratio	Cooling system	Fuel system	Transmission	Front suspension	Rear suspension	Front tyre	Rear tyre	Wheel base	Weight (kg)
65N, T, S TL, TS	1952–57	1 Cyl, OHV	44	43	65	8:1	Air	Weber carburettor	3-speed	Hydraulic fork	Twin shock swingarm				55
98N, T, TS TL, Sport Bronco	1952–62	1 Cyl, OHV	49	52	98	7:1	Air	Dell'Orto carburettor 16 mm	4-speed	Hydraulic fork	Twin shock swingarm	2.50 X17	2.75 X17	1245	87
55/R/E	1954–56	1 Cyl, OHV	39	40	48	6.7:1	Air	Weber carburettor	2-speed	Leading link	Twin shock swingarm	2.00 X18	2.00 X18	1092	45
125TV, TS, Aurea, Bronco	1956–66	1 Cyl OHV	55.2	52	124	6.8:1	Air	Dell'Orto carburettor 18 mm	4-speed	Hydraulic fork	Twin shock swingarm	2.50 X17	2.75 X17	1285	90
85T, S	1957–61	1 Cyl, OHV	45.5	52	85	9:1	Air	Dell'Orto carburettor 16 mm	4-speed	Hydraulic fork	Twin shock swingarm	2.50 X17	2.75 X17	1245	79
175T	1957	1 Cyl, SOHC	62	57.8	175	7:1	Air	Dell'Orto carburettor 22 mm	4-speed	Hydraulic fork	Twin shock swingarm	3.00 X17	3.00 X17	1320	103
175 Sport	1957–60	1 Cyl, SOHC	62	57.8	175	8:1	Air	Dell'Orto carburettor 22.5 mm	4-speed	Hydraulic fork	Twin shock swingarm	2.50 X18	2.75 X18	1320	106
48 Sport	1958–65	1 Cyl, 2 stroke	38	42	48	9.5:1	Air	Dell'Orto carburettor 15 mm	3-speed	Hydraulic fork	Twin shock swingarm	2.25 X19	2.25 X19	1180	54
100S	1958	1 Cyl, SOHC	49	52	98	9:1	Air	Dell'Orto carburettor 18 mm	4-speed	Hydraulic fork	Twin shock swingarm	2.50 X17	2.75 X17	1320	89
125S/T/TS	1958–65	1 Cyl, SOHC	55.2	52	124	8:1	Air	Dell'Orto carburettor 20 mm	4-speed	Hydraulic fork	Twin shock swingarm	2.50 X17	2.75 X17	1320	100
175TS Americano	1958–60	1 Cyl, SOHC	62	57.8	175	7:1	Air	Dell'Orto carburettor 22 mm	4-speed	Hydraulic fork	Twin shock swingarm	2.50 X18	2.75 X18	1320	108 (118)
200 Elite Americano TS	1959–65	1 Cyl, SOHC	67	57.8	204	8.5:1	Air	Dell'Orto carburettor 24 mm	4-speed	Hydraulic fork	Twin shock swingarm	2.75 X18	3.00 X18	1320	111
200 Motocross	1959–60	1 Cyl, SOHC	67	57.8	204	8.5:1	Air	Dell'Orto carburettor 27 mm	4-speed	Hydraulic fork	Twin shock swingarm	2.75 X21	3.00 X19	1380	124
250 Monza	1961–68	1 Cyl, SOHC	74	57.8	249	8:1	Air	Dell'Orto carburettor 24 mm	4/5-speed	Hydraulic fork	Twin shock swingarm	2.75 X18	3.00 X18	1320	125
250 Diana/ Daytona	1961–64	1 Cyl, SOHC	74	57.8	249	8:1	Air	Dell'Orto carburettor 24 mm	4-speed	Hydraulic fork	Twin shock swingarm	2.75 X18	3.00 X18	1320	120
250 Scrambler	1961–67	1 Cyl, SOHC	74	57.8	249	9.2:1	Air	Dell'Orto carburettor 27 mm	4/5-speed	Hydraulic fork	Twin shock swingarm	3.00 x19	3.50 (4.00) X19 (X18)	1350	109 (120)
48 Brisk Piuma	1962–67	1 Cyl, 2 stroke	38	42	48	6.3:1	Air	Dell'Orto carburettor 12 mm	1-speed 3-speed	Hydraulic fork	Twin shock swingarm	2.00 X18 (X19)	2.00 X18 (X19)	1160 (1170)	45 (52)
80 Setter	1962–64	1 Cyl, 2 stroke	47	46	80	7.1:1	Air	Dell'Orto carburettor 15 mm	3-speed	Hydraulic fork	Twin shock swingarm	2.25 X18	2.50 X17		62

The
MOTO GUZZI
Story

Third Edition

VELOCE

IAN FALLOON

Ducati Bevel Twins

1971 to 1986 Authenticity and Resotration Guide

When the great Ducati engineer Fabio Taglioni designed the 750 Ducati in 1970 there was no way he could comprehend how important this model would be. The 750, the Formula 750 racer and the Super Sport became legends, and this book celebrates these machines in year-by-year, model-by-model, change-by-change detail. An absolute must-have for any Ducati aficionado.

Paperback • 27x20.7cm • 1500 colour pictures • 288 pages • ISBN: 978-1-787111-81-3

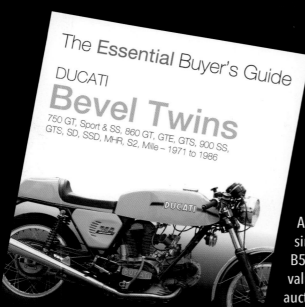

Ducati Bevel Twins

The Essential Buyer's Guide

Stop! Don't buy a Ducati bevel twin without first buying this book!

All you need to know about buying a used BSA unit single, from the very first 250cc C15 to the final 500cc B50. Get the low-down on model histories, relative values, points to look for, plus advice on paperwork, auctions and restorations, and more.

Paperback • 19.5x13.9cm • 160 colour and b&w pictures • 64 pages • ISBN: 978-1-845843-63-2

The Moto Guzzi
Sport & Le Mans Bible

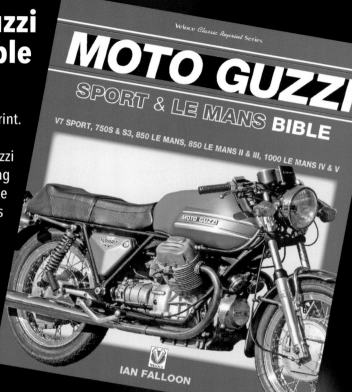

A Veloce Classic Reprint.

Lino Tonti managed to take the large V7 Moto Guzzi touring engine and create a spectacular sporting motorcycle, the V7 Sport, in 1971. This remarkable machine evolved into the stylish 850 Le Mans. This book is a year-by-year account of development and specification changes of a great series of motorcycles.

Paperback • 25x20.7cm • 160 colour and b&w pictures • 160 pages • ISBN: 978-1-787110-95-3

Laverda Twins & Triples Bible

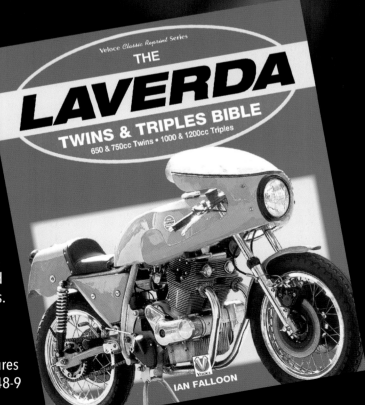

Reprinted after a long absence! A successful racing programme led to the release of the legendary 750SFC, the 1000cc triple, and then the spectacular Jota and new generation RGS during the 1980s. Containing year-by-year, model-by-model detail, this book is essential reading for both owners and enthusiasts.

Paperback • 25x20.7cm • 222 colour and b&w pictures • 160 pages • ISBN: 978-1-787110-48-9

INDEX